AF326939

Bright Stars

For Juno Bobby Bryan, my perfect little star.

First published in 2021 by Frances Lincoln,
an imprint of The Quarto Group.
The Old Brewery, 6 Blundell Street
London, N7 9BH,
United Kingdom
T (0)20 7700 6700
www.QuartoKnows.com

A catalogue record for this book is available from the British Library.

ISBN 978 0 71125 173 1
Ebook ISBN 978 0 71125 174 8

10 9 8 7 6 5 4 3 2 1

Designed by Mariana Sameiro

Printed in China

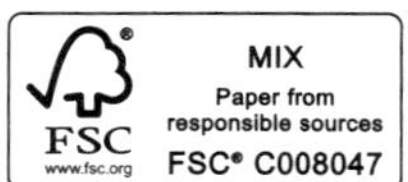

Bright Stars

Great Artists Who Died Too Young

Kate Bryan

Illustrations by Anna Higgie

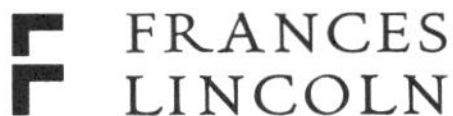

FRANCES LINCOLN

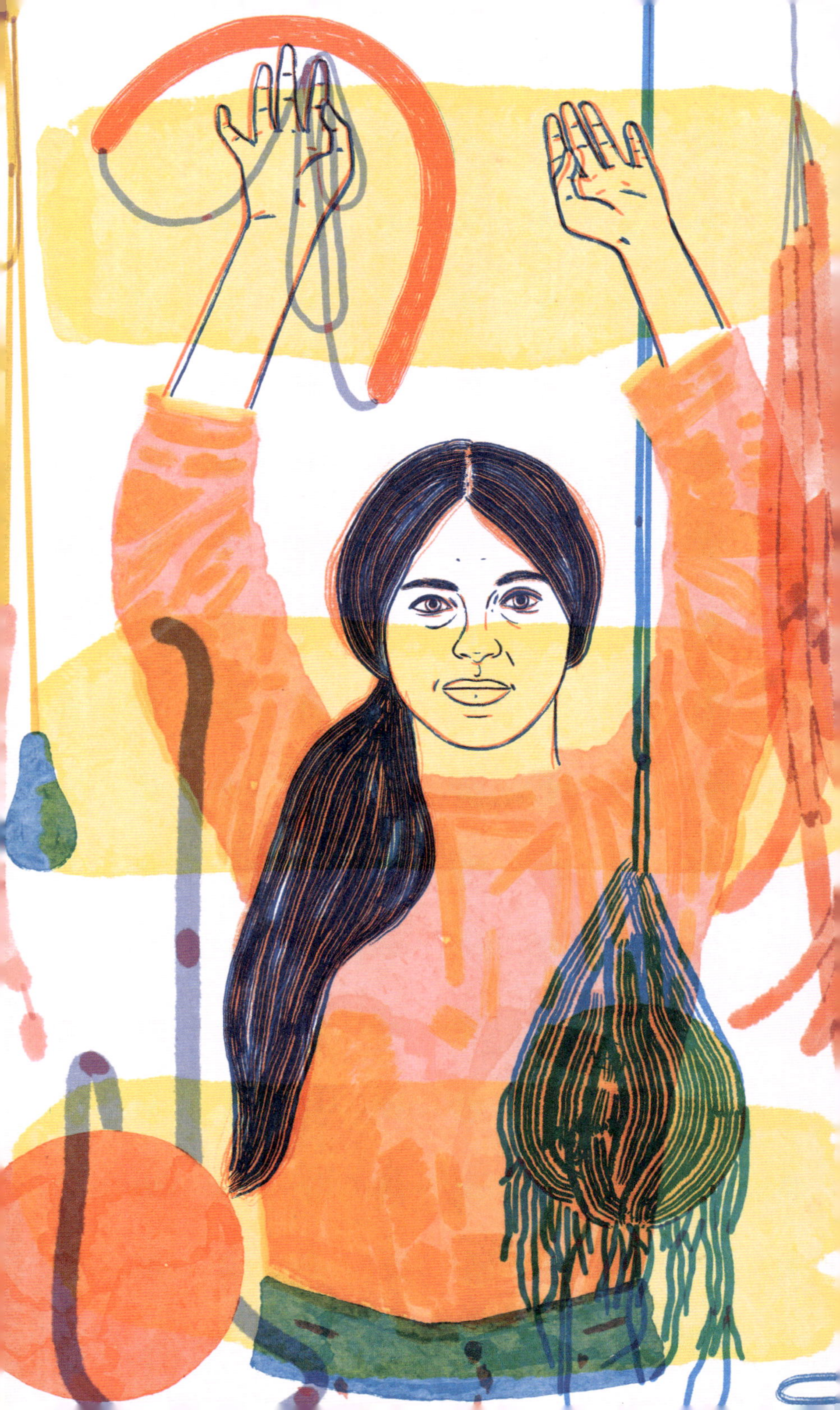

Introduction

True Artists Never Die

This is a book about legacy and how art history is made. It features some of the most famous artists in the world and some of art history's most compelling mythologies. I have selected these thirty artists because I believe them to be great, but they are united by much more than their talent. Each artist in this selection died around the age of forty and I seek to address whether this is mere coincidence or whether there is something in their dying young that ultimately propelled them to greatness.

Today's culture has a fetish for youth. In other realms like film and music, youthfulness has long been a prized asset, emphasised and commodified. Artists, on the other hand, usually need longer to develop their talent, secure a foothold, climb the ranks and emerge as a master – we do not think of Michelangelo, Rembrandt, Artemisia Gentileschi or Titian as fresh-faced painters. In the art world, the concept of a young, successful artist would not feature in any dramatic way until the 1980s when Keith Haring and Jean-Michel Basquiat were hailed as bright stars in a newly minted and art-savvy New York, bursting with new collectors, galleries and critics. Basquiat, in particular, would be unique for the extremely high prices his work commanded while he was in his early twenties.

Alongside this fascination for all things fresh and new was a voyeurism into disaffected youth. The sixties gave us rock-and-roll legends that burned too bright, lived fast and died young. The commercial art world started to build similar mythologies around artists in order to secure the interest and legacy. As a result, I find it fascinating to consider whether these artists would have had the ability to carve out a space for themselves in our collective imagination without the legends that circulate to prop up their stardom after their early departures. Would we have come to know Amedeo Modigliani and Vincent van Gogh anyway without the sensationalism of their deaths? I have tried to detangle the mythologies that surround many of these artists, in some cases obscuring the important truths about their art.

Early death did not mean the same thing straight away for these artists. Like Raphael, it might have canonized them immediately, but for others like Charlotte Salomon it buried some of the most absorbing art made in the twentieth century for decades. I consider our fascination for rediscovering artists who were either hiding in plain sight, like Johannes Vermeer and Caravaggio, or literally hidden in the attic, like Gerda Taro and Pauline Boty. This book reflects on whether an artist can control what happens to their work after they have passed away and whether a painting might speak on behalf of its maker. It asks what revisionist work we can collectively undertake together to help secure legacies for those artists who have been left in the margins of art history.

The thirty artists presented in this book span five hundred years of art history, hail from several countries and made art in incredibly diverse ways. Most died either in their twenties or thirties and therefore had a limited time in which to build a distinct body of work, make an impression and secure a legacy for their practice. I was motivated to create this book because I was struck by the fact that so many of my absolute favourite artists enjoyed so few years making art: ten years for Vincent van Gogh; only six years making paintings for Amadeo Modigliani; seven for Ana Mendieta and eleven for Jean-Michel Basquiat. And I have already lived longer than all of them. And yet, despite this they all manage to resonate and be a source of huge inspiration globally today.

Working in the contemporary art world I am conscious that it is extremely important for an artist to protect their practice. From tedious archival work to celebrated museum shows and exhibitions, there is always an ambition – however explicit – that the artwork created should remain when the artist has departed. Artwork that is destroyed, damaged or neglected can generate feelings of great loss and this book reveals a deep instinct to protect the creations of those undefended by their makers. In 1988, two years before his death of AIDS-related complications, Haring expressed that his practice was a 'kind of quest for immortality. Because you're making these things that you know have a different kind of life. They don't depend on breathing, so they'll last longer than any of us will. Which is sort of an interesting idea, that it's sort of extending your life to some degree.' Exactly one hundred years earlier Theo van Gogh, an art dealer and brother of Vincent, shared the same sentiment: 'Painters being dead and buried, speak to a following generation or to several following generations through their works. In the life of the painter, death may perhaps not be the most difficult thing.'

The artists presented here are divided into five themes to help navigate their stories through common ground. The first theme deals with the twisted romance of dying young, the artists who burned bright and fast. The second features artists who have come to be defined or understood through the prism of their death. I have tried to untangle mythologies so that we might better understand and be sensitive to each artist's career. Next are the pioneers, the artists who made work far ahead of their time. They may have died before they were fully understood and, remarkably, their work perfectly encapsulates our current concerns and they fit beautifully into today's cultural landscape. Then we have those artists who were battling in their lifetimes: whether with illness, real conflict or with themselves, and artists who found salvation and peace in their art making. Finally, we have the unfinished stories, the artists who are still securing a permanent legacy, either because they passed away recently or because their names faded away after their premature departures. I hope this book might in some small way help to contribute to the strengthening and continuation of their artistic legacies.

Where would these artists' legacies be without the people who fought to have them recognized? The book demonstrates time and time again that there is nothing guaranteed about an artist's legacy. It so often depended upon a dedicated torchbearer who fought to create a space in the history books for an artist. In the case of Van Gogh, it was the determined and strategic manoeuvring of his sister-in-law Jo Bonger that helped to secure his legacy. For Vermeer it was a scholar two hundred years after his death. Even an artist famous in their day needs a champion as testified to by Pauline Boty who fell out of sight and was recovered decades later by an art historian, David Alan Mellor. Too often women are left out of the narrative and it was the feminist scholars Lucy Lippard and Rosalind Krauss who helped shape our understanding of Eva Hesse and Francesca Woodman respectively.

There are many artists who were sadly left out of this selection of thirty as I wanted to present as diverse a range of stories as possible. So many artists who I admire and would have loved to have written about did not make the final list. These include Angus Fairhurst, Ren Hang, Franz Marc, Bob Thompson, Henri Gaudier-Brzeska, Isaac Rosenberg, Antonio Sant'Elia, August Macke, Raymond Duchamp-Villon, David Wojnarowicz, Rotimi Fani-Kayode, Matthew Wong and Mikalojus Konstantinas Čiurlionis. I have endeavoured to make the selection as compelling as possible with as much variety across media, art scene and life story. The span of the book means the presence of artists from under-represented backgrounds is thin the further back in time we travel. Despite this, more than a third of the artists in the book are women. Looking at artists born in the last hundred years, one third are artists who are either Black or Latino and three identify as queer artists. A further four are from Jewish families. This lends us the gift of varied narratives and helps allow for a broader consideration as to why some artists have been held back or overlooked.

What do I consider to be too young to die? After careful consideration I alighted on the upper age limit of forty. This is well into adulthood, but most artists do not begin to work professionally until their early twenties and so would have had less than two decades to make an impact. I was too weak to be ruthless and make the upper age limit exactly forty because I could not resist including three artists who I love so much, Vermeer, Chadwick (both forty-two) and Mapplethorpe who died aged forty-three. When considering artists working hundreds of years ago when the average age of death was much younger, it still made sense to include Raphael, Caravaggio and Vermeer. This is because Raphael's great rival and Caravaggio's namesake, Michelangelo died aged nearly ninety. And another two great Dutch masters, Rubens and Rembrandt died twenty years after Vermeer. I also exercised extreme caution when including artists who passed away in this century. I have done so out of huge admiration for their careers and with the blessing of their families.

Finally, I have endeavoured to create a book that considers a group of artists who died too soon, but that does not dwell on death. It is not morbid but celebratory. There is a romance to leaving artwork behind to speak for creator, a refutation of the finality of death, a celebration of the enduring quality of art over the failings of the human body. It is a kind of belief in afterlife borrowed from religion. As I engaged with these artists, I found it to be a great comfort and impossible to resist the narrative that true artists never die.

One

Burning Bright

Keith Haring wrote in 1989 that it is 'Important to do as much as possible as quickly as possible. WORK IS ALL I HAVE AND ART IS MORE IMPORTANT THAN LIFE. I always knew, since I was young, that I would die young...' He had just been diagnosed with HIV in the early years of the New York AIDS epidemic and although dying young was something he seemed strangely mentally prepared for, he had foreseen an instant death rather than a disease. Haring had always worked with a furious intensity and he burned even brighter once he knew exactly how limited his time was. I have always felt that his passion, energy and creative fury is tangible in the work he has left behind. The same is true for other artists that burned bright, knowing that they died young has coloured a posthumous reading of their work. We think of Caravaggio, Keith Haring, Jean-Michel Basquiat and Dash Snow as forever wild, young and without the inevitable sobriety, reflection and slower pace that sets in with middle age. There is something about the tragedy of all that wasted talent that becomes alluring to audiences over time and this has certainly been emphasized by those who benefit from building the reputations of these artists. Despite the macabre mythology-making that came later, it is true that these artists lived in the middle of their own era's cultural vortex and did so with an intensity most of us can only dream of.

Jean-Michel Basquiat died two years before Haring, an artist who had also come of age in the same extraordinary time when New York was birthing a thrilling art playground against the backdrop of a broken-down, neglected city. For me, Basquiat remains a beguiling mix of pure arrogance – often proclaiming he would be the most important artist of his generation – and sad insecurity, shrinking away from social order and plunging further and faster into the drug abuse that would eventually kill him aged twenty-seven. Basquiat is something of a rockstar of the art world, listed alongside Jim Morrison, Jimi Hendrix and Janis Joplin, all of whom died alcohol-and-drug related deaths at the same tender age. Like Haring, who also used the streets of New York as his first canvas, Basquiat had a compulsion to make art; it seemed to pour out of him. But unlike the endlessly positive and giving Haring, Basquiat was self-contained and it became depressingly clear to those around him that he was trapped in self-destruct mode.

The ultimate bad boy of art history, Caravaggio lived in another extraordinarily fertile place and period for art: Rome of the early 1600s. His biography presents him time and time again as an artist who lacked any social graces and repeatedly acted as his own worst enemy. He remains an enigmatic figure for delivering us a radical new kind of art that fused a sacred pathos with the profane. We know that Caravaggio lived through torment, violence, despair and so his paintings dealing with beheadings, prayer and conversion seem more urgent and vital. Like Basquiat nearly four hundred years later, Caravaggio was the star of his generation, but he too burned too bright; his genius was extinguished while on the run for murder aged just thirty-eight and he left behind a paltry amount of work, albeit they were all masterpieces.

Unlike Caravaggio's acclaimed treasures, Dash Snow leaves behind a legacy that is not entirely certain. He shared many of the same self-destructive tendencies with the Baroque painter as well as his fellow New Yorker, Basquiat. His overdose in 2009 came a generation after Basquiat, but before he had firmly established a secure foothold in the art world. His work, full of doubt, anger, political paranoia as well as intimacy, joy and the recklessness of youth, instantly transports us to a particular time and place in New York's history. The fact that he held conventional art world systems at arm's length has meant a lack of critical assessment and an insecure posthumous position. His inclusion here, although he is by no means as established the names he sits alongside, is important to me since he and his work have come to stand for the last days of true bohemia in New York. His anarchic attitude, refusal to accept his enormous inheritance and distaste for the encroaching digital world make him seem positively antique and yet he only died just over ten years ago.

It is interesting to note that all of the artists in this section were uncomfortable with the traditional art world model. They either resisted the commercial aspect of art or would not bow down to the elite that could secure them success. Their careers were very much on their own terms, they all made work first and foremost that sprang from their unique experience of the world and satisfied them as an extension of their lives. They were all disruptors of a kind that only fuels the flames of their mythologies. As these chapters will attest, there is a long-standing twisted romance in dying young – so much so that Haring created work from the outset with a premonition of his early death. As for Basquiat, Caravaggio and Snow, we all know that a compulsion exists to fetishize those who live fast and die young. In a way that is just not the case for their peers, these artists have been frozen in time as demi-rock-gods, burning bright in their lifetimes and leaving us with an appetite for more.

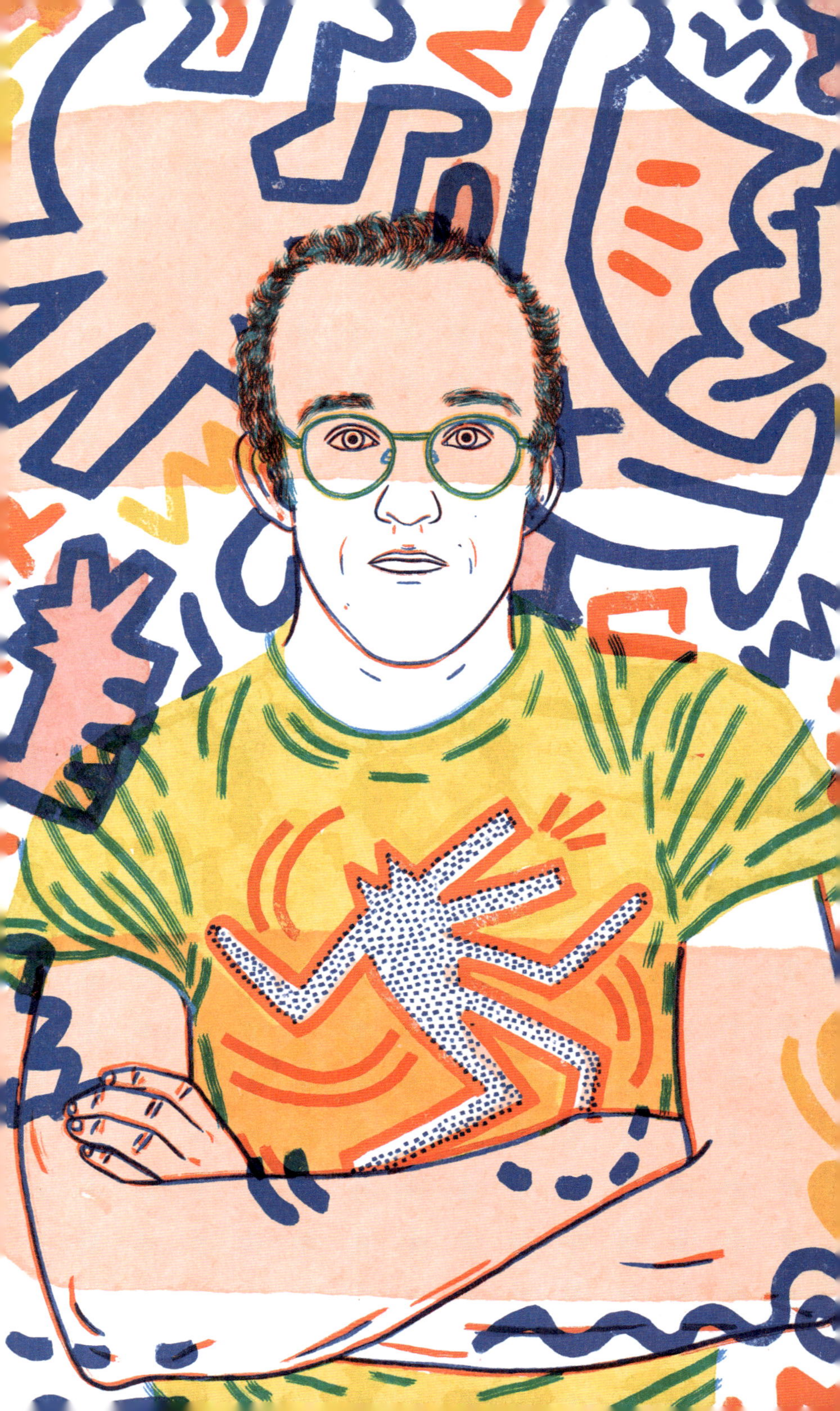

Keith
Haring
1958–1990

Art for Everybody

'There are no regrets. Part of the reason that I'm not having trouble facing the reality of death is that it's not a limitation, in a way. It could have happened any time, and it is going to happen sometime. If you live your life according to that, death is irrelevant. Everything I'm doing right now is exactly what I want to do.' In 1989, the American artist Keith Haring set out these beautifully brave thoughts in *Rolling Stone* magazine about what he believed might be his impending death from AIDS-related complications. He would die in February 1990 at just thirty-one years of age.

Unlike nearly all the other artists featured in this book, Haring had given a lot of thought to the potential brevity of his life and work. Consequently, he was extremely driven, even before he knew he was ill and after he was diagnosed, he ensured that his prolific career would be properly looked after. His concern for longevity beyond the grave was not simply to satisfy his own ego, rather he was very committed to giving a permanent form to his socially motivated practice and using his art to financially benefit charities supporting HIV and for under-privileged children.

Haring had always intended for his art to reach out to people. From the earliest subway drawings he made in New York aged twenty-two, he intended for his images to be universal, to speak directly to the masses. He eschewed what he perceived to be the elitism of the art world in favour of a system that was more democratic, making dozens of public murals, handing out free posters, opening his own shop to sell affordable art and using empty subway ad spaces to make his mark in chalk. It was not simply his delivery that bypassed the upper echelons of the art market, but also the language he employed, so joyful that it has never gone out

"I sort of stepped on some toes..."

of fashion. His imagery still resonates so loudly decades later because of its apparent simplicity: a radiant baby; beating hearts; dancing figures; barking dogs; oppressed people; two men in love. With a clear debt to the cartoons that inspired him as a child, Haring's flair for graphic, reduced lines and strong, brightly coloured and simple forms means his work is endlessly reproducible and has huge commercial appeal. It exists today in museum collections but also among us in the form of a dizzying plethora of products, from skateboards, to badges, to children's colouring books to baseball hats.

The simplicity and ubiquity of his imagery means there is a danger we might underestimate Haring. The art world is notoriously suspicious of anything 'easy', attractive, commercial or instantly popular. Far from an opportunistic marketing wizard, Haring had a deep commitment to socially engaged activity. He was passionate about not just making art that touched the public directly and energetically, but also spoke to them of the pressing issues of the day. Once Haring had established his signature style he quickly adapted and grew his language so it might be used for his own public service announcements. In his short career he used his art like an activist's placard to draw attention to causes as diverse as drugs, South African Apartheid, HIV/AIDS and nuclear disarmament. In 1986 he painted his famous *Crack is Wack* mural on a handball court wall visible to traffic on New York's FDR Drive. Initially the mural was created illegally and Haring was arrested. He had been inspired to make the work after one of his studio assistants succumbed to the crack cocaine problem that swept across New York. Believing the authorities were not acting quickly enough, the artist created his bright orange mural depicting souls taken by crack, personified by a skull and crack pipe. After public outcry his court order was revoked and he was invited by the City's Park department to repaint it with their permission.

Haring was also a committed champion of gay rights and lived an openly gay lifestyle in an era when it was still extremely difficult to do so. In 1987 he created his *Safe Sex* artwork, possibly drawing the happiest condom in art history. He experienced the AIDS epidemic first-hand, helplessly witnessing as a tidal wave swept up so many of his friends and would eventually claim him, too. In 1989, at the time Haring created *Ignorance = Fear* for the organization ACT UP, it is said that one American was being diagnosed with AIDS every minute. Haring's work, now using bold colour and line as a form of anger and protest, was brilliantly deployed as a secret weapon for the activists in what was a fight for survival and compassion.

Haring's work is instantly recognizable and meaningful across the borders of language and culture. Unlike many of the artists in this book, he was internationally successful within his lifetime, exhibiting in more than one hundred solo and group exhibitions throughout his short career. In 1986 alone he was featured in over forty print articles. He worked with the biggest stars of his time from Madonna to Andy Warhol to Yoko Ono, to name just a few collaborators. The subway drawings that had made his name would be stolen and sold within in minutes of the artist creating them. As early as 1982 Haring also discovered that his imagery was being used on retail products in Japan without his permission, before he had even licensed imagery for commercial purposes. He was becoming a victim of his own success and many art critics, no doubt surprised by his unconventional path to the top, derided his value – Robert Hughes the important *Time* magazine critic labelled him 'Keith Boring'. Haring was well aware of systems in play, commenting that he bypassed the critics and 'found my public without them. They didn't have the chance to take credit for what I did. They think that they have the role of finding the artist… and then teaching the public…. I sort of stepped on some toes…'

In 1986, Haring, disillusioned by the manner in which his artwork was traded to serve the interests of a small pool of wealthy collectors, decided to create his own direct channel for art democracy by opening a shop. Designed as if walking into a Haring artwork and accessible to its very core, Pop Shop allowed the public to buy their own Haring poster, badge or t shirt. The tactic increased his fan base but worsened his standing in the art world as collectors feared he was lessening the scarcity and therefore value of his artwork. Haring responded, 'The use of commercial projects has enabled me to reach millions of people whom I would not have reached by remaining an unknown artist. I assumed, after all, that the point of making art was to communicate and contribute to culture.' Haring was happy to defy expectations and his commitment to a non-elitist, open approach to making and distributing art is hugely influential today. As recently as 2019 Banksy opened his own shop in Croydon.

Today young artists can bypass the gallery system and find their own audience by using social media, and Haring, in many ways, is the godfather of this Instagram generation of artists. Haring was a visionary who believed in the goodness of people and the value of art to create happiness and instigate change. He was decades ahead of his time. Thankfully his vision extended to a remarkable legacy in the shape of his foundation.

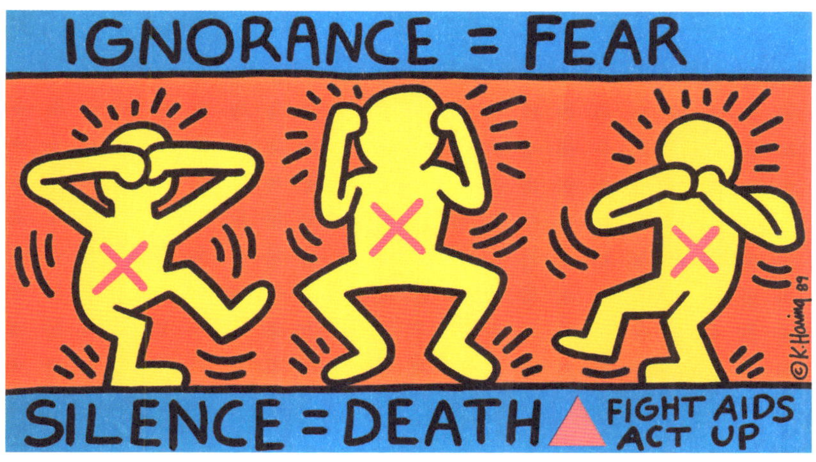

Ignorance = Fear
Keith Haring (1958–1990)
1989, offset lithograph,
61.1 × 109.4 cm (24 × 43 in),
Whitney Museum of American Art,
New York, USA © Keith Haring Foundation

Three decades after his death, the Keith Haring Foundation is still directed by the artist's former studio manager, Julia Greun, who worked alongside the artist for six years. Set in his former studio, the non-profit organization judiciously uses Haring's distinct vocabulary to raise funds in licensing deals to benefit causes close to his heart – a heart known and recognized by millions across the world: still beating, bold and happy.

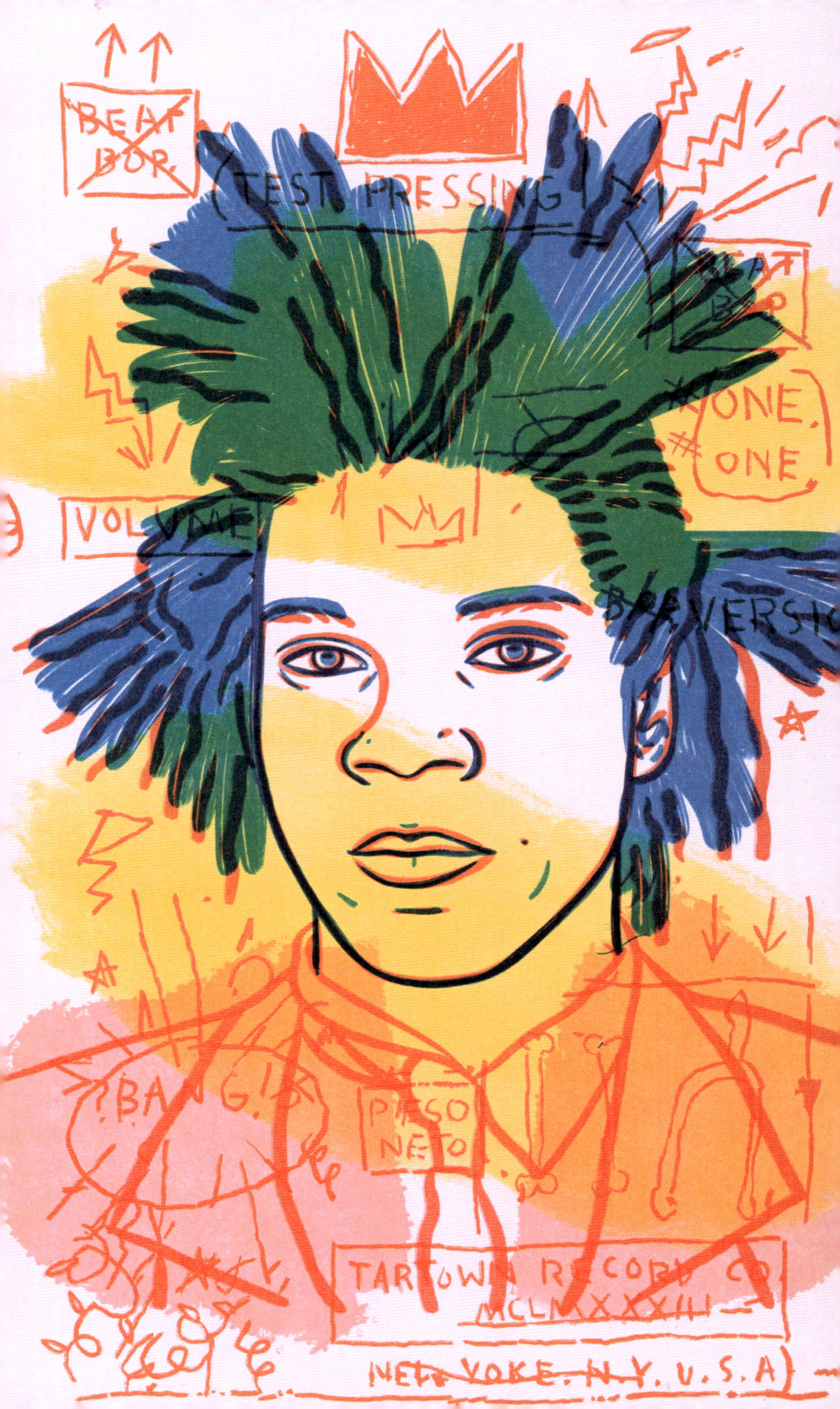

BEAT BOR
TEST PRESSING
BEAT B
#ONE, #ONE,
VOLUME
B VERSIO
BANG!
PESO NETO
TARTOWN RECORD CO
MCLMXXXIII
NEW YOKE, N.Y. U.S.A

Jean-Michel Basquiat
1960–1988

Rock-Star Painter

Of all the artists in this book, it is Jean-Michel Basquiat that suffers most from a dangerous mythologization, so much so that the circumstances of his life threaten to overshadow the power of his art. The mythology of Basquiat is dangerous because it is symptomatic of an art world that is unrelenting and depressingly white orientated. Basquiat's career was explosive, unprecedented, thrilling, terrifyingly ill-fated and it sat at the nexus of race, politics, money and power in 1980s New York. It is said that the eighties were all about greed and speed and the meteoric rise to fame by Jean-Michel Basquiat typifies this alarming commodification of art and culture.

Born to Puerto-Rican and Haitian parents, he suffered from a kind of oblique but endemic racism that positioned him as *the* African American artist, meaning he was a laden with being a signifier of blackness and a lone figure in what was deemed to be an otherwise white art world. When asked if he liked being called 'The Black Picasso', he responded with his typical guarded astuteness, 'Not so much. It's flattering but it's also demeaning.' Basquiat didn't want to be famous because of, or in spite of, his race, why should he suffer the indignity of being seen first and foremost as black? But he did want to be famous. Like his hero Warhol, Basquiat subscribed to the belief that you were nobody unless you were somebody. Even as a teenager, he proclaimed his own future success with a wilful but naive arrogance. He was born in 1960, the dawn of Pop Art and he would become one of Warhol's children who found the spotlight, burned too bright, lived too fast and died young.

Although his career lasted just eight years, Basquiat was prolific and almost pathological in his need to make art. He would sleep on his paintings, walk across them, eat, drink and smoke with them, write phone numbers upon them, they were a physical manifestation of his inner experience and this is partly what gave his work such potency when he first burst onto New York's downtown art scene. However, Basquiat's youthful looking, unrestrained line and colour belied his respect for, and knowledge of, art history. Although he was not formally trained (another fact that the art establishment would marvel at, giving him the additional burden of being some kind of child prodigy), Basquiat spent a lot of time looking at art, beginning with trips as a young child to the Metropolitan Museum of Art (MoMA) with his mother, Matilde. One of his long-term girlfriends Suzanne Mallouk recalled that he had an encyclopaedic knowledge of the MoMA, 'Jean knew every inch of that museum, every painting, every room. I was astonished at his knowledge and intelligence and at how twisted and unexpected his observations could be.'

Basquiat grew up speaking French, Spanish and English and lived in a multi-cultural community in Flatbush. His genius stemmed from his ability to synthesize the complexities of the world around him with a feverish energy, like an elevated form of music sampling. His painting was a raw conduit for his lived experience and his sources were a dizzying concoction of high and low culture: art history books; cartoons; television; jazz; African culture; poetry; graffiti; anatomical books; hobo signs; sport; literature; celebrity; magazines; hieroglyphics; advertising; and the news.

One of his largest paintings, and widely considered one of his masterpieces, is *Undiscovered Genius of the Mississippi Delta* (1983). An ambitious frieze-like span across five canvas panels immediately situates the work as the artist's thunderous response to academic history painting. Basquiat plays with the formal conventions of Abstract Expressionism, delivering intelligently executed passages of raw colour and unstructured form, which is then taken to another level with a rich overload of imagery and text that focuses on African American struggles. From *Mark Twain*, to the *Deep South*, to *Negroes* to *Cotton*, the painting was part of his artistic codex that presented the African diasporic condition alongside

"Death can really make you look like a star"

his personal experience, specifically he includes a self-portrait marking his recent twenty-third birthday in the top left. Using his signature jazz-like repetition of words as well as crossed-out text that can still be clearly read, the artist is not so much making statements as creating rhythm and insisting the viewer pay attention. Basquiat was part of a generation, including Jenny Holzer, Barbara Kruger and David Salle that experimented with text as a visual signifier. To many contemporary commentators his wordplay was connected with his early and brief association with the graffiti movement as one half of the anonymous street bomber SAMO. When Holzer used text, it was postmodern. When a young black man did the same, even if it was on canvas and displayed in a gallery, it was deemed to stem from graffiti, something that Basquiat observed to be a racist slight.

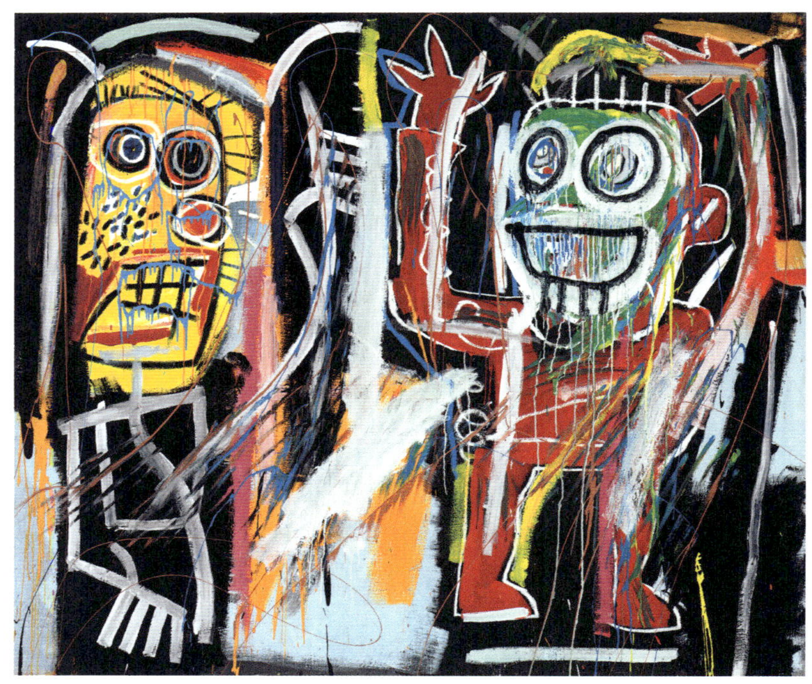

Dustheads
Jean-Michel Basquiat (1960–1988)
1982, acrylic, oilstick, spray enamel
and metallic paint on canvas,
182.8 × 213.3 cm (72 × 84 in),
© Keith Haring Foundation

Basquiat was right to be on his guard. He found success extremely quickly and although he disdained the rich white elite that reigned over the art market, he knew he had entered a Faustian pact with them. Between the ages of fifteen and eighteen he went from being a homeless teenage runaway to a couch-surfing graduate of the liberal City-As-School programme that nurtured those with talent who could not fit the mould of traditional educational programmes. He came of age in the urban dystopia of a broken-down city, first grabbing the attention he craved as SAMO and quickly bursting into the downtown arts scene. He was a regular and charismatic fixture, playing in a band with Vincent Gallo, dating Madonna and partying with Keith Haring. Although his career began with him so broke he would hook up with girls just to have a place to sleep and scavenge old doors to paint on, in less than two years he was selling work for thousands of dollars and famously painting in Armani suits. At the height of his fame, and still only just in his mid-twenties, he was travelling by limo (as a black man in New York he was always mortified he could not get a cab despite his wealth), exhibiting internationally multiple times a year and, depending on which of his dealers you believe, would receive a stipend of somewhere between $700,000 to $1.4 million in cash against sales. Basquiat is arguably the first martyr for the fetish for young talent. Today we presume that anyone investing in art will back emerging or young artists, but in the 1980s this was a new phenomenon. Both speculating on art and buying work that was practically still wet were very new aspects of the art world where previously prices for living artists remained moderate in their lifetime and would sometimes peak after their death.

Basquiat was increasingly paranoid about being used by dealers and collectors, and he came to feel fundamentally misunderstood as an artist and was convinced his friends would betray him by selling art he had gifted them. As an insecure, emotionally unstable young man who had an increasingly estranged relationship with his domineering father Gerald (Basquiat reported serious beatings at his father's hand) he was ill equipped to deal with fame and money. Sales, press, invitations, drugs, alcohol, expensive wine and clothes began to have diminishing returns. Innately compulsive and rebellious, Basquiat was never one for moderation and his life grew increasingly wild and toxic in its consumption levels.

One of the most important and consistent relationships in Basquiat's life was with his hero Andy Warhol, whose orbit he came into as a new young star. Warhol's diaries reveal that they painted together, worked out together, had their nails done and chatted on the phone at length. When Warhol died in February 1987 after complications from gallbladder surgery, a part of

Basquiat died, too. His surrogate father figure, someone who reprimanded him for his drug use and validated his talent, was gone. By 1988 Basquiat felt used by the art world and increasingly isolated himself from friends and family. With a face covered in sores and teeth missing as a result of his gargantuan drug and alcohol abuse, he was a shell of his former self. His art was suffering and the collectors, dealers and critics that had put him on a pedal stool as a demi-art-god now had a mournful disdain of a tragic figure they helped to cultivate.

In August 1988 Basquiat died of a heroin overdose in the studio and apartment space he rented from Warhol. By dying young at twenty-seven, he joined the ranks of other legendary talents that lived the rock-and-roll lifestyle and crashed at the same age: Jimi Hendrix, Janis Joplin, Jim Morrison. In some respects, the spectre of death had drifted over his entire career. He idolized the musician Charlie Parker, who died young as a heroin addict in 1955, and one of Basquiat's signature images was the skull. He painted hundreds, and the motif that spoke of ancestors, history but most importantly death, has become a sick sign of value in the art market. It is said that a Basquiat with a skull will be worth far more than one without. Taking the point to an extreme, in 2017 *Untitled* (1982), a large skull painting by Basquiat became the most expensive work of art ever sold by any American artist, shattering records at $110.5 million. As Warhol once quipped on British Television, 'Death means a lot of money, honey. Death can really make you look like a star.'

The fetishization of the skull as a symbol of his inevitable demise cannot undo the vivacity and sheer force of life that runs through Basquiat's entire oeuvre. These are paintings of the world and about the world; they pulsate with energy. They were a way to exorcise demons, rebirthing the artist's pleasures, dreams and fears into powerful painted incantations. They inspire people the world over because Basquiat, like Van Gogh before him, achieved what he set out to, 'I wanted to make very direct paintings that most people would feel the emotion behind.' Basquiat's legacy is not just financially enormous. Away from the auction rooms, his paintings are some of the most influential works created in the last century. At the memorial service Haring, like a cultural clairvoyant, stated 'Greedily, we wonder what else he might have created, what masterpieces we have been cheated out of by his death, but the fact is that he has created enough work to intrigue generations to come. Only now will people begin to understand the magnitude of his contribution.'

Haring would die two years later as a victim of the AIDS epidemic that was already angrily taking hold of the city. He wouldn't have known that in the decade after his friend's death, museums would reject offers by wealthy patrons to donate works they owned by Basquiat, likely concerned he was a star of the market only. Although he was prolific, of the two thousand artworks Basquiat created only around twenty are in US museums and the UK has no work by Basquiat in its institutional collections. It is depressing to think that he may be forever tainted by money, but I am hopeful that those who perhaps considered him an art world mascot who didn't fulfil on his promise will re-evaluate this view in light of recent events. Not only was *Basquiat: Boom for Real* the most successful exhibition in the Barbican Centre's history, with record-breaking attendance of 215,000 people in 2017, but the Black Lives Matter movement of 2020 has shone a glaring light into the whiteness of museums that is not going away. Basquiat deserves to be academically reappraised: he rewrote the rulebook and left behind an artistic encyclopaedia of his own creation. To stand in front of one of his paintings is to feel him rise from the dead.

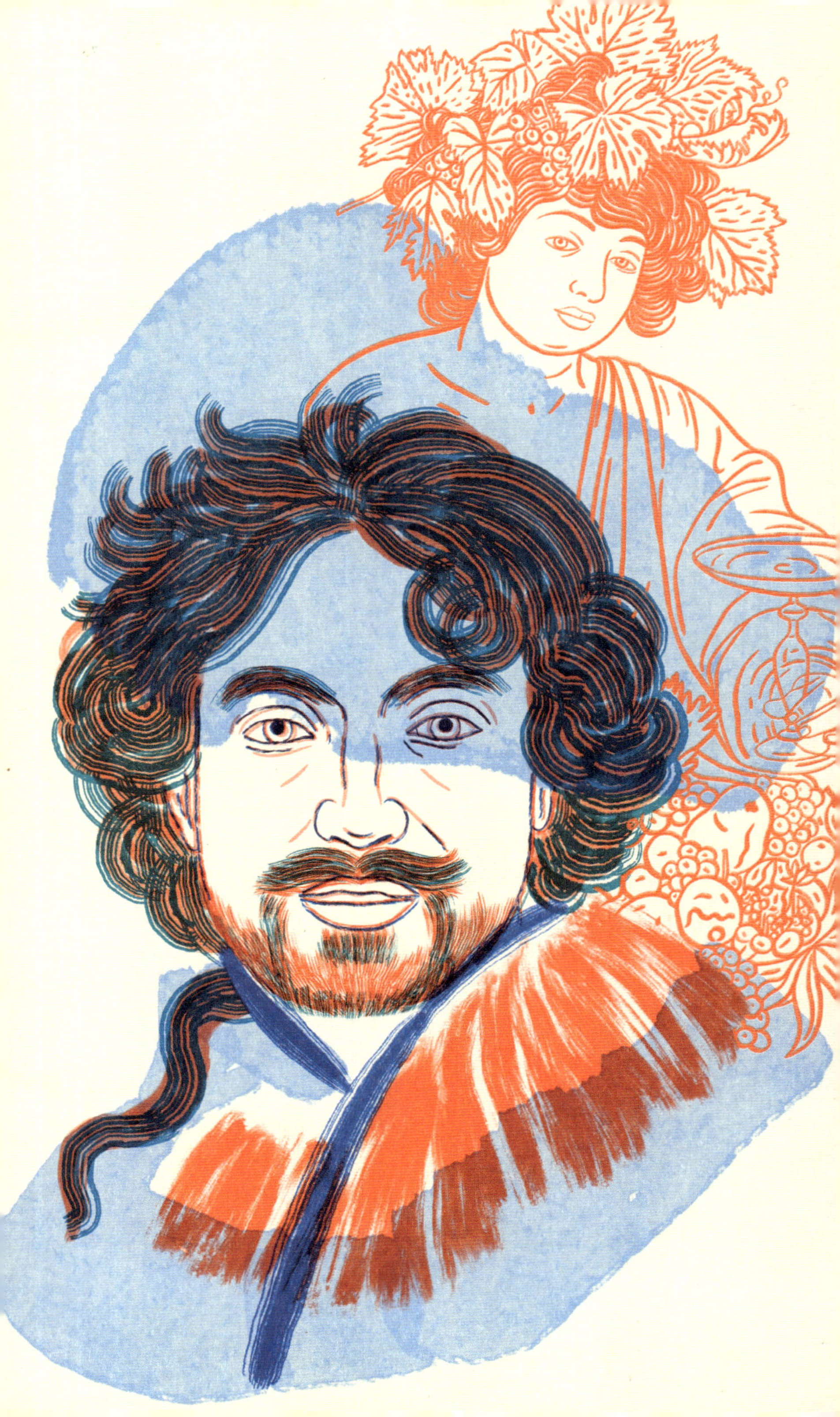

Caravaggio
1571–1610

Art History's Bad Boy

Caravaggio is, in some senses, the first modern painter. Rather than build on the developments of successive generations of artists in the mission to move art history forward in subtle grades, his approach was pure revolution. When we stand in San Luigi dei Francesi in Rome and compare his three panels in the Contarelli Chapel to artwork in the neighbouring chapels that date from the same decade, we are in a position to fully appreciate that the only thing they have in common is the mere materials. Caravaggio's work seems to belong to a different century; in fact, it is a distinct, other world of painting altogether. It would not be until the twentieth century that artists such as Cezanne and Picasso would break with the past in such a decisive manner again.

To synthesize what makes his work so radical and lends him such a staggering legacy some four hundred years later, we should consider two things. Firstly, the manner in which he dramatically built pictures of out light and darkness, as if seeing the world through flash photography. And secondly his atypical, often considered profane, approach to portraying distant and spiritual events as if they were playing out amidst the sweat and dirt of his real world, imbuing the divine with a new humanity.

In *The Calling of St Matthew* (1599–1600) he uses contemporary dress to insert modern-day Romans into the Biblical scene. He dispenses with the idealized imagery of Christ, giving him a realistic face and allowing only a sliver of a halo, which is partially obscured. The dramatic directional lighting that brings the scene to life from its dark background is a precursor to modern photography and theatre. It is hard to comprehend quite how staggeringly original it must have seemed four centuries ago.

The unprecedented departures he made in seventeenth-century painting still astound us today. What is almost equally hard to take in is how brief his career was. Caravaggio is a towering giant of our cultural landscape, filling Italy's churches and the world's museums with devoted crowds. All this, and yet his career lasted only a decade and all that remains is just over forty surviving paintings. (A paltry number when we compare it to Van Gogh, who died at the same age after painting two thousand works over the same length of time.) Dead by the age of thirty-eight, Caravaggio's career was not only brief, it was also volatile. He had no formal studio practice with assistants and he was more or less self-taught, the only artist in this era to forgo drawing completely and work up his masterpieces directly onto the canvas. Just as he broke the rules in art, Caravaggio also broke them in life. He is the ultimate bad boy of art history: of all the great artists, he is the only one to have committed murder and spent half of his painting life on the run.

Given the scarcity of his paintings and the complete lack of preparatory drawings and letters in his hand (which do so much to disseminate the style and attitude of an artist after their death), it is remarkable that Caravaggio has managed to have any staying power. Much of what we know about the man is gleaned from criminal archives, for Caravaggio was often on the wrong side of the law, although there is no doubt he lived in violent times. When Caravaggio arrived in Rome in the late 1590s it was still in ruins from the Sack of Rome in 1527. He lived in the artists' quarter, a squalid abandoned neighbourhood and, although it was illegal, he carried a sword. The court records show he had a temper and was often spoiling for a fight. Although he would come to be supported and admired by cardinals and the city's elite, he never ceased his role in what we might describe in today's terminology as gang culture.

The underbelly of Rome would not just incubate and aggravate Caravaggio, it would also find its way into his paintings. Caravaggio hired prostitutes or labourers to sit for him and scandalized Roman society by portraying the recognizable facial features of known street walkers in paintings where they performed as religious figures such as the Virgin Mary or Mary Magdalene. His motive was likely the pursuit of realism, to transform the idealized, untouchable characters that had long dominated religious painting into more relatable figures. He was also partial to

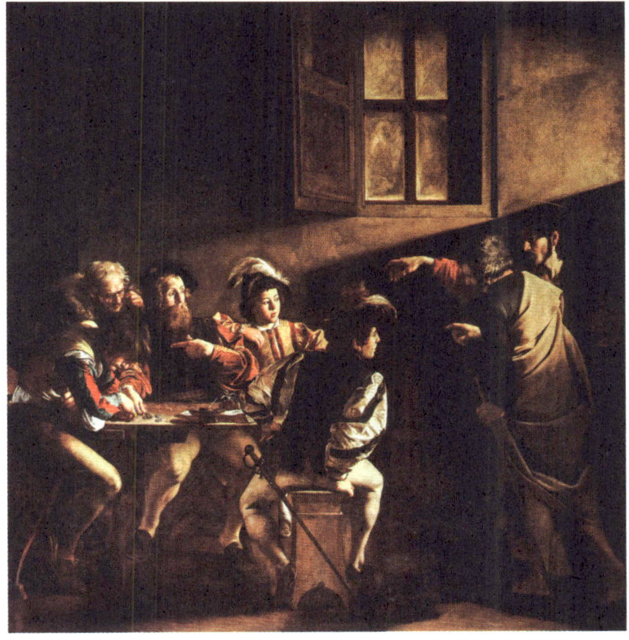

The Calling of St Matthew
Caravaggio (1571–1610)
1599–1600, oil on canvas,
322 cm × 340 cm (127 in × 130 in),
San Luigi dei Francesi, Rome, Italy

violence and gore, depicting numerous beheadings including those of St John the Baptist, Holofernes and Goliath. Caravaggio would certainly have witnessed public executions and brought his testimony to bear in his believable pulsating veins and pools of blood. The Church was outraged by his approach, which included the presentation of saints with dirty feet as if they had walked the filthy streets of Rome.

Although his work was rejected more than once for profanity, the public responded immediately. When a new commission for a church was unveiled, hundreds would arrive to catch a glimpse of his daring new work. His admirers were not simply connoisseurs of art, but also the faithful who saw in his unidealized approach a path to God that resonated with their imperfect lives. Caravaggio was a celebrity in his day, attracting not just admiring young artists such as Artemisia Gentileschi, but also his fair share of jealousy. Several public spats with other artists are recorded, including a court case for libel against him. More dangerous, though, was his feud with Ranuccio Tomassoni, which would end Caravaggio's time in Rome forever.

After an illegal duel in which he murdered Tomassoni in 1606, Caravaggio fled and spent the next four years in exile with a price on his head, dodging assassins as he painted his way from Naples to Sicily to Malta, all the while scheming with opportunistic cardinals for a Papal pardon. After an eventful few years, during which he painted several masterpieces, escaped from prison and survived a near-fatal knife attack, Caravaggio eventually secured a pardon by bartering his desirable paintings with Cardinal Scipione Borghese in return for his help in securing the Pope's good favour. But Caravaggio would never return to the Eternal City. Bad luck and a mystifying ability to self-sabotage followed Caravaggio like a dark shadow. His long-awaited homecoming began in July 1610 when he reached a port in Tuscany, twenty miles west of Rome. There he was promptly detained – most likely a result of his temper. Meanwhile, his ship returned to Naples with his paintings that were to secure his freedom. In spite of his recent six-month convalescence following the knife attack, upon his release he raced on horseback to meet the ship again and retrieve his precious cargo. But he died from either a fever caused by heat exhaustion or a heart attack.

Although buried in an unmarked grave, he did not disappear from the minds of those in Rome. There was an unseemly scuffle to locate and take possession of his remaining paintings. Almost immediately, he became the most imitated artist of the age, even by admirers in Naples, where he had spent only a short time; the paintings that remained on display there had left an enormous impression on the city's artists. The market for his work was so healthy that a school sprang up known as the Caravaggisti and it spread as far as France, Spain and Holland.

Despite this immediate popularity, Caravaggio later fell into the margins of art history for nearly three hundred years. His work was too humane for the indulgent Baroque period and too sensual for the prudish Victorians. The critic John Ruskin derided him as the 'ruffian Caravaggio' and described his work as 'horror and ugliness and filthiness of sin'. He was sidelined, too, by the art market as the birth of modern art connoisseurship correlated to saleability of artworks. With the majority of his small oeuvre in situ in Italian churches and no works on paper, he was not a candidate for inclusion in the boom in art history tomes and monographs from the late nineteenth century onwards. It would not be until the 1950s that Caravaggio emerged from the shadows to take his place as the anti-hero of art history. This was largely down to the efforts of the Italian art historian Roberto Longhi who did much to resurrect Caravaggio's fame and reputation. One of Longhi's pupils was the film director Pier Paolo Pasolini, who would channel Caravaggio's spot-lit, dramatic compositions imbued with the scent of the street in his films. Martin Scorsese has also cited the revolutionary artist as a major influence in his cinematic masterpieces. Perhaps if he were alive today, and able to stay out of trouble long enough, Caravaggio would be a ground-breaking documentary maker, artfully composing dramatic narratives that elevate and inspire the lives of those around him.

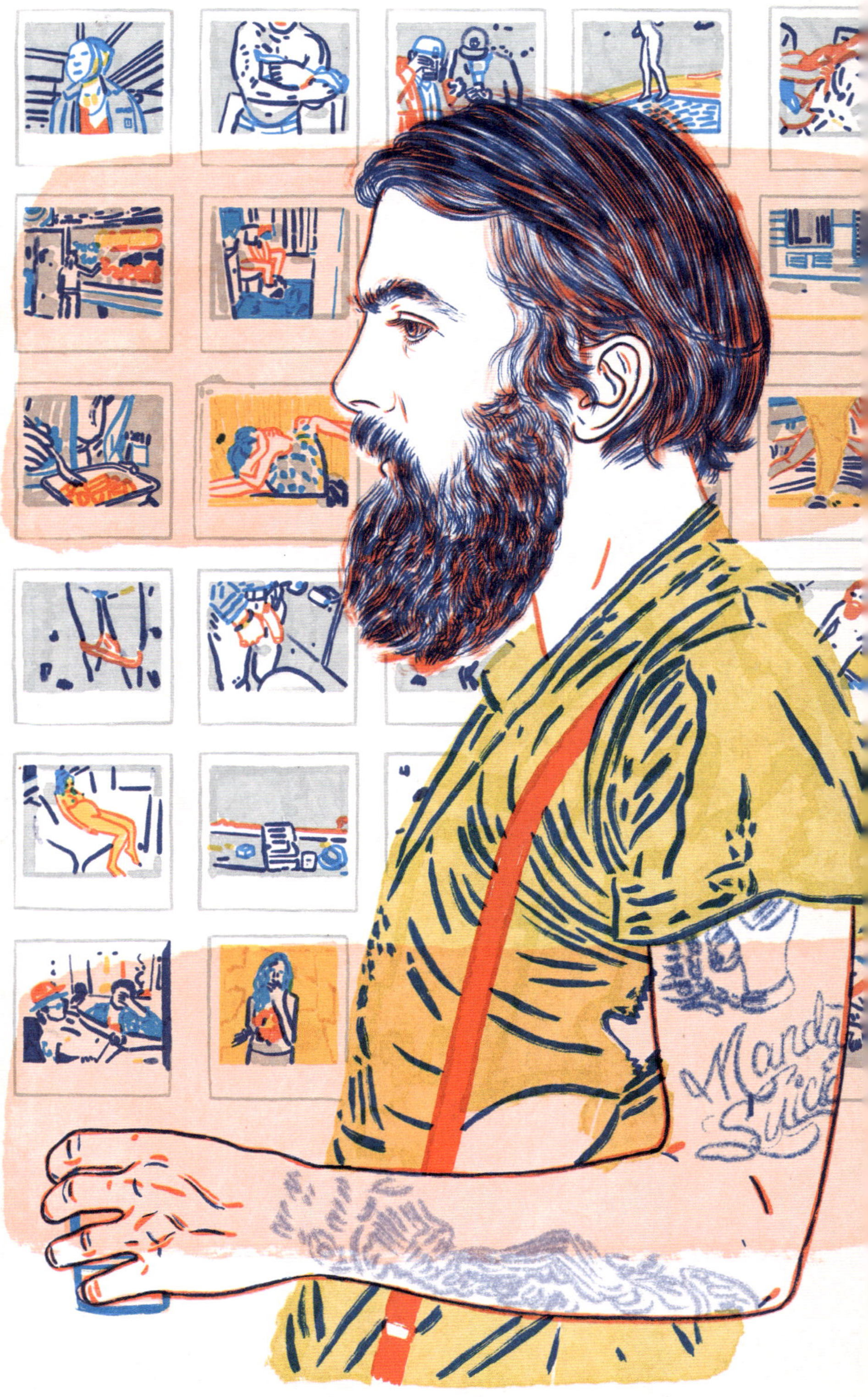
Mandy
Slice

Downtown Rebel

Dash Snow lived his short life engaged in a continual act of resistance. He resisted the mounting wave of digital technology in the first decade of the twenty-first century that was soon to take over every aspect of our world, shunning the internet, email and mobile phones. He resisted authority as a young man, goading both his family and the law with irresponsible behaviour. He defied expectations and opportunities by cutting himself off from his family's staggering wealth and status as one of the greatest art-collecting families in American history. He undermined his health as his substance abuse propelled him towards the drug overdose that killed him aged twenty-seven. He even resisted the word artist, finding it unnecessary to promote his work to an art world he viewed as commercial and inauthentic. Instead of sculptures he used the word 'situations', as if to highlight the casual, throwaway existence of both the work and the man. All of this resistance has met something of a stalemate for his reputation within the art establishment, and the legacy of Dash Snow today sits in purgatory.

There are those who might endeavour to discredit his originality, and it is true that Snow's artwork is dependent on other moments in art history.

His approach is not invented but openly borrowed: the found object; assemblage; collage; Super 8 films; Polaroid and text all show a great debt to Dada, Marcel Duchamp and Andy Warhol. His anarchic attitude was nothing that previous counterculture generations hadn't manifested before. But to posit that there was nothing original or memorable about Dash Snow would be disingenuous. In many respects he may have secured a legacy for himself by his *very* attachment to these vintage attitudes and modes of making. Described by the press after his death as the latest incarnation of a dying New York species, 'the downtown Baudelaire', Snow hurtled into the twenty-first century furious and distrustful of family, the government, the police, the art world, surveillance technology, and created work that clearly manifested his position.

He turned twenty years old not long before the Twin Towers fell on September 11, 2001 and, like it did for the generation that saw Kennedy assassinated, the violence would permeate the American psyche. Along with his best friends, the artists Ryan McGinley and Dan Colen, he came to stand for New York's disaffected youth, his subject was his precarious and dissolute lifestyle as captured in grimy Polaroids. It was McGinley and Colen, today long-established art world names, who have left their wild twenties behind, who encouraged Snow to step into the shoes of an artist. Now exhibited as fine art, Snow claimed he originally created the Polaroids simply to remember where he was the night before. The images are unflinching snapshots of a throw-away world populated by drugs and sex, captured by someone both inciting the subjects and participating, indignantly letting the viewer know that life is cheap, too. But one cannot help but think that if Dash didn't care about these moments, he wouldn't have taken such trouble to freeze frame them, to suspend anarchy in time with a knowing aesthetic.

His friends had 'made it' and Snow was beginning to gain traction: Colen had sold a work for six figures to the lynchpin of the London art scene, Charles Saatchi. Both Snow and Colen exhibited work at Saatchi's gallery in 2007 and went to London for the show. It was there that Colen and Snow made an installation together, not in the gallery but in a Mayfair hotel room paid for by Saatchi. The 'Hamster Nests' were an astonishing concoction of drugs, alcohol, dozens of shredded phone books and newspapers as the two young men purposefully spiralled out of control in their expensive act of bonding and nesting. It may seem that the activity is more closely aligned with rock stars throwing televisions out of windows than it is with performance and installation art, but they would later stage another Hamster Nest at Deitch Projects in New York. Snow took the installation even further by inviting a homeless person to live in the gallery for the duration, a provocative gesture from someone who rejected the enormous wealth and cultural privilege he was born with. The act of transference from hotel suite to one of New York's most important, cutting-edge galleries diluted the recklessness and intensified the concept of ritualized bonding and gave a more recognizable artworld form to their pursuit of total freedom and an insistence on being irresponsible in a heavily burdened era.

The work Snow made in his short career may have appeared throwaway, because he was serious about not being taken seriously. He did not seek approval, praise or acceptance, he was a throwback, a self-styled outsider who was uncomfortable in an era when selling art was no longer seen as selling out. Snow's work was both an expression, and extension of, his own lifestyle of resistance, populated by other kindred spirits, but often referring to a larger world outside the one they made for themselves. Many works, for example, show an obsession with Saddam Hussein. In *Untitled (Saddam Dick)* of 2007, Snow presents a carefully staged image of the splayed legs of a naked man alongside a real human skull and a cut-out picture of the dictator's face, closely positioned to the flaccid penis. More than ten years on, the juvenile aspect of the work's creation has faded to allow the anti-authoritarian attitude to speak volumes about distrust of power systems.

It is perhaps not the content of Snow's work that would make the inner sanctum of the art world twitch, so much as the context. He worked hard to unravel his life so not a thread of privilege remained, but it has been said that this privilege was never forgotten by the New York art scene.

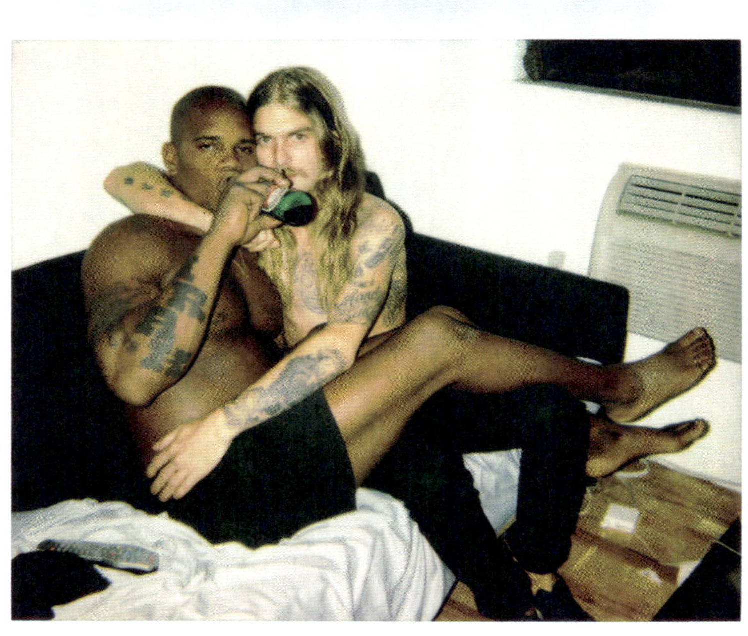

Untitled (Polaroid #141)
Dash Snow (1981–2009)
2003, digital c-print from Polaroid,
50.8 cm × 50.8 cm (20 × 20 in),
courtesy of the Dash Snow Archive,
New York, USA, and Morán Morán

His background was impossible to ignore, his grandmother was Christophe de Menil, heir to the Menil's staggering old-money fortune and one of the greatest American art patrons of all time. Snow grew up around Cy Twombly and Robert Rauschenberg paintings, his family own the iconic Rothko Chapel in Houston. He hailed from American royalty, his aunt was the actor Uma Thurman and to commentators he was a fallen prince. A high-school drop-out who spent time in correction centres as a teenager, he found his way into countercultural circles by way of graffiti. Like Basquiat before him, he was never at ease in the art world. Despite his nihilism, he had a creative compulsion to construct and document his world. He did this not necessarily to understand it, and not even as a catharsis, but more to extend the energy of the moment into something that might capture its power. Unlike Basquiat, he did not live to see his work fetishized by collectors and sold for unprecedented sums. His death in July 2009 came after various attempts to sober up and, sadly, he left behind a young daughter, a fiancé and an ex-wife.

Although, as is the case with so many artists in this selection, it is difficult to disassociate from Snow's biography, his work manages to convey the artist's distinct point of view: his energy, otherness and uncommodified rebel spirit. When we consider his output and perspective from today's highly commercial art world, he represents an extinct breed, not to mention someone who saw our dependence on digital technology coming. There is something prescient about the manner in which he obsessively raked through the detritus of his life, presenting not Warhol's glamour or Duchamp's irony but, instead, a candid, confessional look that is today's Instagram parlance. Snow worked hard to make something out of nothing, to capture a fleeting moment of unrestrained, nihilistic freedom most of us will probably never have the bacchanalian instinct to experience for ourselves.

Two

The Mythology of Death

By the end of the nineteenth century, as part of a wider proclivity for sentimentality, the artist became a figure in society who was romanticized and mythologized. The role had morphed from unknown craftsman in the medieval world, to individualized genius in the Renaissance, to academic master in the eighteenth century. In the industrialized age, the image of the artist began to stand outside of the realm of the rational and 'normal' sphere of activity. Not every artist would attain such a status and, more often than not, they were most likely to do so having attracted only controversy or disdain in their poverty-stricken lifetime and then unknowingly garnered a staggering veneration following their early death.

More than any other artist, Vincent van Gogh has become the poster boy for the myth of the tormented artist and his death inextricably linked to his fame and legacy. He is the leader of this next mythical group of artists who have become legendary since their early demise, and more specifically, have had their work interpreted a certain way because of the nature of their death. Van Gogh is probably the world's most famous and beloved artist and yet he sold almost nothing in his lifetime and worked between bouts of mental illness. His self-mutilation, better known as cutting off his ear, has become a widely shared piece of cultural information even for those who know little about his work. Van Gogh's unstable condition, combined with his (perceived) failure in his lifetime, set the stage for his Goliath mythology: the prodigious misunderstood genius who could face the world no longer and took his own life aged just thirty-seven. As we will see, once an artist's legacy enters into this territory it is very hard to untangle the myth that their death may create.

Three decades after Van Gogh died, the Parisian art world would anoint another young painter as a legendary figure upon his death. Amadeo Modigliani's mythology has no doubt fuelled the flames of his extraordinary popularity today. Considered a reckless bohemian, addicted to drugs and alcohol, who died of tuberculosis before fame found him, he is the artist who left behind a pregnant girlfriend who took her own life shortly after her lover's funeral. Today these grisly events make Modigliani a kind of art historical martyr. His artworks sell for astronomical sums, and there is a major market in forgeries of his work and, like Van Gogh, the reading of his oeuvre is often skewed with the events of his life.

Nine decades after the suicide of Van Gogh, Francesca Woodman also took her own life in New York. Her beguiling photographic work demonstrates a preoccupation with disrupting the wholeness of the female figure (often her own) through blurring and conjuring spectral-like visions. As a very young woman Woodman jumped from a building to end her own life, and it has been difficult for commentators to resist seeing a prefiguration of her death in her work. I have tried to untangle this mythology to get a clearer sense of an artist who defies any easy categorization.

The circumstances of the death of Ana Mendieta have also coloured interpretations of her work. Four years after Woodman, she too fell from a New York building, but the circumstances surrounding her death are more mysterious and uncertain. As an artist who is known for using the imprint of her own body in her practice, there is also an interpretation that sees a strange prefiguration, or echo, before the fact of her early demise in the work she leaves behind. As with Woodman's, I have approached Mendieta's story to reveal her pioneering body of work as separate from the tragic circumstances of her death.

Not long after the deaths of Woodman and Mendieta, New York lost another important talent when Félix González-Torres died of AIDS-related complications in 1996. Keith Haring and Robert Mapplethorpe are also included in this book and these three artists are among the hundreds of thousands who died in the epidemic. Although González-Torres made work that was more specifically related to socio-political concerns than that of Woodman and Mendieta, we should proceed with caution when approaching his legacy solely through the prism of the disease that killed him and many of his friends. While all three deserve their iconic status, it is the mythologizing after the fact of their deaths that I am keen to investigate and unravel.

It is interesting to look at how mythologies were explicitly invented and propagated historically. Raphael is perhaps the best example of this. After his death in the sixteenth century, the eminent Renaissance biographer Giorgio Vasari cemented Raphael's reputation as a man who sought beauty and sensuality in everything he did, going so far as to report that Raphael died of a sex-induced fever. Naturally, centuries later, scholars have cast aside this juicy morsel and viewed Raphael's canon through an academic lens, but it is fascinating to see how Vasari's myth persisted and may even have helped secure Raphael's ongoing importance in modern art.

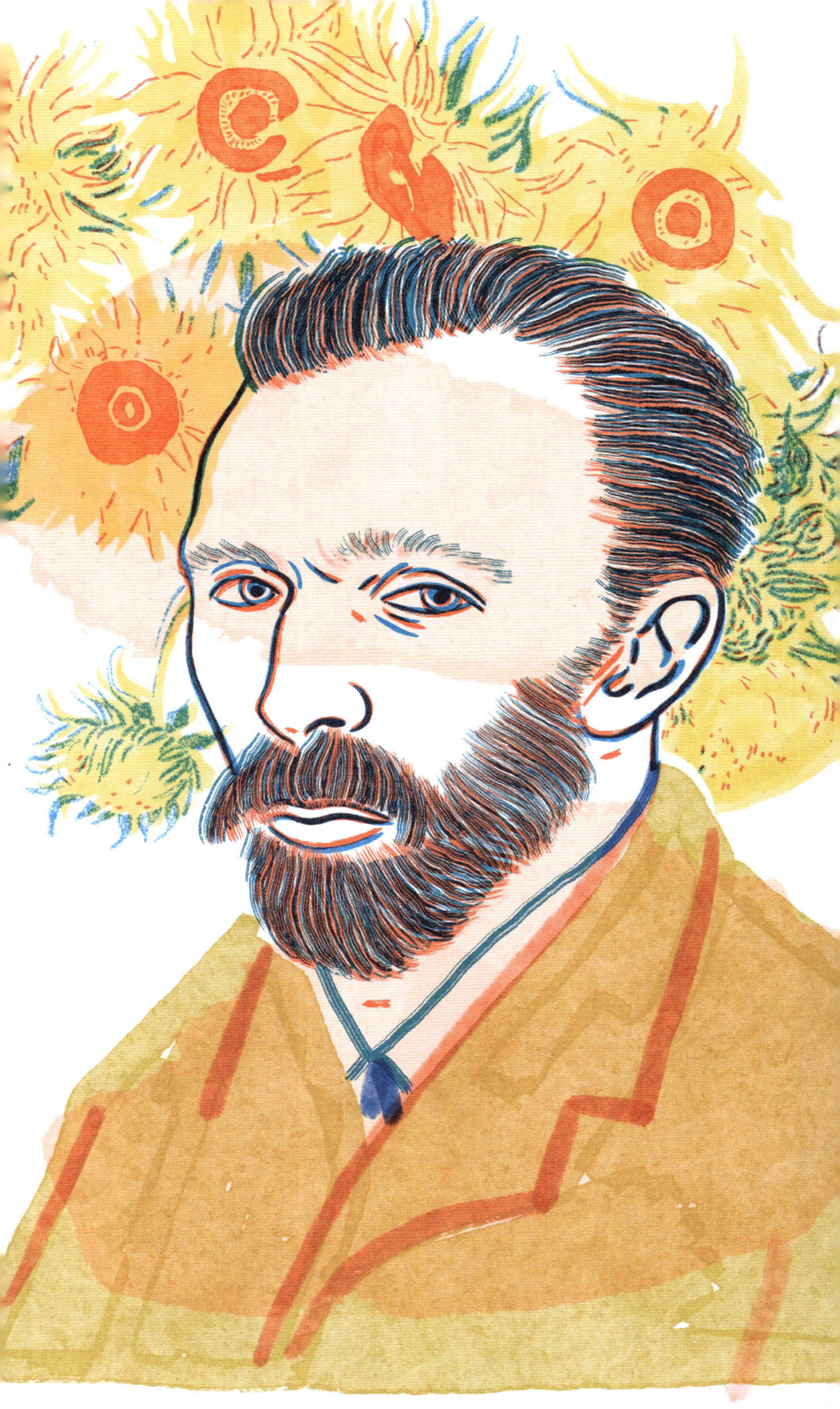

Vincent
van Gogh
1853–1890

Misunderstood Titan

n 1957 Kirk Douglas played Vincent van Gogh in the American film *Lust for Life,* based on the best-selling biographical novel by Irving Stone. The final scene sees Douglas's Van Gogh angrily painting what was then thought to be his last canvas, *Wheatfield with Crows.* Terrifying discordant music accompanies a fraught artist beleaguered by overhead crows, distressed with his art and retreating behind a tree to write a suicide note that reads, 'I am desperate, I can foresee absolutely nothing, I see no way out'. The music stops dead, only crowing can be heard until the camera pans away and a bone-chilling gunshot rings out across the wheatfields. The film won an Oscar, a Golden Globe and played for a record thirty-seven weeks at the Plaza Theatre in New York. Characterizing the protagonist as a madman, unknown, unsuccessful and despairing of his artistic abilities, Hollywood successfully helped to birth the modern mythology of Van Gogh as the ultimate tortured artist.

It will come as no surprise that this version of events, which influenced decades of similar portrayals on stage and on television, was reductive and overlooked the real artist's achievements and intelligence. Although he suffered from serious mental health issues, Van Gogh was not an outsider artist. He was well versed in art history and as a young man over a period of seven years he worked for his uncle's art dealership in The Hague and London. Born in the Netherlands in 1853, he was multilingual: he wrote and spoke fluent French; was proficient in speaking, writing and reading English and was able to read German. He was extremely well read: his letters record some eight hundred literary sources with a special focus for Charles Dickens, who he mentions more than any other writer. Van

"I use colour more arbitrarily in order to express myself forcibly..."

Gogh admired Dickens for his empathetic attitude to those on the margins of Victorian society as he, too, was a keen humanitarian. His letters to fellow artists as well as to his closest confidant, his art dealer brother Theo, frequently include intellectual, rational and insightful commentary, especially on the act of painting. Van Gogh was a sensitive soul but had a sharp mind with serious aspirations for his artistic career.

Van Gogh came to art comparatively late, aged twenty-seven. Despite this, in one decade he produced nine hundred paintings and over a thousand drawings (we might compare this to the modest output of other artists in this book, such as Johannes Vermeer and Caravaggio, by whom we have less than fifty paintings). Across ten years, Van Gogh committed himself to constantly pushing forward, improving, learning, remaking and advancing what his art could be. His art is characterized by expressive qualities that give each painting a charged energy as he best attempts to convey the very nature of things. 'Instead of trying to reproduce exactly what I have before my eyes, I use colour more arbitrarily in order to express myself forcibly... to exaggerate the essential and to leave the obvious vague.' Van Gogh set the stage for modern art that values and creates space for the artist's particular account of the world. Rather than the pursuit of an academic realism (as was the case in the nineteenth century) or a mission to disrupt on solely formal terms (as with the Impressionists), Van Gogh was radical in his vision that art should connect psychologically and convey an emotive force, whether describing a face, a field or a flower.

The intensity of his work, so full of feeling, combined with the knowledge that Van Gogh suffered from mental illness and tragically took his own life, seems to render his reputation helpless in the face of the 'mad genius' label. The ancient Greek philosopher Aristotle set the stage for this reading of Van Gogh with his assertion that 'No great mind has ever existed without a touch of madness.' As harmless as Aristotle may have intended this to be, the notion of the tortured genius is dangerous and denies us a privileged and far more useful perspective in our contemporary culture. In contrast to the portrayal by Kirk Douglas, Van Gogh did not produce his work in a frenzy of madness, his painting was not a physical manifestation of an unravelling mind. Rather, he painted between bouts of illness. Art was his salvation, a reason for him to get better and fight for his sanity. He was not a genius because of his instability, but in spite of it.

Although it is true that Van Gogh did not sell his art in his lifetime (with the exception of one canvas), he was not without admirers. He had famously dreamt of creating an artistic commune and invited the artist Paul Gauguin to join him at The Yellow House in Arles. Although it would end disastrously with the self-mutilation of his ear, there was a brief period when the two men invigorated each other's practice. Van Gogh was a restless person and spent the last two years of his life – by far his most productive – mostly cared for in an asylum at San Remy. Despite this, he was a known figure in avant-garde circles, as testified to by his funeral, held the day after his death on 30 July 1890, where half of the gathered mourners in Auvers-sur-Oise were fellow artists. Upon hearing he had shot himself aged just thirty-seven, letters of condolence arrived from eminent artists such as Henri de Toulouse-Lautrec and Claude Monet. The latter wrote to Theo van Gogh that he was 'greatly affected by your terrible loss'. Camille Pissarro regretted not being able to attend the funeral with his son Lucien, also an artist, and remarked that Vincent's death would be 'deeply felt among the younger generation'.

Theo wrote to their grieving mother shortly after, lamenting that 'if he could have seen how people behaved toward me when he had left us and the sympathy of so many for himself, he would at this moment not have wanted to die'. Compounding the family's loss, Theo died six months after his older brother from syphilis, leaving behind his wife, Jo Bonger, and their one-year-old son, also called Vincent. Although Theo had tried to organize an exhibition of his brother's work before his untimely death, the gallerist Paul Durand-Ruel (renowned for his dealings with the Impressionist market) had backtracked with concerns that the work would not sell. The fact that such a respected gallerist initially agreed is a signifier that these were works with a recognized talent, even if they lacked an existing market. Instead, Theo showed the paintings in his Parisian home to friends and acquaintances. It was the artist Émile Bernard, a good friend of Van Gogh's, who staged the first public exhibition of Van Gogh's work in Paris two years after his death in April 1892. Interestingly, Bernard recounted Paul Gauguin's anger towards the one man show, 'He wrote to me saying that it was not good politics to exhibit the works of a madman and that I was going to jeopardize everything through such a thoughtless act, for him, myself and our friends.' Gauguin, nervous about having his own yet-to-be-fully-understood work tainted by association, was increasingly called upon to discuss his experiences with Van Gogh as word grew around the

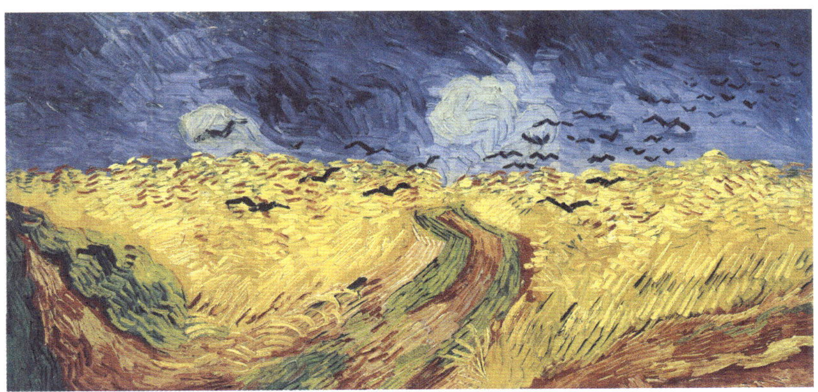

Wheatfields with Crows
Vincent van Gogh (1853–1890)
1890, oil on canvas,
50.5 × 103 cm (20 ×40 ½ in),
Van Gogh Museum, Amsterdam (Vincent
van Gogh Foundation), the Netherlands

late artist. Gauguin was always broke and, in 1895, keen to finance a return trip to Tahiti, he would sell the two sunflower paintings given to him by his friend. Through a dealer they ended up in the possession of Edgar Degas, then in his sixties and a keen collector of great modern artists such as Paul Cezanne as well as a modern master himself.

Less than a decade after Van Gogh's death, there was a small but healthy market among the Parisian avant-garde for his works. But his reputation may have abated, and indeed his large oeuvre been carelessly dispersed or even destroyed, if it were not for a crucial (but woefully under-recognized) person in the making of the legend of Van Gogh, his sister-in-law Jo Bonger. After her husband Theo's death, Jo couldn't face returning to Paris and had her possessions sent to her in Holland. They included the enormous number of artworks that had filled every available space of her small home; as she recounted 'to the great despair of our maid, there were under the bed, under the sofa, under the cupboards in the little spare room, huge piles of unframed canvasses'. Jo's brother began to compile an inventory and advised her simply to dispose of the work to release herself of the burden of dealing with things that had no financial worth. Instead, Jo dedicated her life to championing Van Gogh's paintings and made extremely astute decisions to ensure his work received the attention she felt it deserved.

Jo moved to Bussum in the Netherlands because it was a respected artistic centre, and by 1900 she had organized more than twenty exhibitions for Van Gogh's work and loaned key paintings like the *Sunflowers* regularly. As early as 1892 she wrote in her diary that 'people are beginning to be very interested in the work of Vincent, and there's hardly a newspaper that doesn't say something about him'. She was ambitious to create an international market for the work and offered dealers in various European cities healthy sales commission to encourage them to place the artworks. In 1905 she organized the largest-ever exhibition of Van Gogh's art, a ground-breaking exhibition of five hundred pieces at Amsterdam's Stedelijk Museum. In her lifetime, she sold nearly two hundred paintings and over fifty drawings. Her most significant act in managing Van Gogh's estate was to sell *Sunflowers* to London's National Gallery in 1924. Although she had been extremely reluctant to part with a treasured family possession, she recognized that 'it is a sacrifice for the glory of Vincent's art'. Jo was also responsible for editing a book of Van Gogh's letters to and from Theo, publishing it in Dutch, English and German. Her biographical introduction served as the most useful text on Van Gogh for many years. By publishing the vast correspondence, full of lucid and fascinating insights into the act of creation, details of individual paintings and the details of his artistic challenges, she was keen that Van Gogh's genius would be fully recognized.

In the decades after Jo's death in 1925, Van Gogh would become arguably the most famous and beloved artist in the world. Through a sensationally popular exhibition in 1947 in London (more than five thousand people per day queued to see the show), his paintings would become symbolic of post-war recovery, beacons of colourful hope in war-torn Europe. His name and his work have seeped into popular consciousness in a way that is exceptionally rare. Alongside Michelangelo's Sistine Chapel, Van Gogh's paintings have become a benchmark of Western culture.

Rather than seeing Van Gogh as a failure then, it is apparent that his intention to make work that resonated with 'ordinary people' and that might act as some form of salvation and escape were fully realized. Thanks to the relentless work of Jo Bonger, his work was in a position to resonate globally, across generations and become a touchstone for generations of artists who followed through the emotive door that he opened. To view his artwork through the prism of his death and mental illness is to fundamentally misconceive its power. Hollywood created an undignified portrait of a self-destructive talent, a madman who became an art historical martyr. The reality is that in the twenty-first century, in a climate thankfully more sensitive and understanding of the nuances of mental health conditions, we deserve to reappraise Van Gogh. We should save him from a myth that has become a parody and champion him as an inspirational figure who made a lifetime of masterpieces in ten profoundly important years.

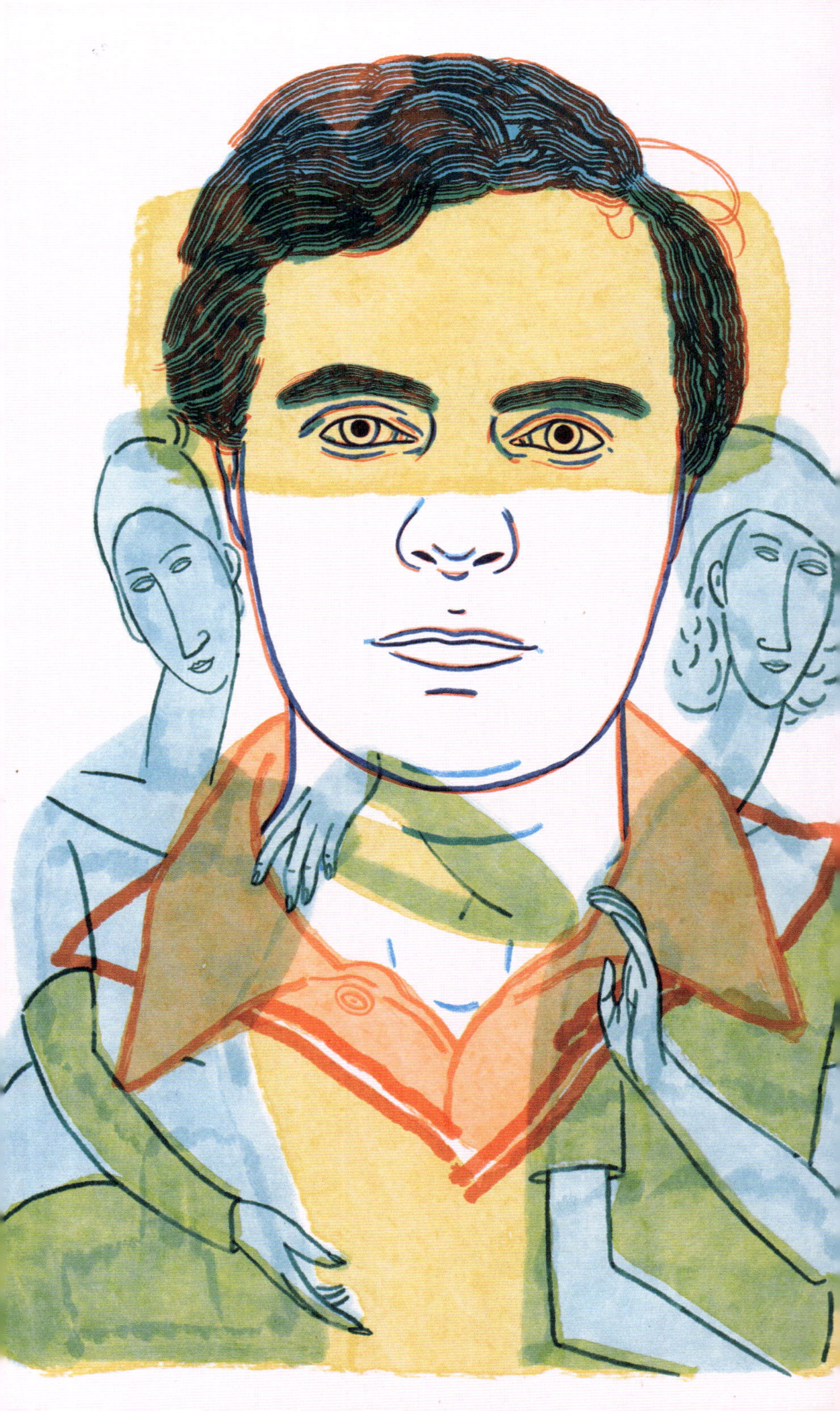

Amedeo Modigliani
1884–1920

'Reckless' Bohemian

The life and death of Amedeo Modigliani has a distinctly mythical quality. For a century his name has stood for a particular kind of reckless bohemianism; live fast and die young. He is thought of as one of art history's ultimate starving artists who did not live to see his work sell for astronomical sums. We imagine him in the typical artist's garret furiously painting his sensual, other-worldly and distinctly modern nudes with no audience, subsisting on alcohol, drugs and scraps of food. Images like this fuel our sentimental love for the underdog, neglected in his lifetime and celebrated after his death. Since the last decades of the twentieth century, Modigliani's fame and the allure of his art have entered a new dazzling realm, culminating in an era where his work sells for more than one hundred million pounds, redefining what an expensive picture costs.

The provocative martyr myth no doubt fuels the flames of his forceful auction record, but the reality of Modigliani's life is quite different from the legend. Although he was never financially comfortable, he did sell work and enjoyed a fair degree of market success. Modigliani was not overlooked: he had a solo exhibition of his work in his lifetime in Paris, as well as showing work in exhibitions in New York and London. He received excellent press from some of the day's most important critics and his work was accepted in the prestigious Salon d'Automne. He benefitted from two devoted art dealers as well as securing serious patrons early in his career. He dressed like a Bourgeoisie gentleman, Jean Cocteau describing him as 'our aristocrat'. Although he was an émigré from Italy, he was not an outsider in France. He became fluent in French and his circle was populated by well-known artists and poets of the era. He was literary even by the bookish standards of the day and a keen poetry scholar.

Modigliani was an adept social creature, very popular among the creative souls of Montmartre and later Montparnasse, but he retained a fierce independence when it came to his style of art. Although he was at the heart of an extraordinary artistic milieu in Paris, unlike most of his peers he did not align himself with any artistic movements – such as Cubism, which flourished soon after he arrived from Livorno in 1906. Like Picasso and several other Modernists, Modigliani was struck by the contemporary obsession for non-Western art. But he uniquely synthesized this interest with many other stylistic sources from art history, which he had been drinking in since he was a child in Italy. His signature elongated necks, oval faces and almond eyes are a blend of sources including the Mannerist artist Parmigianino and the Renaissance master Botticelli, as well as art that would have come from the French colonies in Africa and Cambodia.

Originally a sculptor who was taken under Constantin Brancusi's wing, Modigliani eventually gave up three dimensions to focus on painting in 1914, most likely as a result of the dust aggravating his weak lungs. Modigliani was well known in his lifetime for being a big drinker, so much so that it has become part of his legend that defines him as a reckless genius. But his primary weakness was the tuberculosis that he contracted aged sixteen after already fighting near-fatal pleurisy and typhoid. It has even been suggested that his substance abuse was not only a result of self-medicating his condition but was more than that. Perhaps Modigliani played the drunken fool to disguise his disease since alcoholism was more socially acceptable than tuberculosis, a diagnosis that he kept extremely private.

Modigliani benefitted from a mature and multi-faceted Parisian art scene that had been fast developing since the Impressionists had broken with the long-dominant conservative academic mould in the 1880s. Modigliani was not alone in his garret; Paris was his stage and he was starting to shine. In 1914 he met Paul Guillaume, a precocious young art dealer who, by the age of twenty-two, had already opened his own gallery. The dealer was seven years his junior, had an exceptional eye for talent and would champion his new find, securing inclusion in a group show in New York for his paintings in 1916. That same year, Modigliani met another man who would help secure his position as an established artist. Léopold Zborowski was a Polish poet and would become his main dealer. Zborowski maintained a good business relationship with Guillaume, the two men often traded Modigliani's work and both advocated on his behalf. His new dealer elevated Modigliani's creative output by giving the artist a stipend of fifteen francs per day and paying his models five francs per sitting. He also secured Modigliani's first solo exhibition at Galerie Berthe Weill in 1917. The show, which featured several nudes, has become notorious for being investigated by police on the grounds of indecency. Although nudes had been a mainstay of art history from the classical world to the Renaissance through to Édouard Manet, what made Modigliani's nudes so confronting was the inclusion of pubic and underarm hair. The offending paintings were forcibly removed though, as the legend tells it, the exhibition was not closed. In fact the infamy probably helped drive increased visitors and two drawings were sold.

Zborowski likely saved Modigliani's life by having a physician insist that he leave the city for the south of France in the final months of the war. He left with his common-law wife, Jeanne Hébuterne who bore him a daughter, also called Jeanne. The Midi was prescribed as a retreat for his worsening health, though in actuality the damp air did not help his lungs, but the temporary relocation did remove him from the German shelling of Paris at the time. It was in the south of France that Modigliani, while trying to moderate his drinking, took his painting to another level. It was an exceptionally fertile period that saw him produce over sixty

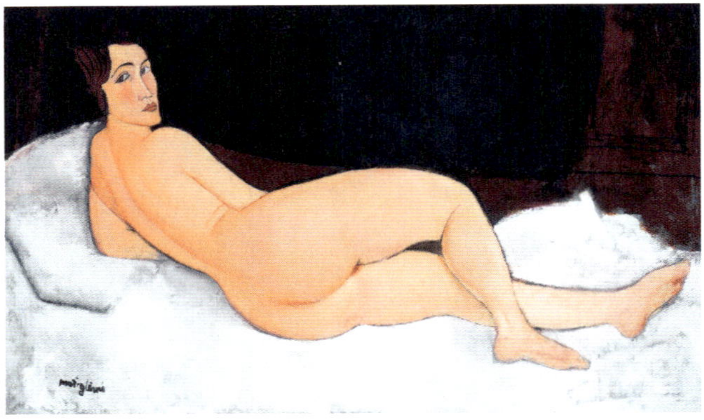

Resting Nude (On the Left Side)
Amedeo Modigliani (1884–1920)
1917, oil on canvas,
90.5 × 146.4 cm (35 ½ × 57 ½ in),
private collection

oil paintings in fourteen months. His work began to show a greater engagement with the natural world and empathy with his sitters who were mostly ordinary people, in contrast to his paintings of those in his inner circle who he tended to portray in a more stylized, detached manner that recalls masks.

Modigliani returned to Paris in spring 1919, eager to re-immerse himself in the art world having recently sold work at Paul Guillaume's gallery. The works he made upon his return are some of his greatest portraits: dignified, elegant, sinuous, sensual and full of conviction. In August his confidence and financial security peaked when his work was included in a major exhibition in London. His paintings received praise from the leading critic Roger Fry and another critic astutely wrote that his paintings bear 'a suspicious resemblance to masterpieces'. Modigliani's health prevented him from travelling to the exhibition, but he kept his newspaper clippings in his pocket and boasted that the huge exhibition of modern French art included more of his works than any other artist, even Picasso.

As his career was surging, his health was declining. His teeth had started to fall out and eventually the tuberculosis would cause meningitis. Jeanne Héburterne seemed powerless to act, respecting his wishes to avoid doctors despite his evident decline. By the time a neighbour intervened and took him to hospital, it was too late. He died on 24 January 1920 aged thirty-five and was buried in the Père Lachaise Cemetery, a mark of respect for a man of good standing. The artist Jacques Lipchitz recalled his funeral: 'I will never forget Modigliani's funeral. So many friends, so many flowers, the sidewalks crowded with people bowing their heads in grief and respect. Everyone felt deeply that we had lost something precious, something very essential.' The day after the service Jeanne committed suicide, jumping out of the fifth-floor window of her disapproving parents' home. She was eight months pregnant.

The circumstances of his death and the tragedy of Jeanne's suicide quickly fuelled the myth of the desperate artist only appreciated after his passing. This took a matter of months rather than years and the interest in his work was quick to follow, with prices for his work quickly doubling. Such was his popularity that his market was soon victim to forgeries and today he is widely regarded as one of the most faked artists in history with a possible one thousand forgeries yet to be seized. Modigliani has left an indelible mark in art history and yet he was only painting for six years between 1914 and 1920. His works resonate because they are distinctive: no one presents the human form quite like him. His nudes are thoroughly modern looking while also being in dialogue with the old masters. In a sense his work is more of a continuation of the art of the past than an abrupt redirection like many other Modernists. His friends and colleagues knew him to be erudite, educated, social, charming, gifted, ambitious and dedicated. They saw his career develop and begin to take off in a meaningful way. Very few would have known he was ill and fewer still could have imagined that his career would come to be defined not just by the facts of his life but by the prices achieved decades later for the mythologized artist's work.

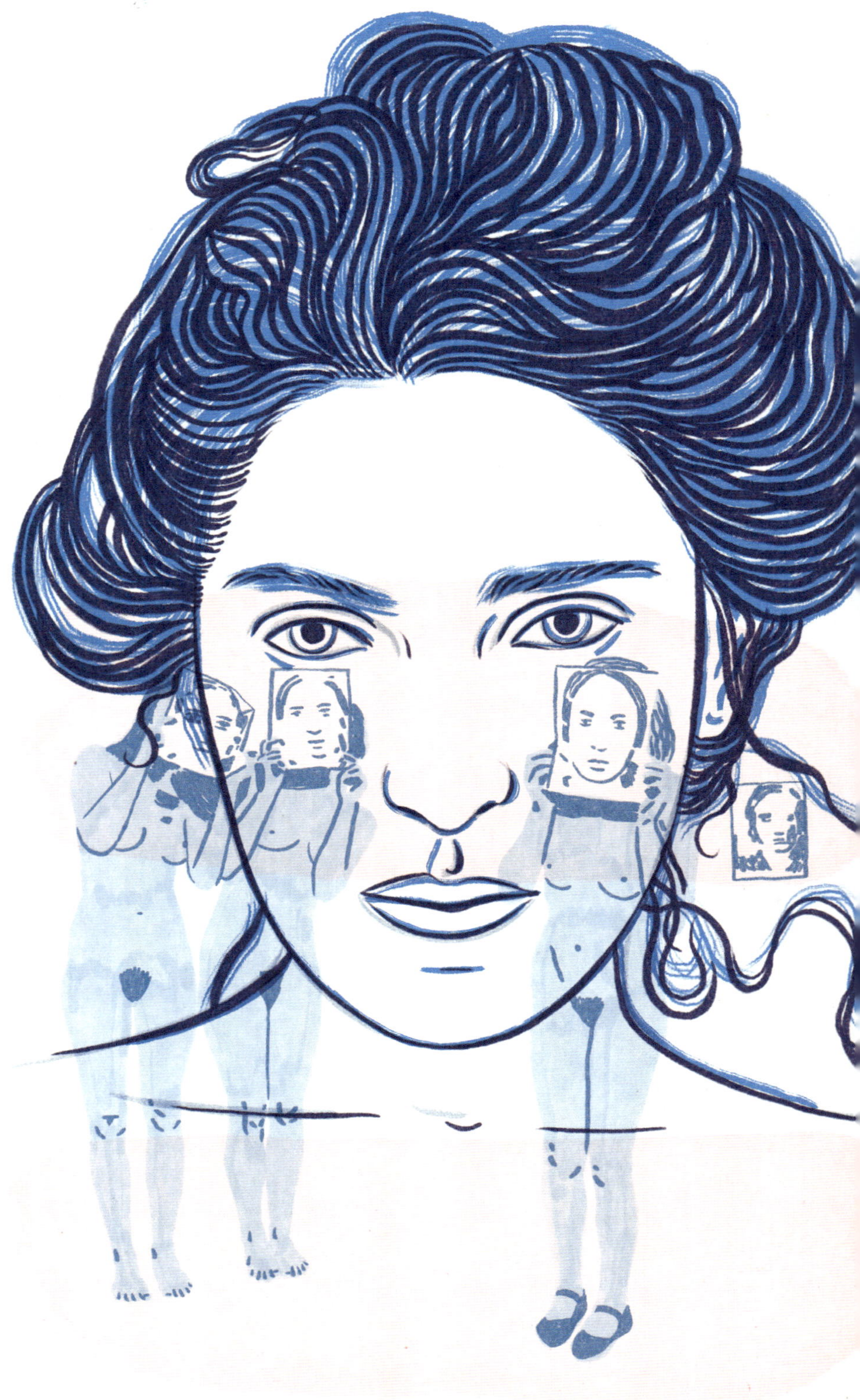

Francesca Woodman
1958–1981

Spectral Prodigy

Considered a child prodigy, Francesca Woodman is a rarity in art history for being widely fêted as an uncannily gifted photographer from her early teenage years. Artist child prodigies are rarely celebrated, unlike in the arenas of sport, science or maths where the phenomenon is more easily recognized and established. An artist may be *technically* gifted in painting or photography at a young age but to have a unique point of view, a sophisticated grasp of psychology and to be conversant with historical references is so rare as to make Francesca Woodman almost singular. Despite being widely celebrated with an almost cult-like status, it is not straightforward to pinpoint exactly who Woodman was as an artist. Her professional career has been entirely posthumous; everything exhibited today was created while she was still a student. The facts surrounding her death also have a strong tendency to overshadow her art, infusing the imagery she created with the knowledge that she took her own life by leaping from a building aged just twenty-two.

Woodman's work was almost all black and white and focused mainly on the relationship between a figure, most often her own nude body, with its surroundings. Her work creates a fluid boundary between the human form and the dilapidated, worn rooms it is placed in. The wholeness of the figure is always displaced through being obscured with an object such as a doorframe or mirror, blurred in movement, or blending into the background wallpaper.

One of Woodman's most iconic bodies of work is Angel Series, created during a year studying abroad in Rome from 1977 to 1978. Woodman employed long single exposures and movement to blur bodies so that they appear as spectral figures. It has been difficult to resist viewing her black-and-white photographs with ghostly apparitions as a prefiguration of the young woman herself. As a consequence of making so many works that centre on dissolving the parameters of the figure, most often her own, Woodman's output has been psychoanalysed after the fact. For decades viewers have searched her artwork for signs of her mental state and clues as to the tragic decision to end her own life.

Woodman's work has also been subject to a lengthy feminist appraisal. This largely stems from the interpretation given by Rosalind Krauss, an American critic who posited that the photographs pointedly resist the male gaze. Krauss saw the work at a modest exhibition at Wellesley College five years after Woodman's death, and it was her critique and sustained interest in Woodman's work that was largely responsible for delivering her art to a wider audience after her death. Interest grew, and by 2011 the Museum of Modern Art San Francisco had organized a solo exhibition of Woodman's work; major international exhibitions have followed, including shows at the Guggenheim New York and Tate Liverpool.

Much of Woodman's posthumous appraisal has been informed by both the circumstances of her death and the strong feminist critique already mentioned. In more recent years, Woodman's parents, both artists themselves, have attempted to redress the balance and undo the mythologization, as they see it, of their daughter's practice. They are keen to emphasize her irony, wit, humour and youthful appreciation of the absurd and surreal. They refute that she had any feminist message, although Woodman's closest friends at the Rhode Island School of Design where she studied between 1975 and 1978 maintain that while they mocked some aspects of the women's movement, they were feminist. Clearly Woodman demonstrates a preoccupation with the human form in her practice and went to great lengths to disrupt its presence, solidity and representation. However, although she most often employed the nude female, her work does not focus on the grand narrative of the female experience. It feels very personal, exploratory, more abstract and ephemeral than that. If we leave feminist theories to one side, we could instead interpret them as formal exercises by an artist who was interested in the capacity of a photograph to bend reality and deliver complex imagery.

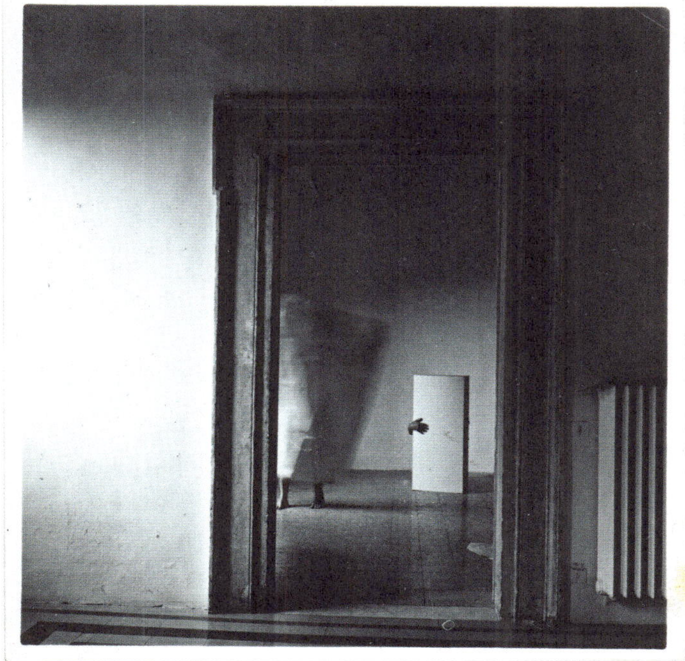

Untitled, from Angel Series, Rome, Italy
Francesca Woodman (1958–1981)
1977, photograph, gelatin silver print on paper,
93 × 93 cm (36 $^{61}/_{100}$ × 36 $^{61}/_{100}$ in),
Tate and National Galleries of Scotland, UK

Woodman employed various props and motifs in her work and seems to have been drawn especially to objects favoured by the Surrealists, such as mirrors, gloves, birds and bowls. Like Man Ray before her, Woodman saw the potential of the camera to deliver an altered, even elevated reality. The photograph could allow the body to be more strange, more unexpected than a painting because of the supposed verisimilitude that a camera offers. During the year she was in Rome, Woodman frequented a bookshop that specialized in Surrealism, Libreria Maldoror. This would

"I would rather die young leaving various accomplishments intact"

later become the site of the first small showing of her work. There may be a debt to the Surrealists, but Woodman has earned her place in the tradition of great Modernist photographers by pushing the conversation forward. In her last journal entry, she wrote eloquently of her capacity for invention: 'This is why I was an artist... I was inventing a language for people to see the everyday things that I also see... and show them something different...'

Woodman died before she was able to gain a footing in the art world. From a cultured family with both parents working as practising artists in Manhattan (her father's work was due to be unveiled at a group show at the Guggenheim the week she committed suicide), she was well versed in the steps an aspiring young artist should take. She had sent her work to various magazines and, to no avail, applied for a grant. Letters and journals reveal that Woodman valued her work and wanted it to live on without erasure. 'My life at this point is like very old coffee-cup sediment and I would rather die young leaving various accomplishments, i.e. some work, my friendship with you, some other artefacts intact, instead of pell-mell erasing all of these delicate things.' Depression took hold of her and she first attempted to take her own life in the autumn of 1980. She survived, moved in with her parents and received psychiatric help and medication. It is believed she stopped taking her medication, and during another bout of illness she jumped from a Manhattan roof on 19 January 1981.

Despite dying at only twenty-two, she had wielded a camera on an almost daily basis for over eight years and left behind ten thousand negatives in the estate managed by her parents. Their familiarity with the art world made it easier for them to understand the importance of exhibiting her work after her death, but it did little to help them come to terms with the fact that she was the artistic genius of the family and she left them too soon. Her father George Woodman passed away in 2017 and her mother Betty Woodman, now in her eighties, is custodian of their gifted daughter's work and watches with awe as it travels the world for international museum and commercial exhibitions. Woodman's work is represented by blue chip galleries and as yet only a quarter of what she produced has been exhibited. The appetite for her practice continues to grow. In a digital age of image overload and fake news, the quiet, prepossessing work of Woodman conjures another parallel world to our own where we suspend disbelief and enjoy the reformulation of the familiar, seduced by decay and strange beauty.

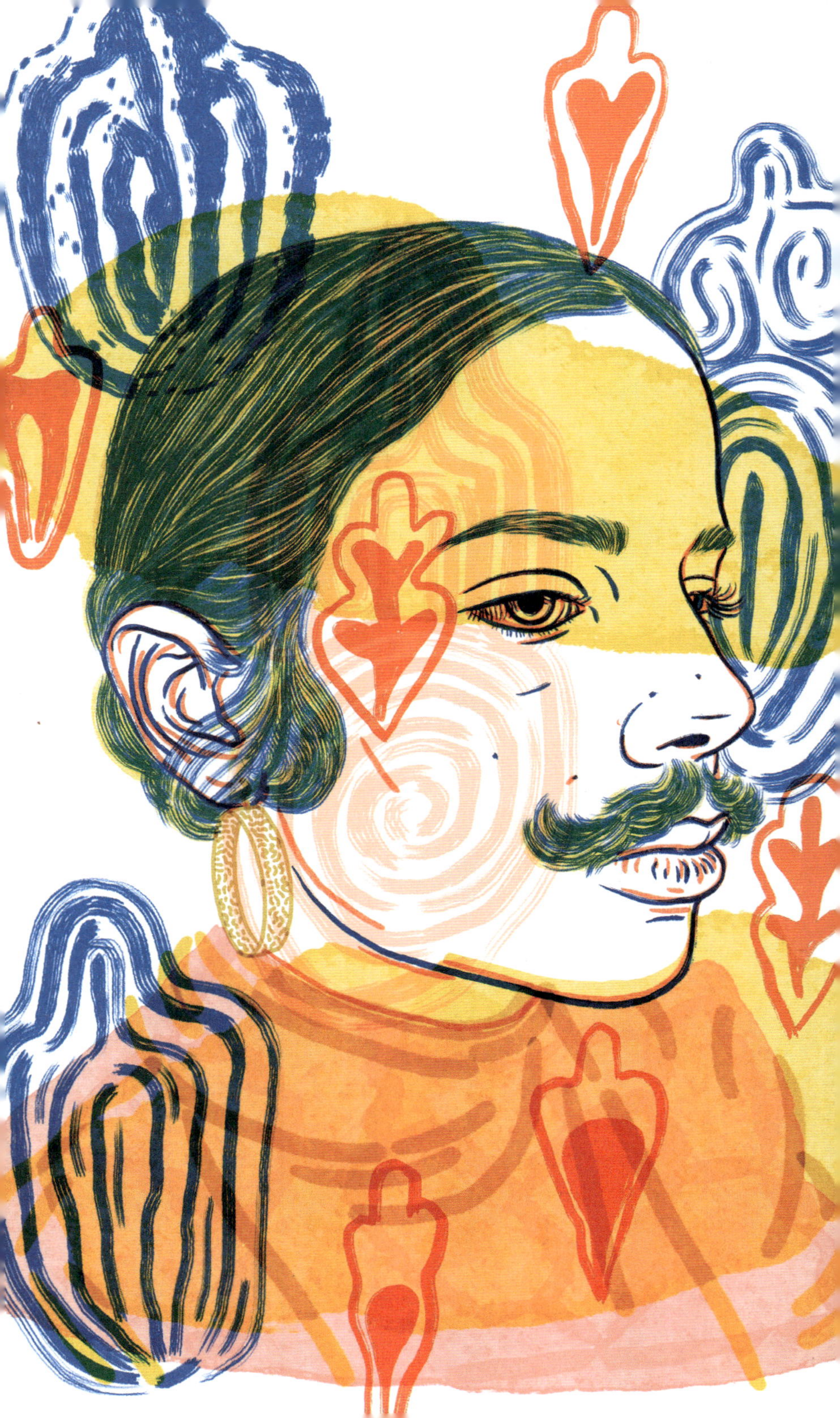

Feminist Pioneer

Ana Mendieta was a pioneer of performance and body art, deftly exploring the boundaries between humanity and the earth in work that transcended her specific circumstances to speak of universal experiences. In her signature Silueta Series she left full body impressions in earth, mud, leaves, fire and flowers, poetically highlighting absence of form. It is difficult to resist seeing a premonition of Ana Mendieta's tragic death in her work. In a cruel turn of events, she plummeted thirty-four storeys from her Manhattan apartment, leaving an imprint on impact. Her dreadful death in 1985, still considered by some as foul play, has been forever entwined with her art in a manner which I believe overshadows her greatness. Mendieta should be widely known and considered as a true pioneer; an artist ahead of the curve who disrupted a male-dominated art world and opened the door for art that unapologetically focused on how to dissolve indifference and unite people.

Mendieta worked predominantly in performance, which she would capture using film and photography. A central preoccupation of her practice was to draw attention to the illusion of separateness and demonstrate the fundamental interconnectivity of all living things. An element of this was her exploration of gender division, marking her out as a key voice in feminist theory. Her work was rigorously experimental; she used her own body and personal background to examine big ideas of absence and presence. Born in Cuba in 1948, Mendieta was only twelve years old when she became a child refugee. She and her sister were sent to America as part of a Catholic operation to secretly take fourteen thousand children out of Fidel Castro's dictatorship. The sisters were separated and endured strict reform schools and countless foster homes. Mendieta would not see her mother for five years and her father for eighteen. As a result of her traumatic childhood, Mendieta was forever between places, an exile from both family and homeland, which gave her a tender and restless spirit. Her exile is a reoccurring theme: Mendieta constantly searches for her body's place in the world and invokes Cuban folk traditions to tether herself metaphorically to 'home'.

As well as interrogating her Cuban identity she also examined her gender. In one image from *Untitled (Facial Hair Transplants)* from 1972, Mendieta presents herself with a convincing, full moustache, created using a friend's beard clippings and glue. The image is not intended to be taken on its own terms; Mendieta documented the whole process to bring the audience into the dialogue about gender constructs and social expectations. Mendieta's work was never explicitly about her own identity or position in isolation, she came to use her body as a metaphor for *every* body. In *Body Tracks* (1982), which has the feeling of a crime scene, the artist created a one-minute Super 8 recording of herself with her back to the viewer, arms stretched above her head in front of a blank wall. As she lowers her arms, a V shape appears as a result of the smearing of her blood-stained hands against the wall. She exits the frame, leaving a gory outline of her disappeared body. In this and other works Mendieta was making enquiries beyond her own self to a wider dialogue about race, displacement, violence and gender among all people. There is a duality at the heart of Mendieta's work between an anxious, fierce energy and a soft, almost Earth Mother-like approach. One performance may utilize flowers or comforting natural materials and the next fire or blood.

The undercurrent of displacement and violence in Mendieta's work has become magnified as part of her posthumous legacy owing to the devastating manner in which she died aged just thirty-six. Mendieta was

"My art is grounded on the belief in one universal energy"

married to the American artist Carl Andre, a leading figure in minimalism. Friends were surprised at their union as they appeared to be almost polar opposites of each other: she was spirited and passionate and made visceral art. Andre, on the other hand, was reserved and more detached, and his practice was clinical. They were known to have a fiery marriage, which often escalated into rows after the couple had been drinking. On 8 September 1985, police were called to their Manhattan apartment, which was in disarray. When questioned, Andre told police Mendieta had 'somehow gone out the window'. A trial followed and many in the New York art world believed that Andre's lawyers were using the kind of emotive work that Mendieta made as a case for suicide to clear Andre's

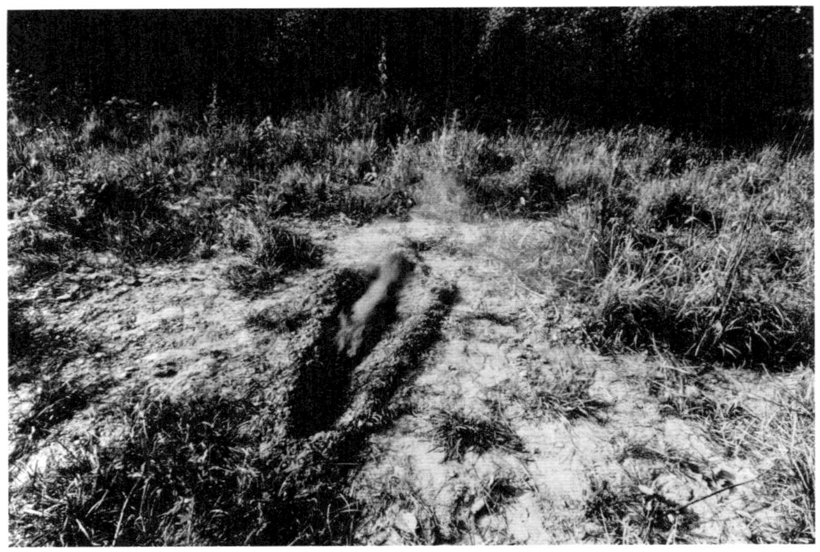

Untitled: Silueta Series
Ana Mendieta (1948–1985)
1978, gelatin silver print,
33.6 × 49.5 cm (13¼ × 19½ in),
The Museum of Modern Art (MoMA),
New York

name. Her friends insisted that suicide was impossible due to her fear of heights and the fact that she was enjoying the first taste of real success in her career. After three years Andre was acquitted due to lack of evidence that he had pushed his wife. Despite the end of the formal legal proceedings more than thirty years ago, the topic has never been fully closed.

Today, a collective known as WHEREISANAMENDIETA still protest outside museums where Andre's work is shown and Mendieta's is absent. The group have taken Mendieta's name to stand for a larger archiving project 'which collects the works from artists who are female, non-binary or people of colour in retaliation to erasure'. Their mission statement and fundamental alignment with Mendieta's name fuels the mythology of the late artist as the patron saint of overlooked and ill-treated women artists. The intention is, of course, extremely worthy and highlights the fact that three decades after Mendieta made important inroads into a male-dominated art world, there is still a great disparity between the success of women artists as compared to men. Thankfully, Mendieta has not been erased from art history. In recent years an intelligent and exhaustive examination of her entire practice has been presented in museums internationally. She has become a touchstone for every subsequent generation of artists who are interested in body politics, performance and earth art. She is certainly a feminist icon, despite her practice having concerns that were much wider than the female experience. Had her time not been cut so drastically short she would now be in her early seventies in the post MeToo era, and no doubt making powerful and emotive work in a divided world grappling with a climate emergency. Thankfully the vitality of her voice stays with us through her ground-breaking art, which serves as an urgent reminder of the interconnectivity and beautiful possibilities available between all living things.

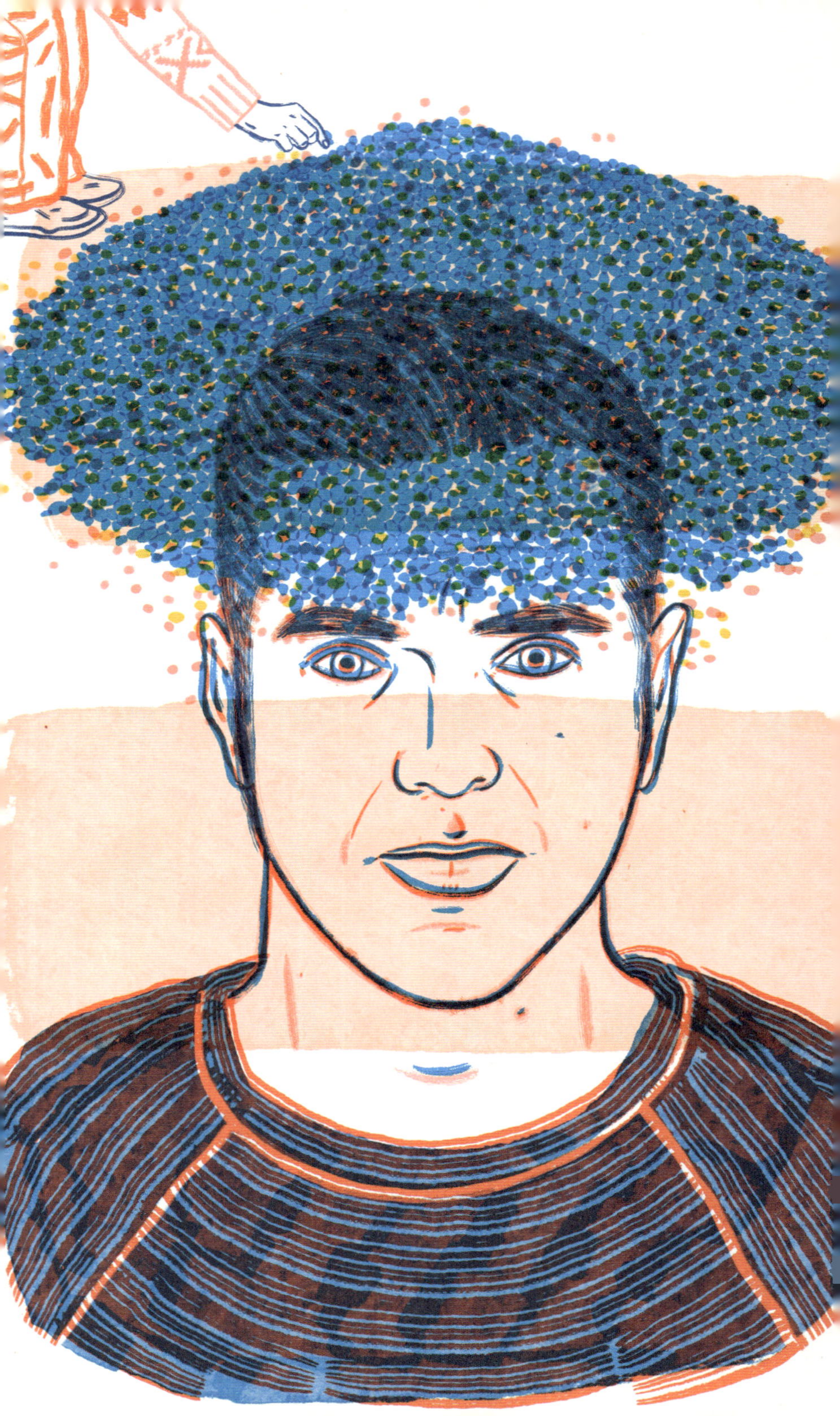

The Personal is Political

The work of Félix González-Torres is unusual for successfully harnessing many dualities. It is both tender and teasing, painful and joyful, solemn and inviting. González-Torres had a gift for softening the hard realities of life in his art so we might bear to consider them. He was by his nature an arts democrat with a gift for teaching and breaking down elitist art world boundaries. His exhibitions dealt with a range of subjects, from poverty to war, from gun violence to sexual desire. Today, the notions of inclusivity and arts activism in contemporary art are so firmly established it is hard to imagine our cultural landscape without them.

González-Torres is one of the forefathers of our inclusive attitude toward art and one of the earliest artists to prize public participation. In New York in 1991, the artist presented a seductive carpet of silver-wrapped sweets directly on a gallery floor. Visitors were invited to take sweets and enjoy them, thereby breaking the most important art world sanction: not to touch the art. Once the offering was consumed by viewers, who were unknowingly becoming participants in the shifting form and meaning of the artwork, the sweets could be replenished. The parallels with the ancient Roman myth of Prometheus (whose liver was eaten daily by an eagle and regenerated at night) raised questions about the essence of art: Where is the original if the ready-made items assembled to create the sculpture are all removed and replaced?

Aged thirty-four, González-Torres was not simply defying gallery conventions and championing the *idea* of art in a Duchampian fashion, he was also forging a droll commentary about the dominant trend for minimalist art. His shiny, monochrome wrappers displayed directly on the floor without a plinth recalled the work of sixties minimalist artists such as Donald Judd and Carl Andre. Their work, which still reigned supreme in the art market, was static, autonomous and emotionless and the younger artist was purposefully subverting these central tennets. His work was instead was participatory, fluctuating and socially engaged. Its political message obscured and revealed only obliquely in the artwork's title. The combined forty thousand sweets (or 'hard candy') were entitled *Untitled (Placebo)*. The title makes reference to the unscrupulous AIDS/HIV drug testing that was taking place at the time and the staggering volume of pills taken by those fighting the disease. The steady consumption of the sweets and the throwing away of the wrappers is a metaphor for a society that ignored the epidemic and especially the plight of gay men.

González-Torres employed a similar strategy to make another conceptual work that dealt with the AIDS crisis the same year. "*Untitled*" *(Portrait of Ross in L.A.)* is an enticing pile of sweets in multicoloured cellophane wrappers. Stacked up in a corner, again the very contents of the artwork could be taken and eaten by the visitors. The meaning and pathos of this work is elevated, somewhat unusually, through its specific mass. At 175 pounds, the sculpture matches the weight of the artist's partner, Ross Laycock at the time of his death from AIDS in January 1991. Looking again with this knowledge, the pert, enticing pile suddenly looks tragic in its unnatural colour, slumped against the wall. This context transforms the festive act of eating free candy in a gallery to a quasi-religious gesture of taking communion from a 'host' body, or

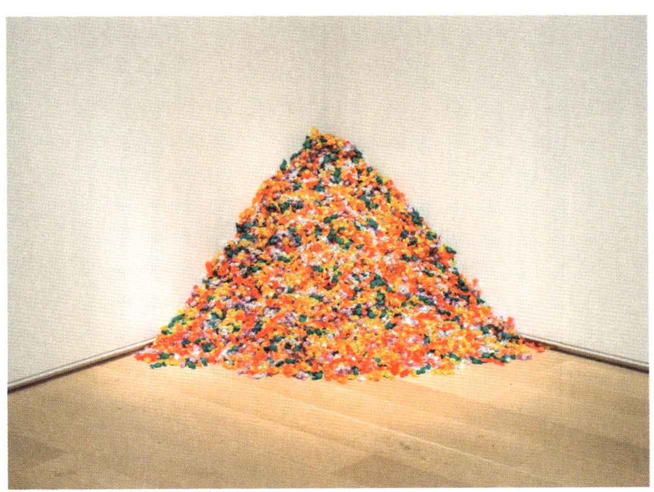

"Untitled" (Portrait of Ross in L.A.)
Félix González-Torres (1957–1996)
1991, candies individually wrapped in
multicoloured cellophane, endless supply,
dimensions vary with installation; ideal
weight 79 kg (175 lbs),
The Art Institute of Chicago, Chicago, USA

even, because the sweet are boiled and therefore need to be sucked, a sexual act. The artist said of this medium, 'You put it in your mouth and you suck on someone else's body, and in this way my work becomes part of so many other people's bodies.'

As conceptual works with multi-faceted meanings, a further veil of poignant significance was added when their creator died five years later due to AIDS. Because of his personal circumstances, and references to them in his practice, it is difficult to view González-Torres's work in a vacuum. The minimalists he parodies remain several steps back from their artwork as people. Despite having an equally serious commitment to form and a sharp eye for presentation, this detachment could never be the case for González-Torres. He belonged to a generation of artists who valued art with a socio-political agenda and considered their identity bound up inextricably with the work they made.

González-Torres was born in Cuba in 1957 and relocated to New York in 1979. He was part of the first generation of artists to make reference to his openly gay status in his practice. However, it is vital that the full complexity of his practice is not subsumed by the facts of his sexuality and death. Such a label would curtail the multi-faceted and far-reaching ideology of his artwork. In his lifetime he was conscious of negating his own biography, he didn't like his portrait being taken, and he used his own story in an oblique fashion that was always as part of a springboard to a wider dialogue. When taken without prejudice on a larger scale, a portrait of the artist's father or life companion who had passed away could also speak more widely of love, family, loss, grief, longing, resurrection and remembrance in the same way as a heterosexual artist tackling the same subject could. In a climate where his contemporaries were making angry or controversial work about the marginalization of queer identity, González-Torres aimed to resist conservative expectations. His work rises above, it elevates the conversation, changes it and turns hate on its head: 'The thing that I want to do sometimes with some of the pieces about homosexual desire is to be more inclusive.'

González-Torres achieved inclusivity not only through his candy offerings, but also by his judicious selection of recognizable, sometimes banal but always magnificently presented ready-made objects. Created in 1994, *Untitled (America)* today hangs as a permanent installation in the stairwell at the Whitney Museum of Modern Art. Comprised of twelve strings of 15-watt lightbulbs, the medium is at once domestic and majestic. The piece can be reconfigured in any way a curator likes and the bulbs, once worn out, will inevitably be replaced. It is shape-shifting, unassumingly resplendent and yet ordinary in its very fabric. The title evokes the artist's (and by extension, everybody's) complex relationship with the United States. González-Torres also harnessed inclusivity by presenting his art outside of the traditional gallery setting using twenty-four billboards across New York in 1992. Appropriated from advertising spaces, the artist presented a black-and-white image of his double bed which has only recently been vacated, the imprints of two bodies still linger on the sheets and pillows. Made following the death of his partner, the sheets are instead a memorial to love and an ode to longing. Like all of the artist's work it works across three levels: unexpected presentation or form; the personal and then the political.

Almost exactly five years after Ross Laycock passed away, González-Torres died in Miami in January 1996 aged thirty-eight. Since his death the fame he enjoyed during his lifetime has been intensified. His work has not only survived a very specific context but moved beyond it to keep delivering new meanings today. His position has been solidified by major international presentations including retrospectives at the Guggenheim, MoMA and Whitney in New York, the Serpentine in London and the Beyeler in Basel to name just a few venues. In 2007, the artist represented the United States at the Venice Biennale, only the second artist after Robert Smithson ever to do so posthumously. Surprisingly, for an artist who defied the notion of a static, and therefore commercially viable work of art, he has also broken new ground in the secondary market. In 2015 a new record was set for his art when one of his candy installations, *"Untitled" (L.A.)*, 1991 sold for $7.7 million.

The year before the artist died, he created one of his final works, *"Untitled" (Golden)*, 1995. Created using strings of glass beads, the artist appropriated a chintzy design feature one might find in fortune teller's living room and transformed it into a resplendent gold curtain. Passing through the large curtain the viewer disrupts the magnificent veil, for a second becoming part of the piece and leaving a ripple of their presence behind. It feels as if the shimmering, vivacious beads are an extension of the artist, here he is in his resurrection drapery of choice, with every visitor ensuring he is endlessly shining, moving and transforming.

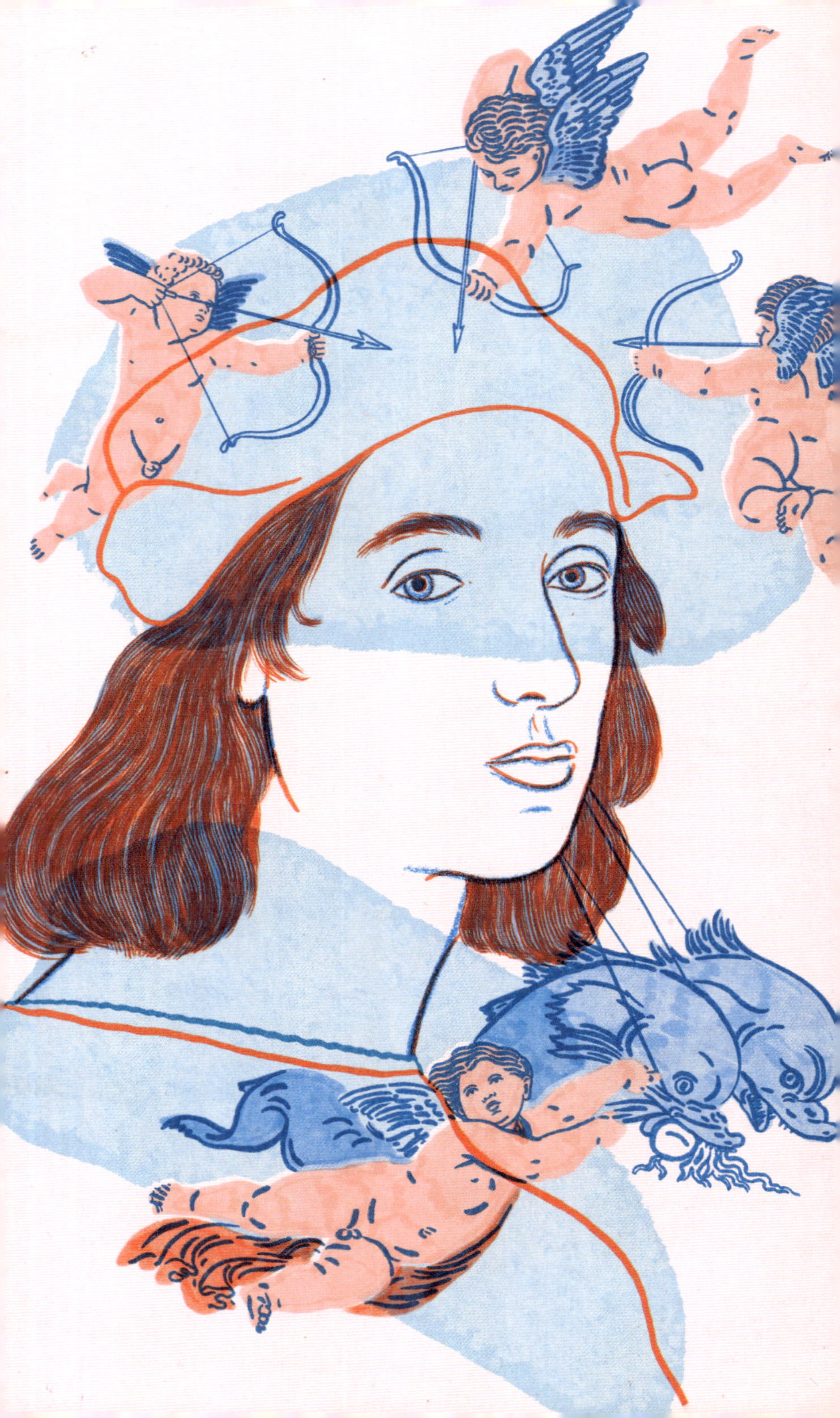

Raphael
1483–1520

Prince of Painters

When an artist dies young, it is not just the work that stops, there also remains a half-finished conversation about who they are as a practitioner. If they are lucky enough to have an established legacy it is the words of others that must form the rest of the dialogue. In the case of Raphael, it was the eminent biographer Giorgio Vasari who established a very particular heritage for the young star of Renaissance Rome. In his seminal work *Lives of the Most Excellent Painters, Sculptors, and Architects* (1568) Vasari recounted that Raphael's career was brought to an abrupt halt aged thirty-seven after a night of vigorous love making with his mistress. As amusing as this might sound to a modern audience, the ideological power of Vasari's detailed tome on the whole of the Renaissance was so powerful that this juicy morsel taken within that context sealed Raphael's fate for centuries as a relentlessly passionate artist who died from a sex-induced fever.

Raffaello Sanzio da Urbino, known as Raphael, is considered part of the holy trinity of the Italian Renaissance masters alongside Michelangelo Buonarotti and Leonardo da Vinci. Contrary to the opinion that it was rare to live beyond middle age in these earlier centuries, Leonardo died aged sixty-seven in 1519 and Michelangelo even older at eighty-eight in 1564. It is therefore all the more remarkable that Raphael secured such a permanent place in the canon of art history given how much shorter his career was. His staying power is largely thanks to his extraordinary relationships with the powerful men of his day, most notably Pope Julius II and his successor Pope Leo X.

Raphael arrived in Rome in 1508 aged twenty-five having already established his reputation as a young and impressive talent. He first learned to paint from his father, who was a leading painter for the refined court of Urbino, and he was supposedly apprenticed to Perugino as young as eight years old. Raphael inherited his father's studio and had secured his own important commissions by the age of seventeen. After four years in Florence where he fully developed his style, Raphael was introduced to the de facto art patron of the Renaissance world, Pope Julius II. Although he was much younger and less experienced than Michelangelo, who was considered to be genius-like even before he painted the Sistine Chapel, Raphael had an advantage over his elder rival: he was a consummate gentleman and social connoisseur. He became known as the 'Prince of Painters', which secured him easy passage through the turbulent political machinations of the early sixteenth century.

While Michelangelo unhappily painted the ceiling that would change art history forever, a few rooms away Raphael was bestowed with the commission to paint the Vatican apartments of Pope Julius II. The masterpiece of the fresco cycle is *The School of Athens*, an undisputed cornerstone of Italian Renaissance art. Against a backdrop of the new St Peter's Basilica, as designed by the artist's great friend Donato Bramante, Raphael brings together all the great Greek philosophers, including Plato, Aristotle, Socrates, Ptolemy, Pythagoras and the so-called 'Weeping Philosopher' Heraclitus, who the young artist impudently gave the recognizable features of his difficult and morose rival, Michelangelo. As well as being an explicit advertisement of the classical world's seismic impact on the Renaissance, the painting is a masterclass in perspective, creating a harmonious, stage-like setting where the dozens of men, each with their own attributes and natural poses, are brought alive from the pages of history into a single, believable space that recedes, full of incident and detail. The painting, which was completed in 1511, established Raphael as one of the leading artists of Rome, then the epicentre of the art world.

Raphael was at the height of his powers and still only in his twenties. Through his relationship with the Pope, Raphael met the richest man of his age and the Pope's personal banker, Agostino Chigi. Chigi commissioned Raphael to paint frescoes thoughout the ground floor of his residence, today known as the Villa Farnesina. Vasari recounts that while undertaking the commission, an infatuated Raphael insisted that his mistress be able to live with him at the villa. She was the same woman that the biographer implicates in the early demise of the artist. Who Raphael's mistress was, and the intensity of their secret affair, has been a source of fascination since Vasari sealed the artist's fate as being fatally sensual.

The woman in question was Margherita Luti, who is also known from historical texts as La Fornarina – long considered to mean the daughter of a baker. However, a recent article has strongly demonstrated that the word, created from the Italian words *forno* (oven) and *fornaia* (woman baker) alludes to the female sexual organs and therefore what was actually at play was an ancient nickname for a prostitute. Regardless of the facts, what is critical to Raphael's reputation is that for hundreds of years this woman has been a central part of his biography. Raphael's lover was also his muse and two paintings survive that are commonly accepted as representing Luti, the most tantalizing of which is known as *La Fornarina* (1518–19). Dressed in an ornate headdress and wearing an armband that bears the painter's name, the dark-haired woman stares directly out, holding one of her revealed breasts. The painting demonstrates the characteristic quality of the artist, the search for a kind of perfect beauty. Raphael's own words survive on the subject of beauty, specifically his desire to procure it with his own eyes: 'to paint a beauty, I should have to see a number of beauties, provided Your Lordship were with me to choose the best'. These kinds of comments and the sensuality of the painting, combined with Vasari's report of Raphael's death, have resulted in a certain infamy for *La Fornarina*. In 2001, in an attempt to further unlock the mystery of this great love story, the painting was X-rayed. It was revealed that originally the woman wore a square-cut ruby ring on the third finger of her left hand, which was painted over, perhaps after Raphael's death to keep their possible betrothal secret.

The fairy-tale quality of Raphael and La Fornarina's story is enhanced when we learn that Raphael was formally engaged to the daughter of a powerful cardinal. As was common, the fine young man would have been expected to marry well in order to elevate and cement his social standing. A relationship with the daughter of a baker, or indeed a prostitute, would always have to be kept in the shadows. La Fornarina was very much a secret mistress, however poorly kept that secret turned out to be.

In a strange twist of fate, Raphael died on his birthday – 6 April 1520 – which was also Good Friday. He was thirty-seven years old and was given a funeral fit for the Prince of Painters. It was extremely grand, well attended and culminated with his burial at the most exceptional monument in Rome, the Pantheon. The inscription on his tomb reads 'Here lies that famous Raphael by whom Nature feared to be conquered while he lived, and when he was dying, feared herself to die.' While Raphael was clearly regarded as one of the most significant and respected artists of his day, his position in history was still by no means guaranteed. His rival Michelangelo would go on to work for another forty-four years and leave behind a gargantuan legacy that secured his place as a master without comparison. In the modern world Leonardo would find a captive audience that was in deep sympathy with his inventive and widely interrogative mind. By contrast, Raphael's signature to pursue beauty at all costs, could have become out of step with a rational, intellectual and modern-thinking world. One factor that has clearly helped Raphael stay in the minds of future artists and art lovers is Vasari's characterization of him as an improbably sensual artist who died in a paroxysm of love. In 1820, Turner paid homage to Raphael by depicting him in a view over Rome from a balcony in the Vatican. The Renaissance

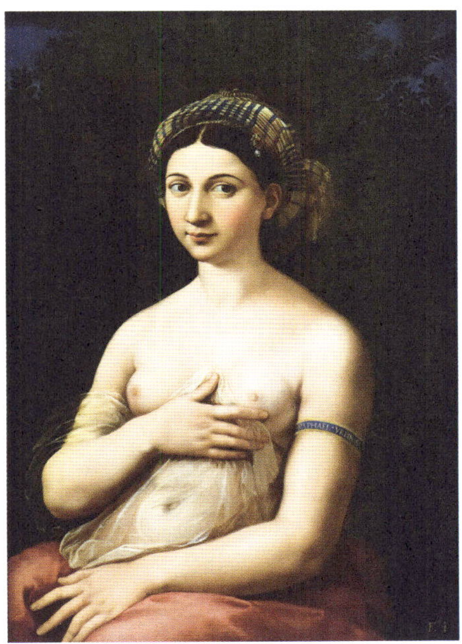

La Fornarina
Raphael (1483–1520)
1518–1519, oil on wood,
85 × 60 cm (33 × 24 in),
National Gallery of Ancient Art in
Barberini Palace, Rome, Italy

artist presents his paintings to his mistress La Fornarina; clearly Turner was titillated by the idea that Raphael was kept company at the Vatican by his illicit lover. A century and a half later and the relationship also fascinated Picasso who created an entire series of pornographic etchings that centre on Raphael and La Fornarina. Picasso takes the imagery one step further by explicitly depicting the couple in the throes of erotica in front of the Pope. Vasari could never have known the seeds he was sewing for centuries to come, preserving the affair of La Fornarina and Raphael as one of the most provocative couplings in art history.

Three

Pioneers

Some artists make work at the start of their careers that is so radical it cannot be fully accepted for decades. In the normal course of a long profession, their art would likely come to have a permanence and a consistency that would help to contextualize any disruptive beginnings. Through perseverance might come a belated respect, or at least there will have been time for an audience to play catch up. When an artist dies young, especially someone who made work that side stepped the accepted norms of the era, it may mean their art becomes paralyzed in the system. Without its maker to advocate and expand ideas, it will take longer to find acceptance and be appreciated. The artists in this section are all pioneering and whether they died three hundred and fifty years ago or thirty years ago, their work shares the privilege of effortlessly encapsulating our current cultural climate.

The French artist Yves Klein was an extremely radical thinker, determined to reduce all art making to nothingness, to the void. His career lasted just seven years and had he continued to make work I am sure he would have been widely celebrated in his own age instead of only years after his death. Although his work is now fêted at auction, this adulation is focused on his signature International Klein Blue, the colour he patented. His oeuvre was incredibly pioneering and yet his reputation today reduces him to one concept and he is still largely under-appreciated intellectually. Klein anticipated Minimalism, conceptual art, performance art and our current fascination with mindfulness and meditation.

Likewise, Gordon Matta-Clark is also one of several artists in this selection who died while making work that was extremely ahead of the curve. Not only was Matta-Clark's practice in seventies New York pioneering, but he was also decades beyond his time for his distrustful attitudes towards civic 'renewal', and prescient in his appreciation of graffiti. Something of a cult figure today, Matta-Clark created a new art form, by turning architecture into sculpture. Using abandoned buildings as ready-made objects, Matta-Clark would create interventions such as slicing a perfect American home in two. As if a knife had cut through a cake, his temporary forms (only available to appreciate through his documentary photographs) feel at once unbelievable and conceptually tight, and scores of subsequent artists would be influenced by his subversion of space and form. In his appreciation of ideas and interventions that questioned civic authority, Matta-Clark was an early example of the artist in the mode of social activist, which is so prevalent in today's culture.

A heady mix of decay and excess formed the backdrop for the practice of Robert Mapplethorpe. New York in the seventies was a city on the verge of ruin, but it would become a kind of underground creative mecca, a space for countercultural ideas and expression. Matta-Clark and Mapplethorpe were part of a generation that resisted conventional narratives and shone a spotlight on new forms and subjects. Matta-Clark was a pioneer for creating an entirely new medium that we are still coming to terms with, whereas Mapplethorpe was making disruptions by using existing art historical language. Famous for his BDSM (sexual behaviours involving physical restraints, unequal power and bondage) imagery, he is often considered a provocateur and his legacy is entwined with the arts censorship battles of the nineties that followed his death. But Mapplethorpe's story is far more subtle than this and his art was pioneering for its role in elevating the discipline of photography into a fine art form. Were it only for shock value, his work would not continue to resonate so well today.

Another artist whose work fits very comfortably into our current cultural and psychological landscape is Egon Schiele. Schiele created an aesthetic that almost perfectly expresses the modern moment, a remarkable feat considering he died a century ago. A master draughtsperson, Schiele made an unrelenting enquiry into the human figure, conjuring strange, unflattering and sometimes contorted bodies. Bereft of any contextual details such as a window, bed or landscape, his subjects seem to exist only on his page. Often explicit and frequently erotic, Schiele created works

"A woman who sought a life beyond the traditional feminine sphere"

that were completely out of step with the conventions of Vienna in the first decades of the twentieth century. The works feel as if they were made for today: he created a series of self-portraits with a piercing psychological quality and his figures could be described in our vernacular as gender fluid.

Like Egon Schiele, Paula Modersohn-Becker also broke new ground within the genre of self-portraiture. She would create what is most likely the first pregnant self-portrait in modern art, a subject still rarely featured today. Born in Dresden in 1876, the artist's journals reveal her to be a woman who sought a life beyond the traditional feminine sphere.

After she married, she wrote, 'And now, I don't even know how I should sign my name. I'm not Modersohn, but I'm no longer Paula Becker anymore either. I am Me, and I hope to become Me more and more. That is surely the goal of all our struggles.' Modersohn-Becker struggled against the prevailing tide and was excited to break new ground as both an artist and a mother. Sadly, it was mismanagement of childbirth that caused her early death and the end of her important career as a modernist painter. Still not as widely significant as she deserves to be, she has become a figurehead for contemporary artists such as Jenny Holzer who have rediscovered her work.

Amrita Sher-Gil is another modern artist who is slowly being put back into the picture in this century. Born in 1912 to an Indian father and a Hungarian mother, Sher-Gil was raised in India but her determination to become an artist was so strong that, aged just sixteen, she convinced her family to relocate to Paris so she might follow her dreams. Despite language barriers, not to mention her age and gender, Sher-Gil would become an established and respected painter with a haunting take on modern figurative art. Like Schiele and Modersohn-Becker before her, Sher-Gil would also innovate using self-portraiture. She was in a singular position of appreciating Western trends such as Gauguin's fetish for Tahiti, while also speaking to that otherness herself. She took many lessons of the European avant-garde back to India with her after she relocated back there, providing a rare link between these two cultures at that time. She did not die before she was discovered, in fact the vast majority of her oeuvre became the core of New Delhi's National Gallery of Modern Art. Since her death she has slowly gained wider recognition outside India and her work is proving to be an absolutely vital addition to the story of modern art.

Sher-Gil is emerging from the shadows, albeit slowly. Vermeer, on the other hand is so much in the spotlight that it is hard to imagine a time when he wasn't one of the world's most celebrated artists. He may have created the sensationally famous, *Girl with a Pearl Earring* (c. 1665) but little is known of the Dutch master's life. Never an established artist beyond his home city of Delft, Vermeer's work was usually attributed to other artists after his early death. As with Van Gogh, Vermeer's modern reputation is largely thanks to a single torch bearer. In Van Gogh's case it was his sister-in-law, Jo Bonger. In the case of Vermeer it was someone who lived in a different city, the German scholar, Gustav Waagen. Two hundred years after his death, Vermeer's work would enter the canon, he would be widely praised as an artistic pioneer and he would be credited with creating 'the Mona Lisa of the north'.

Robert Smithson was also an artist whose work was lost, but rather than falling between cracks in the archives and art history, his work was literally lost to nature. A pioneering land artist, his career is largely defined by one work, *Spiral Jetty*, which was created directly in the Utah landscape in 1970. Smithson was a leading light in a new generation of artists who wanted not only to take their work out of the conventional gallery context, but also to commune directly with nature in their creations. *Spiral Jetty*, a work of staggering scale, was created using thousands of tonnes of basalt rocks in the shoreline of a lake, and it therefore showed signs of deteriorating before it was even finished. There is a duality in his work between the immense physical labour required to materialize his idea and the contrasting serenity of seeing something beautiful slowly disintegrate into nature. Smithson's art undermined the long-held notion of art as a static, precious and eternal thing. He is a pioneer, like the other artists in this section, as his work anticipated our current fascination with experiential art and the performative nature of objects.

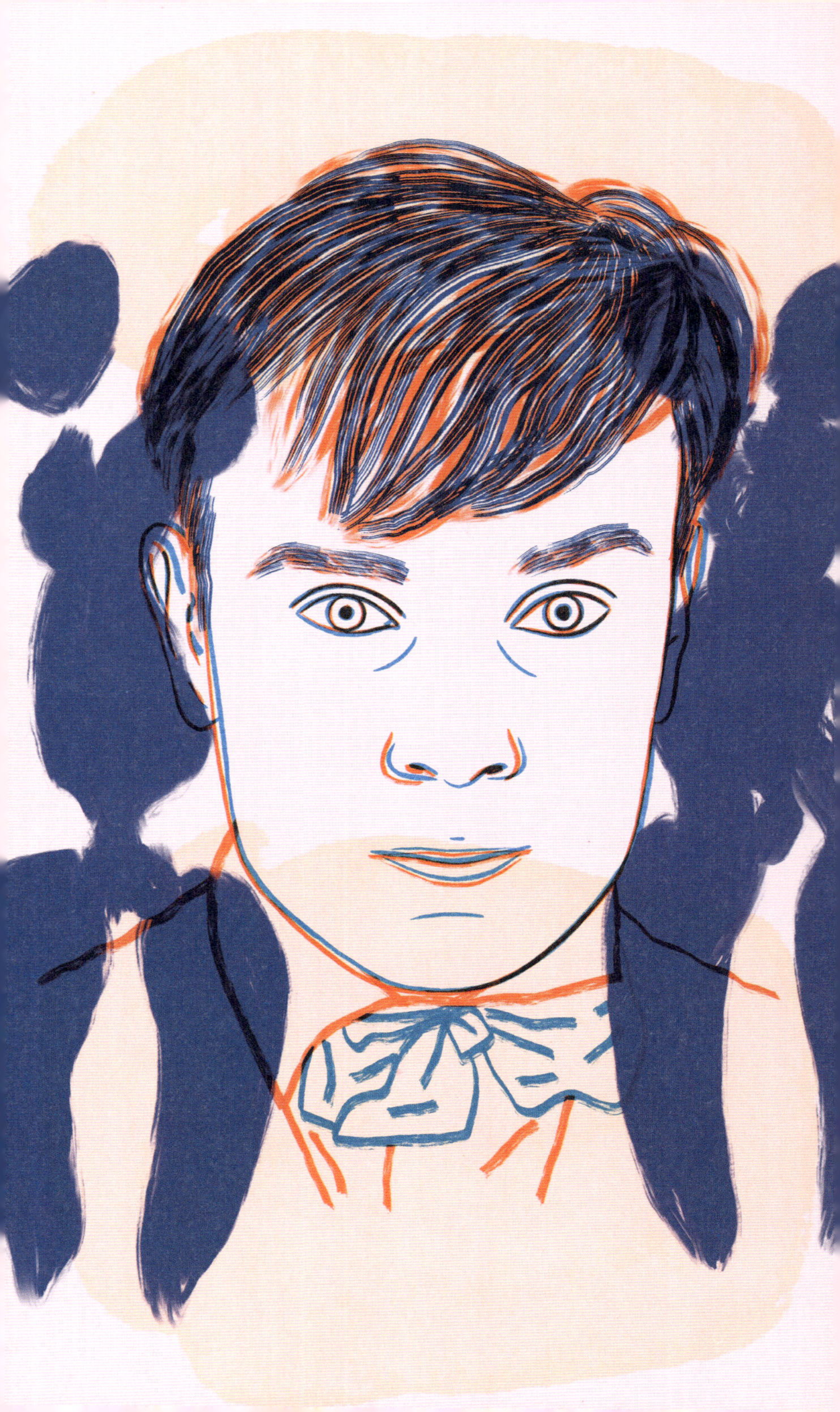

The Blue Shaman

Yves Klein was successful in securing a strong legacy for his art despite his short-lived career. Those who have encountered his work even briefly will know him as the man that patented a colour, inventing International Klein Blue in 1960. One might be irritated by the prospect of an artist 'creating' their own shade of blue and using it endlessly in abstract monochromatic canvases. There is an arrogance to owning a colour, something that is considered universal, and from the viewer there might be a lingering sense of suspicion as to where the artfulness is; is this a case of the emperor's *blue* clothes? Klein was probably too successful in the exploitation of his colour, known as IKB, because this has become his singular myth and legend: the man that made and exclusively used his very own blue. His success with the concept and work dealing with IKB has come to overshadow the complexity and depth of his practice more widely. Because, in fact, the fundamental touchstone of his art was not about a single shade of blue in his name but about a shamanistic and spiritual search for the infinite, or the void.

Born in Nice in 1928, Klein received no formal art training, though his parents were both painters. He accumulated an arts education from being in their orbit and from time spent in an art-framing shop in London. He arrived in the city aged twenty-one, eager to improve his English, and while working at the framers began to handle materials such as gesso, pure pigments and gold leaf that would later appear in his mature work. It was, in fact, in his South Kensington flat that Klein staged his first thrown-together exhibition of gouache monochromes on leftover pieces of white cardboard scavenged from the shop. Before Klein would establish himself formally as a painter, he would become accomplished at judo. He travelled to Japan in 1953 where, aged twenty-five, he became a fourth-degree black belt, the first Westerner to achieve such a status in the martial art. Although this might seem merely a tangential sporting achievement, it is in fact vital to his way of thinking and helped to develop the central tenet of his later artistic career.

As a result of judo training and his time in Japan, Klein was fascinated by the Zen Buddhist concept of *Śūnyatā*, meaning 'emptiness'. This is the notion of the 'non-self', a proposition whereby there can be no permanent self, for we are all constantly changing and any sense of one fixed identity or place is a deception. Klein's interest in illusions and notions of emptiness found fullest expression in one of his most radical works, an intervention that survives only in documentary fragments. In April 1958 Klein emptied a Parisian gallery, painted the entirety of the space white and added a blue window with a blue arrival curtain. The rumours about the exhibition (no doubt generated by Klein himself) were so strong that over three thousand curious visitors queued for the private view, to be greeted with Klein's cultivation of a void. In 1960 he staged the first performance of *Monotone-Silence Symphony,* a radical musical score where one single note is played by the orchestra for twenty minutes followed by the same length of silence. Klein was exploring what nothingness would look or sound like, how it might make one look and feel towards it.

In a ground-breaking artwork, Klein created a precursor to Photoshop in his now iconic image, *Leap into the Void* (1960). The image shows the artist elegantly flinging himself from a second-floor window, suspended in

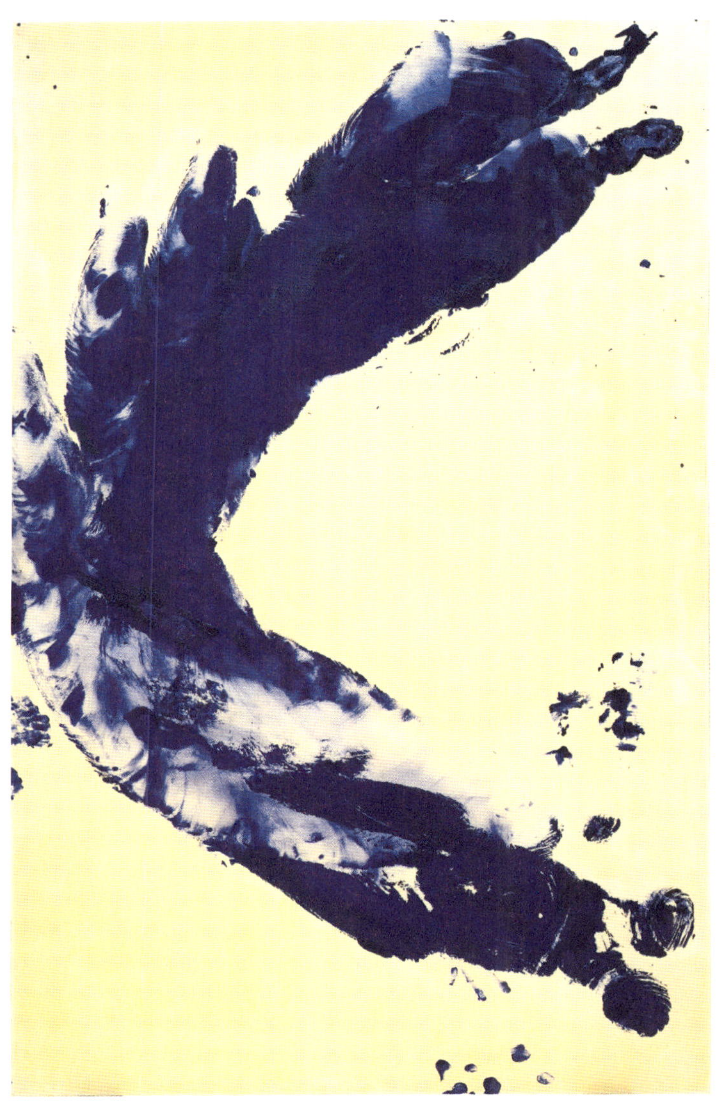

Anthropometry: Princess Helena
Yves Klein (1928–1962)
1960, oil on paper on wood,
198 × 128.2 cm (78 × 50 ½ in),
The Museum of Modern Art, New York, USA

air before he presumably crashed down to the Parisian street. In reality, his friends caught him with a tarpaulin, an aspect that was removed in the darkroom. Klein published the image in his own newspaper with the headline 'A man in space!' Klein's work was radical and he consciously courted controversy, but he was not simply a joker; he was a complex avant-garde thinker, confronting what he saw was a great mystery and his actions, while often amusing, were underpinned by a serious spiritual intention.

He continued to investigate 'the void', making various artworks that attempted to remove the artist from the art object in a kind of disavowal of the self, as espoused by Zen Buddhism. He removed the frames from his monochromatic paintings and installed the paintings several centimetres in front of the wall so the viewer could feel immersed in them, somewhat released from the trappings of the art gallery. In his Anthropometries series of 1960, Klein removed the paint brush to create paintings by assisting naked female models to submerge their bodies in paint and lie down to print their form. The endeavour was a European riposte to the 'action painting' that was then fashionable in New York. Klein was later the subject of a damning critique by feminist scholars for the perceived exploitation of his nude participants.

In these Anthropometries, and almost all other works, Klein used only his unique shade of blue, IKB. For Klein, blue, as the colour of the sky and the sea, could represent the infinite. It was the most highly prized colour in Italian art, always the most expensive pigment and therefore the choicest colour for the Virgin Mary's robes. Surprisingly unrepetitive, the hundreds of paintings and sculptures that Klein made in this single colour are powerful because his blue is the most perfect shade. Created using raw pigment blended using synthetic gels instead of oil or acrylic, Klein's colour has not diminished and the hue remains bright. To stand in front of a Klein painting is to be almost therapeutically bathed in blue. By working with this intense colour in an entirely abstracted fashion, or one that removes the artist's hand, is a way of conjuring silence and forcing concentration upon the viewer.

In 1962 the artist suffered a fatal heart attack; he was just thirty-four and had been working for little more than a decade. Sadder still, there is some speculation that the formula used to create his intense blue suspensions, now so fetishized by art collectors, may have been toxic and contributed to his early death. Today, Klein's search for transcendence is in step with our culture's mass appreciation of mindfulness, but the artist was largely misunderstood in his lifetime and he did not profit from his work in any meaningful way. For the past two decades, however, the prices reached for his work at auction have steadily risen from the millions to the tens of millions.

Klein was ahead of his time, his work influenced minimal art, performance art and conceptual art. After his death, the American artist David Hammons picked up the thread of Klein's Anthropometry paintings and developed it using his own grease-stained body pressed against paper. Klein also continues to be a source of inspiration for major artists working today: Anish Kapoor has invented and retains the sole rights to use the world's blackest black pigment (in an attack on what he perceives as Kapoor's selfishness the younger artist Stuart Semple has created the world's pinkest pink and made it available to all); James Turrell's enormous light installations owe a debt to Klein's attempt to submerge the viewer in a void and many artists working in a fake news era will continue to refer to Klein's 'faked' leaping photographs. Klein's potency as an artist has not been extinguished and it goes far beyond his blue legacy that stays with us, the pigment as brilliant as the day it was created.

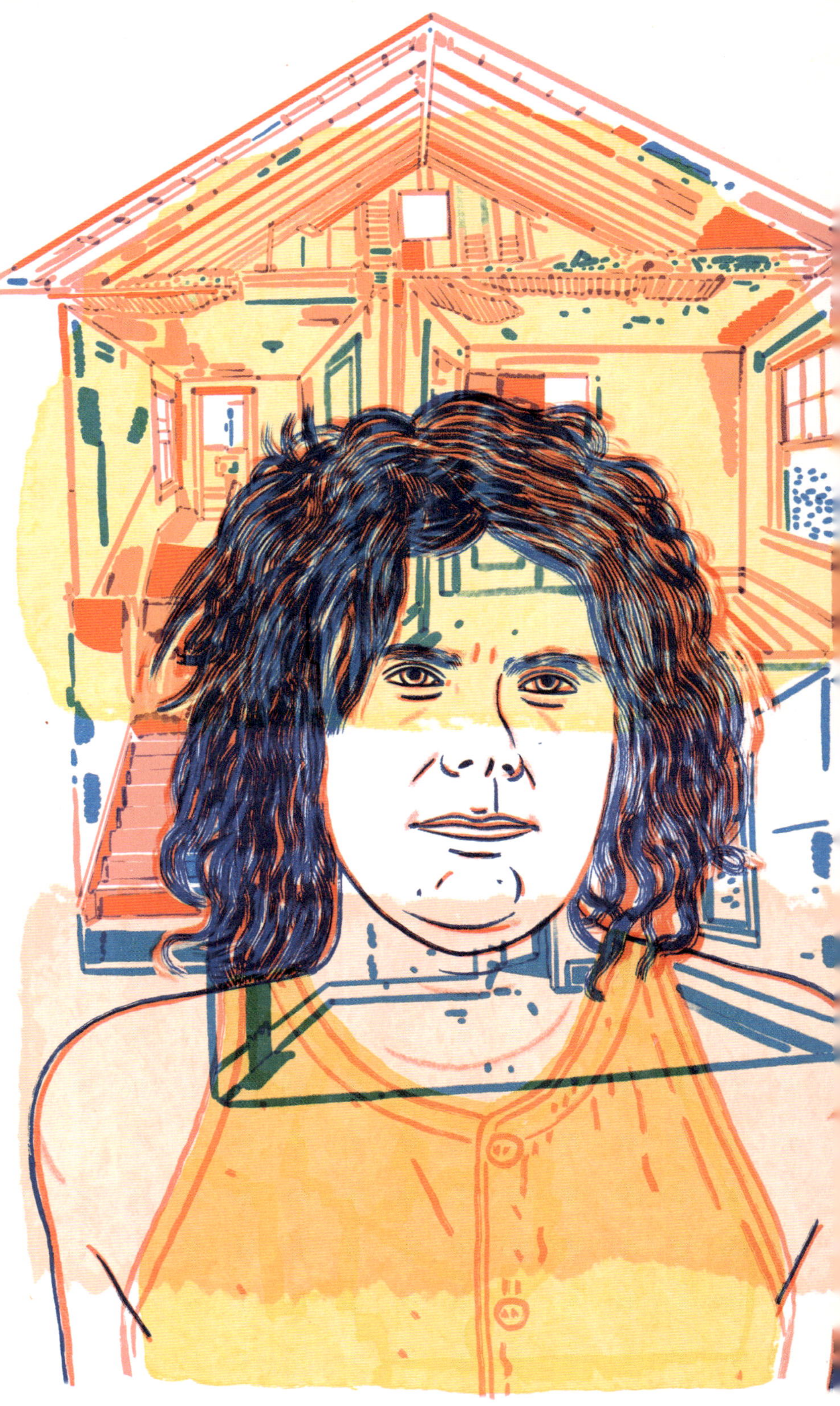

Dissident Anarchitect

———

Of all the artists included in this book, it is possibly Gordon Matta-Clark who leaves us with the most tantalizing prospect of what he could have gone on to achieve had his career not been cut so short. Dead at the age of thirty-five from pancreatic cancer, in just ten years this restless and soulful spirit created staggering work that is still influencing generations of artists internationally. He was a cult figure of 1970s New York, so it's surprising to learn that for someone with so profound a legacy, none of the interventions he created physically exist anymore. We are left with only his meticulous records.

Matta-Clark is known for cutting into buildings: transforming piers, homes and warehouses into a radical kind of sculpture using hacksaws, blow torches and sledge hammers as his artist's tools. His reinventions through destruction were often described by the artist as a kind of 'anarchitecture' – a word formed by the compression of anarchy and architecture – which neatly expresses his complex relationship to the urban landscape. Formally trained as an architect at Cornell University, he graduated in 1968, a year of student rebellion and protests across Europe and North America. Against the backdrop of this unrest the young architect turned away from the path paved by his education. He was disillusioned with the promise of urban renewal and the dogmatics of social planning as espoused by figures such as Le Corbusier in France earlier in the century. He belonged to a generation that distrusted the government and turned to a more grass-roots attitude to civic renewal. Matta-Clark would never design and build from scratch in the manner expected of a formally trained architect. Instead, abandoned structures and buildings would become his raw material and playground for playful interventions.

Matta-Clark initially used the crumbling New York borough of the Bronx as his blank canvas. By the mid 1970s the city's housing administration had effectively cut off any resources for the area, which was largely populated by the city's poorest minority citizens. The plan was to allow the systems and structures to fester to such an extent that people moved away out of desperation and the land could eventually be reclaimed for lucrative redevelopment. Dismayed by what he described as the 'fallacy of renewal' Matta-Clark turned his back on his architectural training's supposed usefulness and instead looked at these abandoned buildings as raw material for an artist. In the series Bronx Floors of 1972–3, he illegally removed small rectangular or square sections of domestic floors or ceilings, as if simply punching a hole through several sheets of paper. The work existed in two modes, the physical displaced floors, which are now museum-worthy artworks and the void in the building where the furtive subtraction had taken place, at least while the buildings still stood before demolition. The piece plays with the duality of construction and deconstruction and made an aggressive act normally undertaken by a builder for a practical purpose into a simple artistic gesture that allowed for a completely different reading of one of the most familiar kinds of spaces, a family home.

Matta-Clark quickly amped up the scale of his interventions and in 1974 he would cut an entire house in half. Often cited as his masterpiece, *Splitting* is comprised of a typical New Jersey home that the artist has sliced down the middle, leaving a gap of one inch by sawing two parallel incisions down the walls, door and window frames and staircase. He engineered the split so that the house could remain upright but inevitably would sag and settle off centre when his work was complete. The property was bought by his art dealer friends as an investment before the whole area was scheduled for clearing as part of a redevelopment programme. The context within which he was able to make his work was clearly an important part of the narrative for Matta-Clark. It wasn't simply that he had to rely on abandoned buildings because of a lack of budget or motivation to seek approval, though this was probably a reality too, but it was also that situating his interventions somewhere near the transition from neglect to lucrative improvement was an important backdrop to his work.

Matta-Clark was extremely forward thinking, considerate of the power of civic action and the value in the individual critiquing the system at large. His cutting projects may not have created new homes or any conventional sense of value in what had been abandoned but they are valuable as a creative statement about the power of the imagination and the refusal to ignore the most blighted corners of New York. He also applied his radical way of thinking to a practical outlet, a restaurant he co-founded with Tina Girouard and Carol Goodden in 1972 called FOOD. A meeting place for like-minded souls, it served affordable food to artists and the community in what was then an unloved neighbourhood, SoHo. Guest artists would set the menu, among them Joseph Beuys, Donald Judd and other names today regarded as giants of the twentieth century. Today it is better understood as an experimental artistic project or even a piece of conceptual art, a precursor to artists who work with food such as Jennifer Rubell and Gina Beavers and a prefiguration of the world's most critically lauded restaurant, elBulli, being included in *documenta* in 2007, where the world's greatest art is exhibited every five years.

Matta-Clark was also prescient in his appreciation of the graffiti that began to appear like a rash throughout New York's boroughs and was arguably one of the first people to acknowledge tagging as a visual and physical act of reclaiming the city by those who felt excluded from the mainstream. The artist made a series using black-and-white photographs

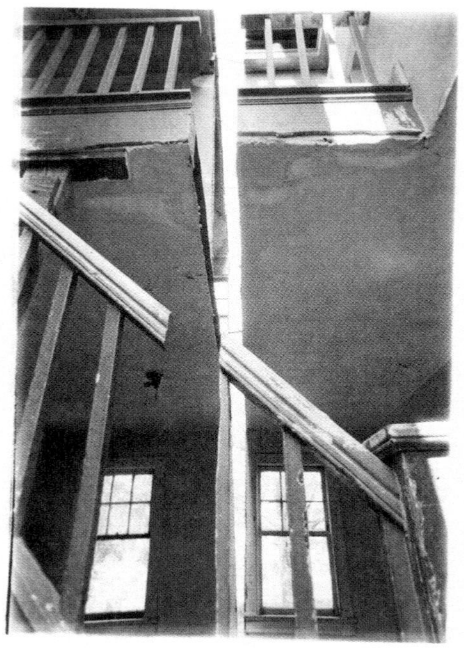

Splitting
Gordon Matta-Clark (1943–1978)
1974, printed 1977, gelatin silver print,
25.4 × 20.3 cm (10 × 8 in),
Whitney Museum of American Art,
New York, USA

of graffiti-laden walls and trains, with carefully hand-coloured tinting for the tags. It would be several years before graffiti gave birth to its own art stars, Jean-Michel Basquiat and Keith Haring, who would be subsumed by the art world hungry for something new, this time their illicit subculture activity of tagging.

In 1977 Matta-Clark, who was quickly being recognized as one of the most potent young thinkers in the city, was awarded the prestigious Guggenheim Fellowship in order to realize a resource centre for youth residents in the Lower East Side. The centre was to be designed and built by the young citizens themselves under the guidance of their free-thinking mentor Matta-Clark. Sadly, the project, which would have been the artist's first work with permanence built into the design, did not come to fruition as he died of pancreatic cancer less than a year later.

Matta-Clark is regarded as a pioneer for many reasons. He was an early sceptic of the motives for urban renewal espoused by government officials, recognizing the human and creative cost of what would become mass gentrification in the decades after his death. He understood that graffiti was not a passing phase and had creative legitimacy some forty years before a work by Banksy sold for nearly ten million pounds. We can see echoes of this radical spirit from the seventies in many of today's museum stars, such as Rachel Whiteread's preoccupation with interiors and negative space, Theaster Gates's socially motivated projects, Hank Willis Thomas's activism as art, and Roni Horn's reassembled drawings. Matta-Clark's practice is exhibited in museums internationally today, thankfully the artist kept extremely focused and interesting photographic and film documentation of his projects, knowing that many would last only weeks at best. Experiencing his archival dedication is especially poignant as we know, but he did not, that his career would be short-lived too. His legacy continues to grow as artistic inheritance continues to drip feed scores of young artists, writers and architects. Plans are underway to honour one of his most ambitious and beautiful pieces of urban sculpture, *Days End*, which was created by cutting large apertures into the decrepit Pier 52 in 1975, letting the sunlight pour in and creating a dramatic new kind of temple facing the water. The Hudson River Park, built next to the new Whitney Museum of American Art, features an installation by David Hammonds that honours the former site of the historic pier by representing it as a metal frame outline. Named *Days End*, it gives at last a permanent memorial to one of the city's brightest and dissident creative souls.

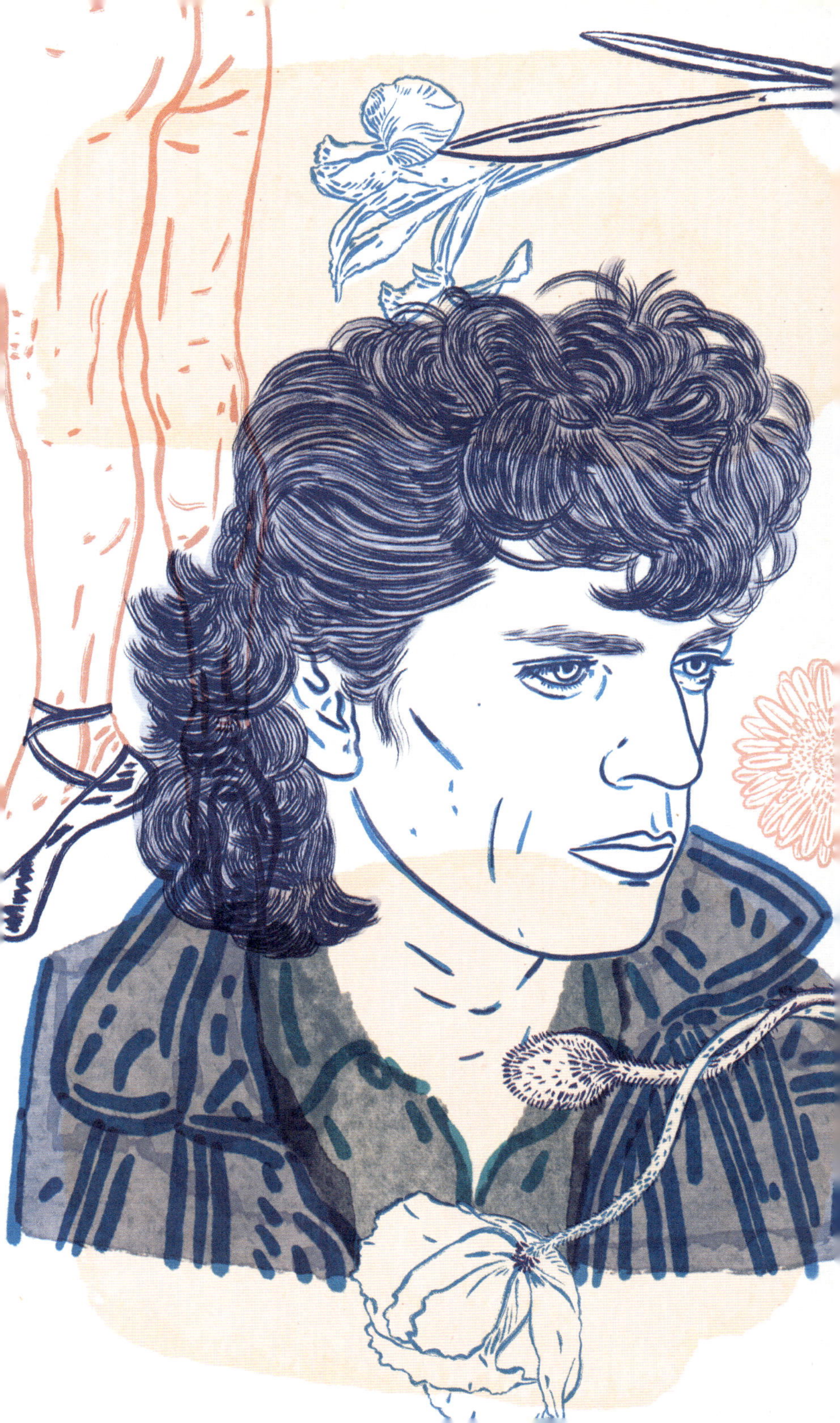

Robert
Mapplethorpe
1946–1989

Elegant Provocateur

n the late 1980s Robert Mapplethorpe's art became indelibly entangled with what is known as America's Culture Wars, a reckoning where liberal and conservative values collided spectacularly. His photographs of gay men engaging in sex acts, or simply kissing, were literally waved on the floor of the United States Senate in a dire warning about the state of American values. Mapplethorpe himself had died a few months earlier, and that his premature demise was due to complications from HIV/AIDS only added fuel to the Republican fire. In the years following his death, Mapplethorpe's photographs were placed at the centre of debates about indecency, race, sexuality, gender norms and the AIDS epidemic. But his work, even the unprecedented BDSM imagery, was not as simple as a rejection of 'good taste' and bourgeois acceptability. Although he was both radical and a pioneer, Mapplethorpe used existing principles and classical ideals. What Mapplethorpe created was a kind of transgression from within that helped secure his place in the twentieth century art canon.

Although he did not consider himself a political artist, Mapplethorpe was no stranger to tension. Even before a censorship war developed around his work, in his lifetime he worked to legitimize photography as a fine art form. His life is particularly interesting because it charts two parallel progressive movements (which would become entwined for him): one within the art world as galleries, critics, museums and artists debated the significance of photography within the hierarchy of art mediums; and the other externally, as the gay community began to create turning points for LGBT rights in the late sixties.

Born in Floral Park in 1946, Mapplethorpe remarked that 'I come from suburban America. It was a very safe environment, and it was a good place to come from in that it was a good place to leave.' He was an outsider and left his strict Catholic family to study art at The Pratt Institute in Brooklyn, where he dropped out before finishing his degree. In 1969 he found his place among the creative misfits of New York's Chelsea Hotel. He lived there in a small room with his muse Patti Smith, who would first be his lover and then, after he came to terms with his homosexuality, his lifelong soul mate as they each pursued their creative passions with fervent dedication. Broke but ambitious, they were drawn to the Chelsea Hotel for its long-held reputation as a gritty incubator for those who would become cultural legends including Mark Twain, Jack Kerouac, Joni Mitchell, William S. Burroughs, Stanley Kubrick, Jim Morrison, Bob Dylan, Marianne Faithfull and Jimi Hendrix.

With romantic unbuttoned shirts (or no shirt), beaded necklaces, leather jackets and long hair, Mapplethorpe may have dressed like a rock star and indulged in the associated lifestyle, but his artistic intentions were uncompromising. He was serious and often introspective, he felt destined to make great art although he wasn't certain what form his contribution would take. Originally, influenced by Joseph Cornell and Andy Warhol, Mapplethorpe made collages and assemblages using pre-existing materials from books and magazines, including pornography. He became dissatisfied with his appropriation of other people's work and began to take his own photographs to use as the basis for his collages, which he felt was more honest. It was his Chelsea Hotel neighbour, the filmmaker Sandy Daley, who gave Mapplethorpe his first camera, a Polaroid, in 1970. The young artist

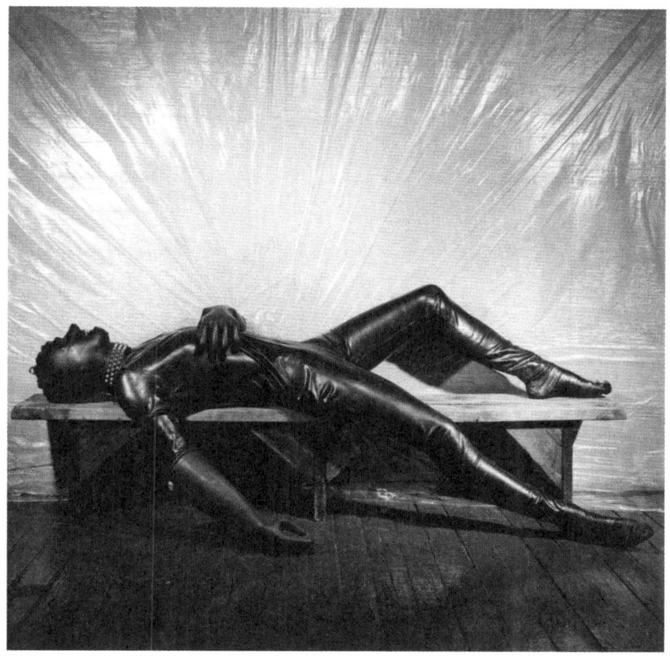

Joe / Rubberman
Robert Mapplethorpe (1946–1989)
1978, gelatin silver print,
50.8 × 40.6 cm (20 × 16 in),
© Robert Mapplethorpe Foundation

realized that the Polaroid was the medium in and of itself and made very few collage works with his own photographs as he had intended. Instead Mapplethorpe began creating fine art photography, eschewing the trend for documentary style, gritty or reportage camera work that would come to dominate the next decades. His work was intentionally preconceived, he wasn't aiming for candid intimacy like Nan Goldin or street action like Garry Winogrand. He also fiercely rejected the lingering belief that a camera was utilitarian and put every subject, including himself, Patti Smith and their bohemian circle, religious objects, flowers and still lives through an exacting aesthetic process that said as much about the artist as it did the person or thing being portrayed. Despite the variety among the staggering volume of work he produced, Mapplethorpe's oeuvre was unified by being predominantly black and white and most of all by his driving aesthetic mission to make his subjects uniquely his own.

In the late 1970s Mapplethorpe turned his camera's attention to New York's BDSM scene, introducing explicit and extreme sexual acts in his image making. His *X Portfolio* included an audacious self portrait, in which the artist strikes an extraordinary pose, his naked buttocks at the high centre of the image, his torso almost impossibly swerving around so that he might look back directly at the viewer. Wearing a leather waistcoat, boots and chaps, the artist holds a leather whip, the thicker end of which is inserted into his anus. He does not break his gaze, it is an image that harnesses power, subservience and voyeurism. There is a formal mastery at work here with Mapplethorpe's attention to grey scales, signature strong shadows and beautiful passages of light on the white stage and wooden floor. That something deemed so taboo is presented as composed, knowing and controlled further complicates the viewer's assessment of a self-portrait that both stands apart from and relates to art history.

Although Mapplethorpe is now often known for what he called his 'sex pictures' he found it challenging to exhibit the works in his lifetime, despite their formal and technical brilliance. For Mapplethorpe, these explicit works were an intrinsic part of his creative output and he regarded them in the same light as his other subjects such as his magnificent floral series, which isolate individual flowers and lend them a highly stylized and almost unreal quality. In 1988 he explained that his rationale for the BDSM work was not to aggravate audiences, 'I don't like that particular word "shocking". I'm looking for the unexpected. I'm looking for things I've never seen before … I was in a position to take those pictures. I felt an obligation to do them.'

Though Mapplethorpe enjoyed the spotlight, his motivations were not anything like the pure sensationalism that would follow in contemporary art of the nineties. His art was one of quiet orchestration not noisy accident. The BDSM pictures are not of intimate sex acts captured by a voyeur, they are staged with genuine BDSM participants and are some of the most pristinely composed images in his era. In the 1980s Mapplethorpe focused on two new bodies of work, female body builders, mainly his muse Lisa Lyon, and black muscular men. In both series he endeavoured to extend the boundaries of idealized beauty, seeking a controlled and detached kind of perfection in his subjects akin to ancient sculpture.

Mapplethorpe certainly leaves behind a provocative legacy. He was an artist who sought to elevate, ritualize, formalize and stylishly disrupt through his choice of both publicly accepted and unaccepted subjects. When Mapplethorpe was diagnosed with AIDS in 1986, he was an established name with international gallery representation, and in 1988 the Whitney Museum of American Art in New York mounted his first American retrospective exhibition. After setting up his own Foundation to promote photography at the institutional level and support AIDS-related medical research, Mapplethorpe died aged forty-two at the height of his artistic powers in March 1989.

Though his multivenue touring exhibition *The Perfect Moment* was thrown into the spotlight of the Culture Wars in 1990 due to a cancelled venue in Washington, DC and an obscenity trial for the director of the Cincinnati venue, ultimately the exhibition and thereby Mapplethorpe were victorious. However, these events resulted in the artist's work being seen through the prism of controversy. Consequently, it has since been asked whether Mapplethorpe's relevance will survive when his images no longer have the power to shock. I would argue there is no sell-by date upon which the world will catch up with the artist's singular vision. He successfully challenged what could and could not be art. The power of Mapplethorpe's work does not reside with an ambition to shock, confront or irritate. His practice was about the discovery of something new, whether forbidden or not, and his legacy is one of a pioneer, charting uncomfortable and beautiful territory, for his subjects but also his medium.

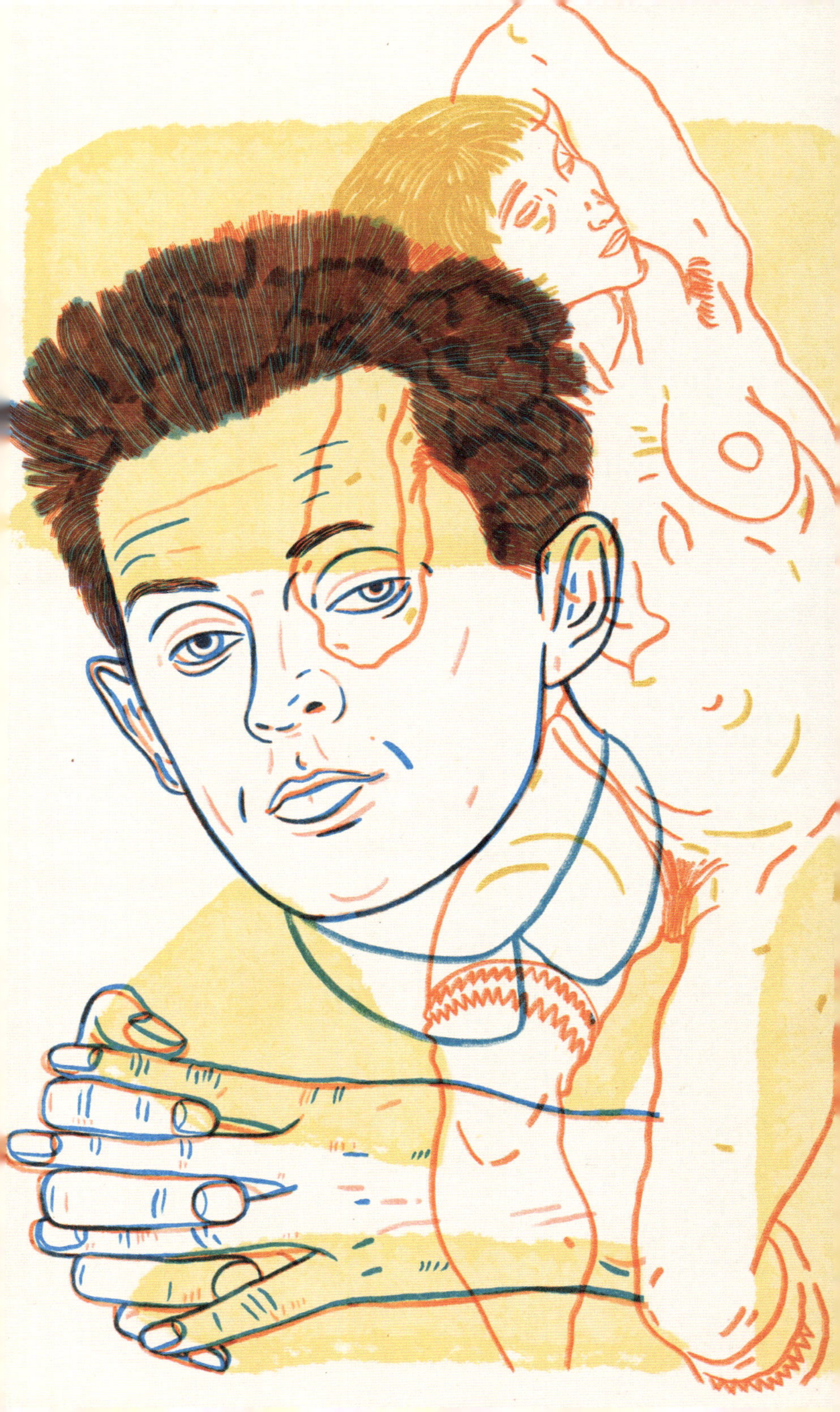

Psychological Draftsman

A long with Van Gogh and Modigliani, Schiele is an early modern master who has reached a cult-like status in the present age. Unlike the other two lionized artistic figures, Schiele is not renowned as a painter but rather a master draftsperson. His line is instantly recognizable, at once layered with the mastery and verisimilitude of centuries of fine art drawing and simultaneously fragile, broken, disjointed. His compositions are a radical departure from the academic life drawing that dominated Europe at the turn of the twentieth century. His figures are placed into difficult positions, seen from unexpected perspectives, sometimes twisted, never comfortable or simplistic in presentation. They are isolated on plain white backgrounds, as if they exist only in his art, forever contained in the nothingness of his abstract spaces.

Born in 1890 in Lower Austria, Schiele came of age in the Vienna Secession, a period dominated by the opulent and decorative brilliance of Art Nouveau. His hero was Gustav Klimt, to whom his early work owes a great debt. By the time the two met in 1910, Klimt already recognized the young man's genius, delighting a twenty-year-old Schiele by responding to a request to exchange artworks, 'Why do you want to exchange with me?

You draw better than I do.' The two remained close for the next eight years before the older artist died of pneumonia in February 1918, whereupon Schiele proclaimed him 'an artist of unbelievable accomplishment…His work is a shrine'. Although he would always view Klimt as a master, soon after meeting him, Schiele would build upon the symbolist beauty of Klimt's painting, pushing the envelope further with expressive, erotic and psychological work that dared to give artistic form to a society newly baptized in psychoanalysis and the intellectualization of sex.

Schiele's work has a heightened psychological feeling, his artwork is visibly removed from the 'real world' there are no markers of place or time. His art can be linked to the astounding development in attitudes towards the self and sexuality as delivered by Vienna's very own Dr Sigmund Freud. Before Freud, introspection was believed to deliver knowledge of oneself. Freud would dismantle this comforting thought and instead posit that parts of our own minds can remain unknown to us. This is perhaps most explicitly interrogated in Schiele's staggering attention to his own face. Alongside two of art history's masters of the self-portrait, Rembrandt and Albrecht Dürer, Schiele is considered one of the greatest exponents of the genre, producing over one hundred representations of himself. *Seated Male Nude* (or sometimes called *The Yellow Nude*) of 1910 is a dramatic departure in the history of self-portraiture; Schiele does not so much present himself as dissect himself. His jaggedly described unsexual nude body hovers over the white canvas. The gouache that gives his flesh its burnt yellow tone and red raw nipples, eye sockets and genitalia is secondary to the intensity of the line. His feet and hands have been done away with and his face is obscured. Schiele in this, and other works, was deconstructing his own image and selfhood, constantly reworking the trope of the artist's self-portrait in his innovative and unsettling approach, revealing the instability and illusion of the idea of one knowable self.

One aspect of the human condition that is almost obsessively explored in Schiele's art is sexuality. Schiele's nudes mostly fall outside the accepted norms of decency. Rather than lying supine like classical goddesses, his

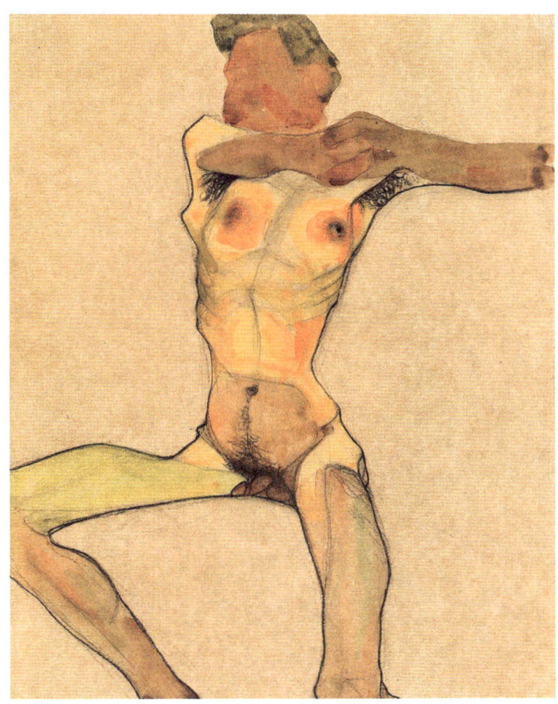

Male Nude, Yellow
Egon Schiele (1890–1918)
1910, gouache, watercolour and chalk on paper,
45.3 × 31.5 cm (18 × 12 ½ in),
private collection

dangerously young females are offered up, not nude but rather graphically naked or half-dressed in stockings. Schiele has often been cast as a sexual deviant owing to his pornographic tendency to explicitly depict vaginas, which are more traditionally hidden between demurely closed legs. Rather than considering him as objectifying the female form, some modern viewers relish his celebration of 'real' womanhood. He created independent sexual beings as opposed to the centuries-long tradition of male artists portraying women as sensual offerings for their benefit.

However, his erotic drawings and paintings are by no means widely accepted today: in recent years a Viennese tourism advertising campaign featuring his nudes had to be censored and images of his work are routinely taken down on social media.

Unsurprisingly, Schiele's work caused the artist serious problems in his lifetime. In 1912 he was arrested and tried for sexual misconduct with a minor. The unsubstantiated charge was dropped but he was found guilty of exhibiting erotic drawings where they could be seen by minors – since Schiele's studio had become a curiosity to the local kids. One of his pornographic works was destroyed by the judge who held it over a candle flame in court, and Schiele served twenty-four days in prison. Schiele's career was not irrevocably damaged by the affair, rather his art was well exhibited and he enjoyed a degree of commercial success. In fact, after Klimt's death, he was already becoming very wellknown and was positioned to take the crown as the Prince of the Viennese art world. He organized the forty-ninth Vienna Secession Exhibition, which opened around the time Klimt died, designed its poster and exhibited to such acclaim that word of his daring new work reached international press outlets. It was the apotheosis of his career; Klimt had passed him the torch but he only held it for a matter of months. In October the same year, Klimt's wife Edith died of the Spanish Influenza that was sweeping across Europe and Schiele would follow her to an early death a few days later on 31 October 1918 aged just twenty-eight.

At the age of nineteen, Schiele proclaimed his great ambition: 'The new artist is and must at all costs be himself.' He was successful at being entirely himself as a creator, and slowly but surely his progressive work has lived beyond its maker, finding a sympathetic audience among subsequent avant-garde artists who saw in his approach a defiant and hungry search for a new means to tackle the human figure – now they, too, were looking at the human condition. Schiele's treatment of the figure became a great source of inspiration to generations of artists as diverse as Francis Bacon, Jenny Holzer, Jean-Michel Basquiat and Tracey Emin.

His work remains an almost inexhaustible well of inspiration. There is nothing calm or art historically familiar in his presentation of both male and female figures. There is nothing straightforwardly sexual either, he plays with the binary motions of masculine and feminine. In some of his self-portraits he portrays himself as small, weak, vulnerable and yet knowing and conversely, his imagery of women can be hard, angular and fierce. His vision of sex is complicated, messy, dangerous and taken to the point of utter intoxication. Taken as a whole we might now understand Schiele's artwork to be proto-gender fluid. This particular aspect of Schiele's work allows for his continually increasing posthumous fame. Originally lauded as one of art history's favourite complex early modern masters, he is now ever-more relevant a century after his death for being light years ahead of his time. His legacy is a prolific body of complicated expressionist work that cannot be fully understood; it is enigmatic and seemed to be so even to him. Schiele shows us the inner forces at work in all of us, he presents clever and beautiful demons at play in both the sitter and the voyeur. He implicates everyone. If his work looks contemporary today, it is because, I believe, it is. Once possible to pick up as erotic ephemerae at flea markets, it has taken decades for Schiele's work to make sense in the linear narrative of art history. With psychic forethought, his achingly modern drawings, full of difficult beauty, angst, sexual discovery and gender fluidity have quantum leaped from the Vienna Secession into our postmodern world where they seem at ease.

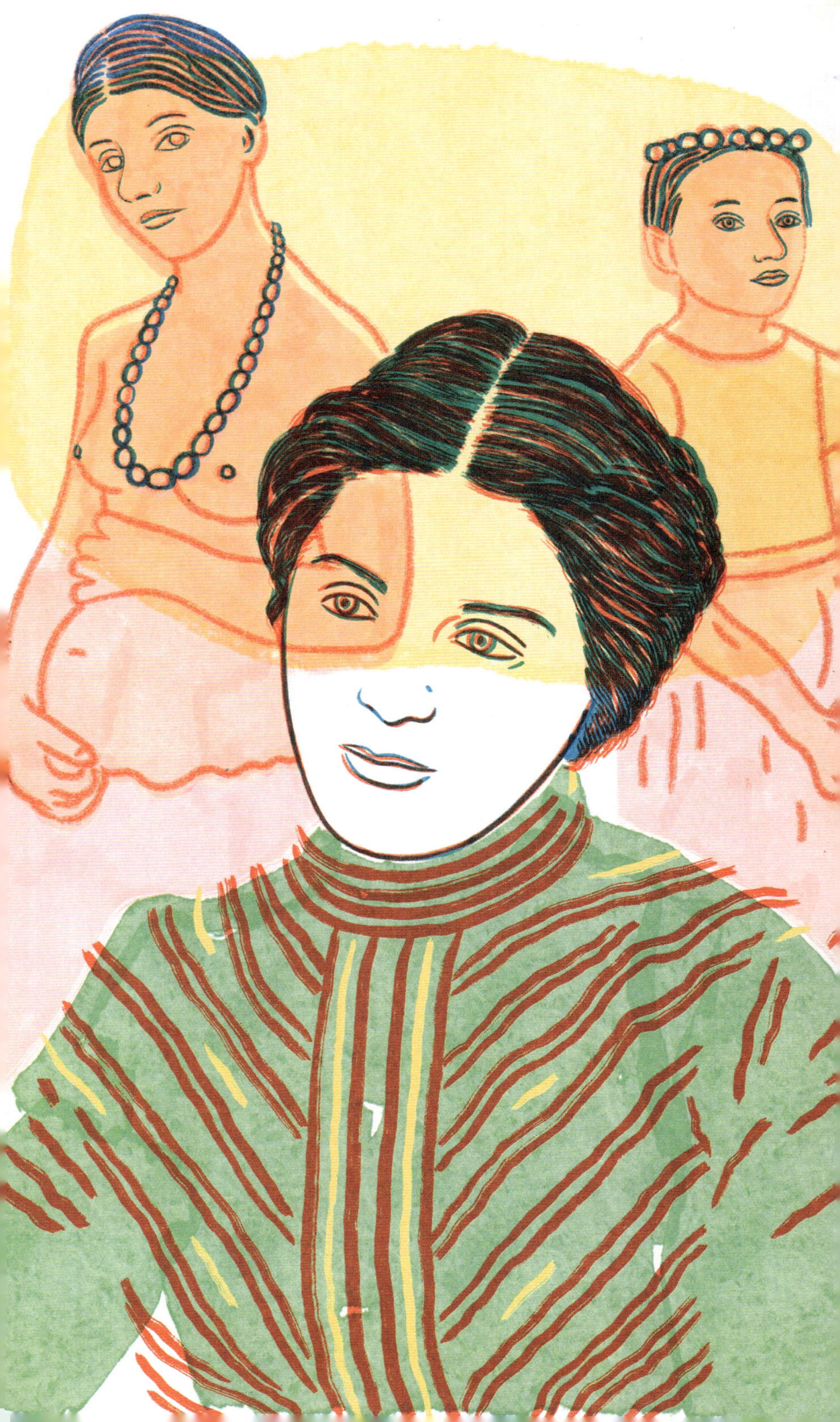

Paula Modersohn-Becker
1876–1907

The Boundless Pre-Feminist

We are so accustomed to the narrative that women did not have real power and freedom before the women's movement of the 1970s that it is sometimes a jolt to hear pre-feminism voices remonstrating against inequality. It is as if, somehow, the frustrated thoughts, unheard feelings, unfulfilled desires and psychological complexities of women only came into being once the feminist movement granted permission. But, of course, on reflection, this is a nonsense; the antagonism may have been repressed but it existed. Paula Modersohn-Becker was an exceptional artist who, in the first years of the last century, vehemently denied the social obligations of womanhood to pursue her unashamed ambition to be a successful artist. Her voice, expressed in a large volume of letters and journals, rings out across the decades to us today as a powerful reminder of the stifling limitations placed upon women of her era. Furthermore, the startling work she created with a furious intensity is a marvellously vital addition to the male-dominated story of Modernism.

Her paintings, kept in the margins of art history for so long, present us with a radical vision of womanhood. In 1907 Picasso undeniably broke new ground with his original treatment of the female nude in *Les Demoiselles d'Avignon*, but in the same time period Modersohn-Becker was painting the first nude self-portrait in art history by a woman artist. To encounter Modersohn-Becker's work for the first time, as many are still doing, is a revelation. Her style is not like anyone else's. While it's safe to say she belongs in the Expressionism camp, her take on form, shape, colour and attitude towards her subject of choice, namely women, is entirely her own. Classically trained, like many artists of the period, she slowly unpicked the threads of her academic life drawing education to reorganize her practice in her own highly individualized way. Her subjects are painted in an elegantly clumsy fashion: bold shapes, flat forms with non-delineated but readable features. They feel intimate yet exotic, bold but not overwrought. Her *Self Portrait* of 1906, which shows her as a half-length nude wearing a large amber necklace against a floral backdrop, still packs a punch over a hundred years later. It synthesizes Paul Gauguin's primitive obsessions, Henri Rousseau's naivety, Fauvism's freedom with colour, the formal experiments of Paul Cézanne and then enters into a new territory of its own. She has crafted herself into a rare presentation: part supplicant nude as painted for centuries by men; part independent modern woman; part artistically exotic creature whose cat-like eyes look away peacefully. It's a beguiling mixture that makes for an irresistible painting and if we needed an icon for the dangers of excluding women from the canon of art history this could well be it.

Born in Dresden in 1876, Modersohn-Becker's career did not come easily. Although she showed such early promise that her parents consented for her to attend art school in London aged just sixteen, she was soon after coerced into a two-year governess programme to secure a future job. During her training she continued to take art classes and when she graduated, she convinced her father to let her attend an art school for women in Berlin. He agreed to only a short stay, which she managed to extend to two pieears. In 1898 she was thrilled to be able to move to Bremen to join an artist's colony in Worpswede. Not content to focus only on nature, Modersohn-Becker started to visit Paris regularly from 1900. After returning from her first trip, she became engaged to colony artist Otto Modersohn, at which point her father asked her to relinquish her ego and sent her to cookery school so she would make a good wife. Her husband Otto was a widower whose first wife had died just months before, leaving him with a two-year-old daughter. Now a young stepmother, Modersohn-Becker never fully adapted to family life and clearly one reason she married was to secure financial security, as she was still dependent on her increasingly despairing father. Her diaries reveal that 'it is my experience that marriage does not make one happier' and note that she was delighted when Otto was away so she could eat simply and spend more time painting and less time cooking.

In 1906, after years of visiting Paris for solo trips to attend art classes, Modersohn-Becker left Worpswede for good without saying goodbye. She painted furiously, dismissing her mother's appeals for her to return to her family: 'Now I am beginning a new life. Don't interfere, just let me be.' Her diaries record that she was confident in her new painting, stating: 'I am becoming something – I am living the most intensely happy time of my life.' It was beginning to pay off, her work was included in exhibitions and she received excellent reviews. Her decision to focus on her art at all costs was radical for her time but not without inner turmoil. One of the most fascinating paintings of this period alone in Paris is *Self-Portrait on Sixth Wedding Anniversary*. Again, she is nude from the waist up wearing the same amber necklace. She looks out to the viewer and holds her pregnant stomach. It's a fascinating presentation not least because, in reality, she was not pregnant. At once harmonious in its serene golden tonal qualities, it also shows the messy side of life and puts us in touch with the agonizing decisions about motherhood and women's choices a century ago that feel unbelievably relevant today.

Unlike her contemporary Gauguin who sailed to Tahiti and cut his ties with his wife and young children, Modersohn-Becker reconciled with her husband who joined her in Paris in late 1906; they later returned to the colony. Having never before then consummated their marriage, she now found herself pregnant. Unsurprisingly, this did not deter her from her practice and she vowed to be both a mother and a successful artist. I think she would be

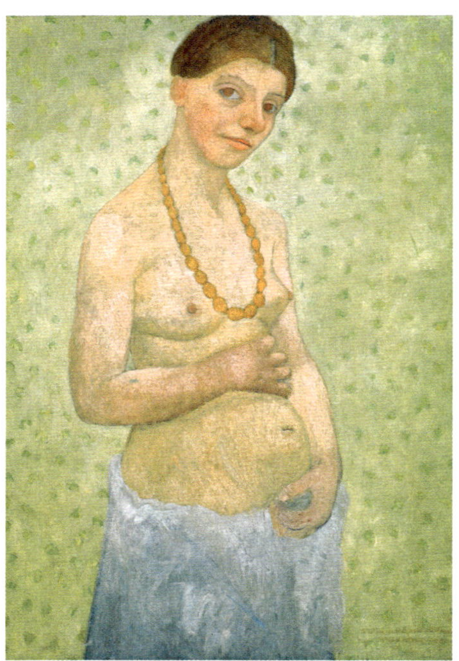

Self-Portrait on Sixth Wedding Anniversary
Paula Modersohn-Becker (1876–1907)
1906, oil on card,
101.8 × 70.2 cm (40 × 27 ½ in),
Paula Modersohn-Becker-Museum, Bremen,
Germany

horrified to realize the struggle to 'have it all' is still very much present in
women's lives and that unidealized imagery of women is still not the norm. In
this regard her paintings are uncompromising in their authentic presentation
of womanhood. Her painting of 1906, again before she herself became
pregnant, *Reclining Mother-and-Child II* portrays a moment of poignant
tenderness between the two without sentiment or idealization. The mother
reclines on the ground, her large breasts, gently rounded stomach and pubic
hair visible while her child feeds lying alongside her. This is not the upright

Madonna and suckling child enthroned as a pair of centuries past, it is the kind of untidy and yet instinctive breastfeeding pose only a woman would portray.

On 2 November 1907 this daring artist became a mother to a daughter and she instantly loved her new perfect nude model. Shortly after the birth she complained of pains in her leg and was ordered to take bed rest. Two weeks later she got out of bed, fell to the floor, proclaiming 'What a pity' and died aged thirty-one years old. She had suffered a postpartum embolism, which bedrest had made fatal: as she stood up, the blood clot travelled to her heart and instantly killed her. Modersohn-Becker never fulfilled her dream of becoming a mother with a successful painting career. Her works would, however, have a major public outing thirty years after her death, though one of the most unpleasant kind. Reviled by the Nazis as 'lacking in femininity and so vulgar', her work was among paintings by Pablo Picasso, Paul Klee, Piet Mondrian, Marc Chagall and Wassily Kandinsky in the Degenerate Art Exhibition of 1937. In this perverse manner her work was featured in the exalted company of the great modern masters. Modersohn-Becker's letters and journals were published after her death by her mother and she became the first female artist to have a museum in her honour. An Expressionist architectural gem, it narrowly avoided being destroyed by the Nazis and today has the largest holdings of her work.

Modersohn-Becker remains a hidden treasure of art history, though several books and exhibitions have emerged in this century to bring her into the canon. To the artists who have already discovered Modersohn-Becker, she has become a talisman, a singular visionary who signalled that women artists were not only valid but had a distinct perspective long overlooked. She was loved by Frida Kahlo, and today for Tracey Emin and Cindy Sherman she is a vital pioneer. Jenny Holzer went as far as to say, 'I was encouraged and frightened by her story' and that the artist's reinvention of motherhood in art influenced her Venice Biennale presentation in 1990. Modersohn-Becker's work is fundamental in presenting a fuller account of the development of avant-garde painting, helping us to build a more cohesive (and less male dominated) picture of the march towards Modernism.

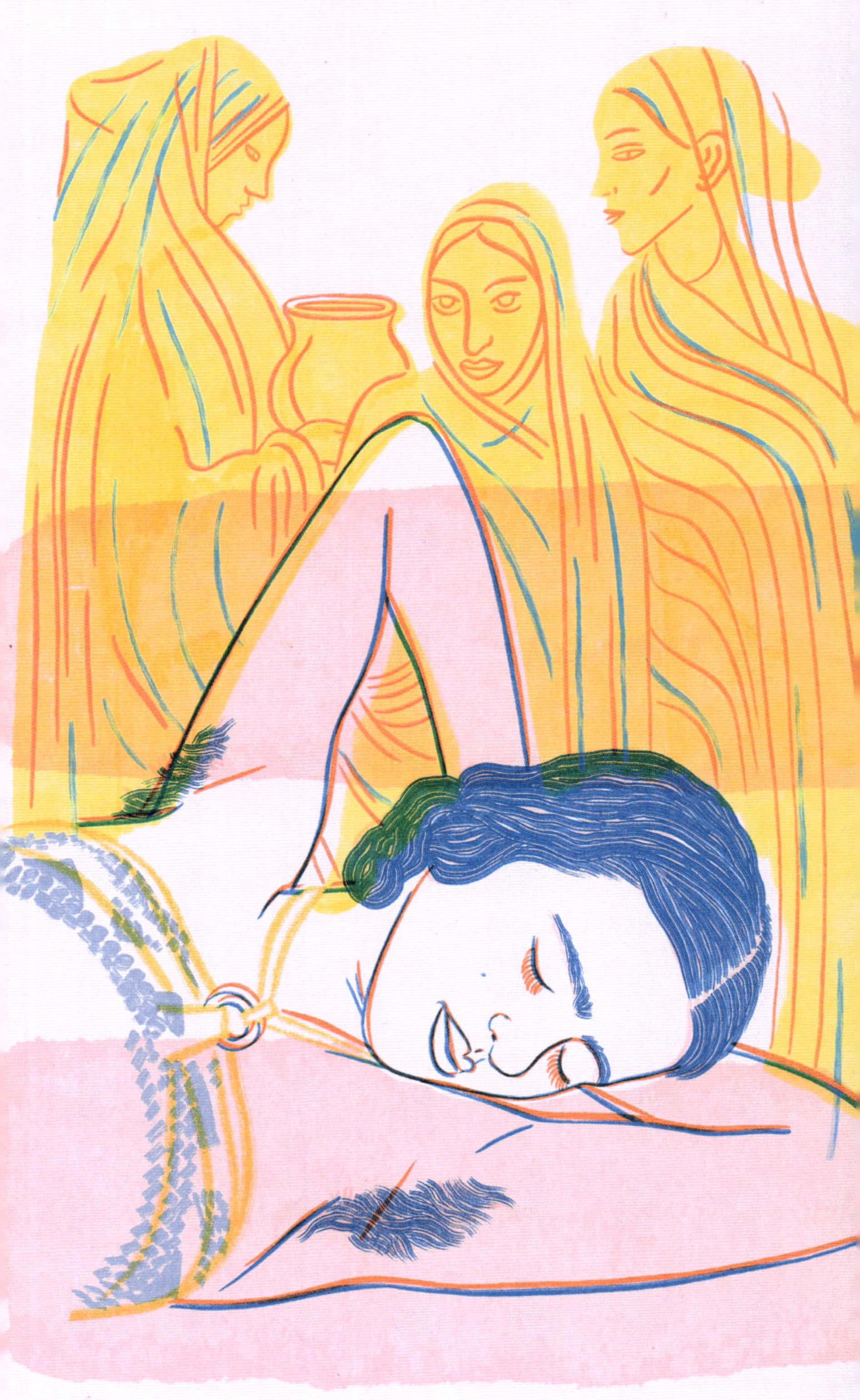

Master of 'the Other'

'Little by little I realize that every person carries within herself a calling against which it is hopeless to fight.' So assured was Amrita Sher-Gil that, aged sixteen, she convinced her parents to relocate from India to Paris so she could study to pursue her ambition to become an artist. This would be a remarkable move for a family to undertake today, let alone in 1929 for the sake of a daughter. Not only would Sher-Gil find early success in the Parisian art world, her work would also go on to help lay the foundations for modern art in India. Her approach to depicting women as independently minded with a range of authentic emotions was pioneering compared to the Indian conservative mainstream that portrayed generic women as happily obliging in their domestic servitude. As an artist with both European and Indian heritage as well an impressive knowledge of both cultures, Sher-Gil occupies a singular space in art history and today her work commands record-breaking prices at auction.

Born in Hungary in 1913 Sher-Gil's father was a Sikh scholar and her mother from an affluent, cultured Hungarian family. The family moved to Simla when she was eight years old. Sher-Gil broke the mould from a young age: she was expelled from a Catholic school in India for protesting against the bigotry and narrowmindedness of the school. Her mother recognized her artistic talents early on, and spurred on by her intellectual brother and Amrita's uncle, she advocated to move her two daughters to Paris so Sher-Gil could attend art school. At the École nationale supérieure des Beaux-Arts in Paris the teenage artist quickly found a strong footing, drawing nudes from life and already turning away from a realistic classical tradition. Her work was awarded the gold medal at the prestigious annual exhibition Grand Salon of 1933 and she was welcomed as an associate member of the institute, which allowed her to exhibit two paintings there every year. For a young woman – who was still a student and an outsider – this was an extraordinary accomplishment.

The five years Sher-Gil spent in Paris would not only provide a brilliant education in the epicentre of the art world, but also a closeness with the European avant-garde and culture of bohemia. Multilingual – she was speaking fluent French within her first year in Paris – she was an avid reader and applied the lessons of the Impressionists and Post-Impressionists in her practice. *Self Portrait as Tahitian* (1934) is one of many striking portrayals of herself. In the three-quarter-length painting she is nude from the waist up, turned almost to profile. Paying a direct debt to Paul Gauguin's exotic images of Tahitian women, there is a solemn quality to the expression and a flattened approach to form. The colour is subdued and the backdrop of a Japanese print is a further nod to Post-Impressionist influences. Where Gauguin's paintings are problematic for their appropriation of another culture under colonial control, Sher-Gil's vision is free from inelegant assumptions. As a young woman familiar with both European fine society and colonial rule in India, she was able to present a complex range of issues from the position of being part of 'otherness' and also a voyeur to it herself through the avant-garde art she admired that co-opted Primitivism. As would become her signature, the young woman's face is far away, neither condoning objectification nor inviting it. She was a master at capturing psychological depth where others might only achieve beauty.

Had Sher-Gil remained in Paris she would most certainly have continued on her upward trajectory in that exciting milieu. What makes her art even more compelling and adds a further layer of resonance is that after five years she returned home to Lahore, then a magnet for India's legendary writers, creatives and intellectuals. In the 1930s she wrote that she was 'haunted by an intense longing to return to India, feeling in some strange inexplicable way that there lay my destiny as a painter'. Her first painting upon her return won a gold medal from the Bombay Art Society. *Group of Three Girls* (1935) shows a further reduction in form, and movement away from her classical life drawing education. The painting is intense in colour, composition and mood. The women are set against a dark earthy backdrop, their robes moving from a light green through to orange through to the striking earthy dark red of the woman closest to the viewer – a sensual colour that would come to be a signature of her work in India. Each woman is alone with her thoughts, the shadows on the wall behind perhaps a reminder that they are on view and contributing to a distinct sense of unease. Sher-Gil was a critic of the subjugation of women in India; as young as twelve she wrote in her journal of a young thirteen-year-old bride whose wedding she attended who had been married off to a thirty-five-year-old man with two wives already. Sher-Gil ruminated on the episode, describing the child bride as a 'helpless toy'.

Sher-Gil is often compared to Frida Kahlo due to the emotional reservoir lying just beneath the surface of her figurative work, not to mention the forcefulness of her personality and independence of mind against all odds. When Sher-Gil returned from bohemian Paris to India, she did so with a reputation as a young woman with an appetite for sex, and rumours circled about her possible relationships with women. The myths of her intense love making and disregard for conservative values have been laboured over by writers, perhaps in an effort to draw comparisons with iconic women from history. However, as with Kahlo, I don't think we need to indulge in the myth of the 'harlot painter', her work stands for itself as a vital contribution to the canon that, for too long, overlooked those who

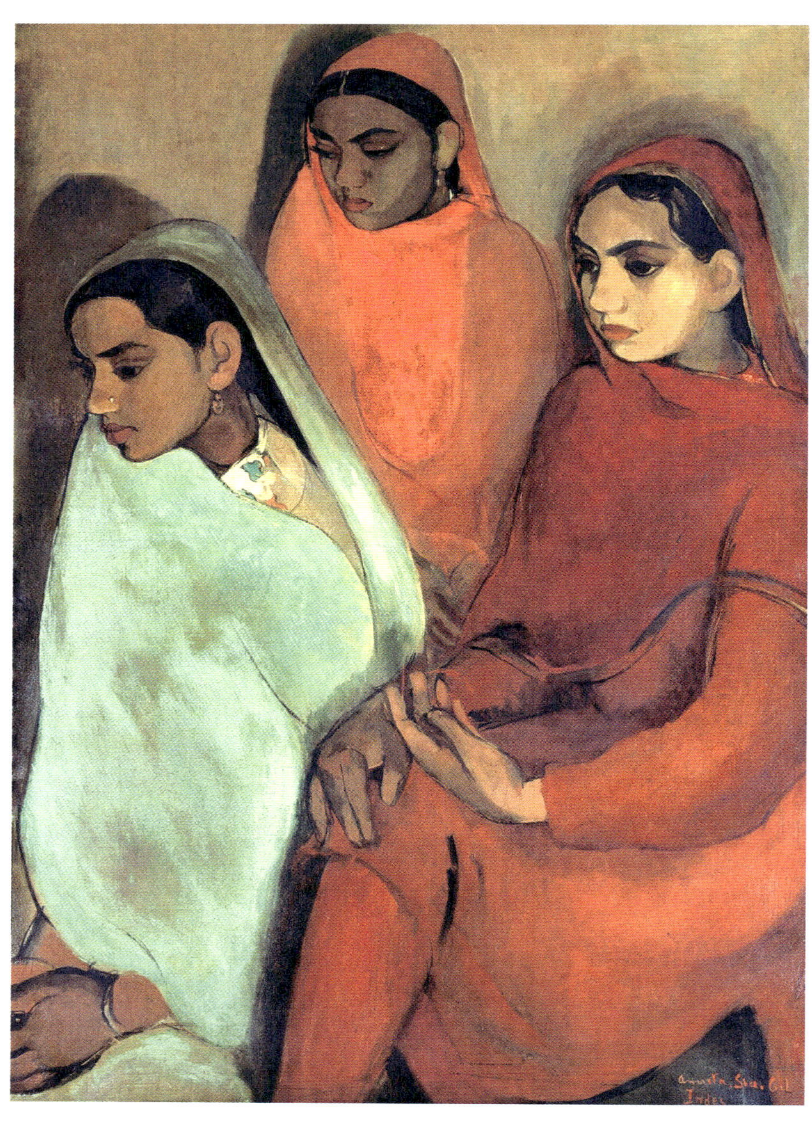

Group of Three Girls
Amrita Sher-Gil (1913–1941)
1935, oil on canvas,
92.5 × 66.6 cm (36 ½ × 26 ¼ in),
National Gallery of Modern Art, New Delhi, India

were not white males. What is more impressive are the words she leaves us with that show she had an enormous self-belief and drive and the words of others that repeatedly talk of how she had a special energy. She was a worldly, intellectual painter who lit up the room.

Her death in 1941, aged just twenty-eight, sent shock waves through the cultured society of Lahore. There is no clear answer as to what caused her sudden demise. Her husband (she married her first cousin, Victor Egan) reported that she had eaten something that caused dysentery or peritonitis, but other reports from friends shortly after her death claim that he was covering up a failed abortion. Sher-Gil passed away a matter of days before her first major solo show in the city was due to open and so she didn't witness the impact that her work would have on the India she had felt so strongly she must return to. Because the planned exhibition did not happen and she died so young, most of her 143 paintings remained in the possession of her family. Her husband would later donate forty-five pieces to the New Delhi's National Gallery of Modern Art, creating the core of the modern collection.

Sher-Gil would become emblematic of modern India, although, as is the fate for many women artists, even those revered in their home countries, it would take decades for her work to start to receive the international attention it deserves. In 2007, Tate Modern hosted an exhibition of her work, and in the past decade Sher-Gil's work has come to auction rarely but always to spectacular reception. In 2015 a self-portrait sold at Christies in London for £1,762,500. Salmon Rushdie selected Sher-Gil as the basis for a character in his novel *The Moor's Last Sigh*, explaining that she was 'the figure that, so to speak "gave me permission" to imagine her personality, to invent a woman painter at the very heart of modern art in India – to believe in the possibility of such a woman'. Soundly rooted in the thrilling principles of European Modernism and updated to harness the sensitivities not only of the Indian experience, but of a female perspective, Sher-Gil's work remains unparalleled.

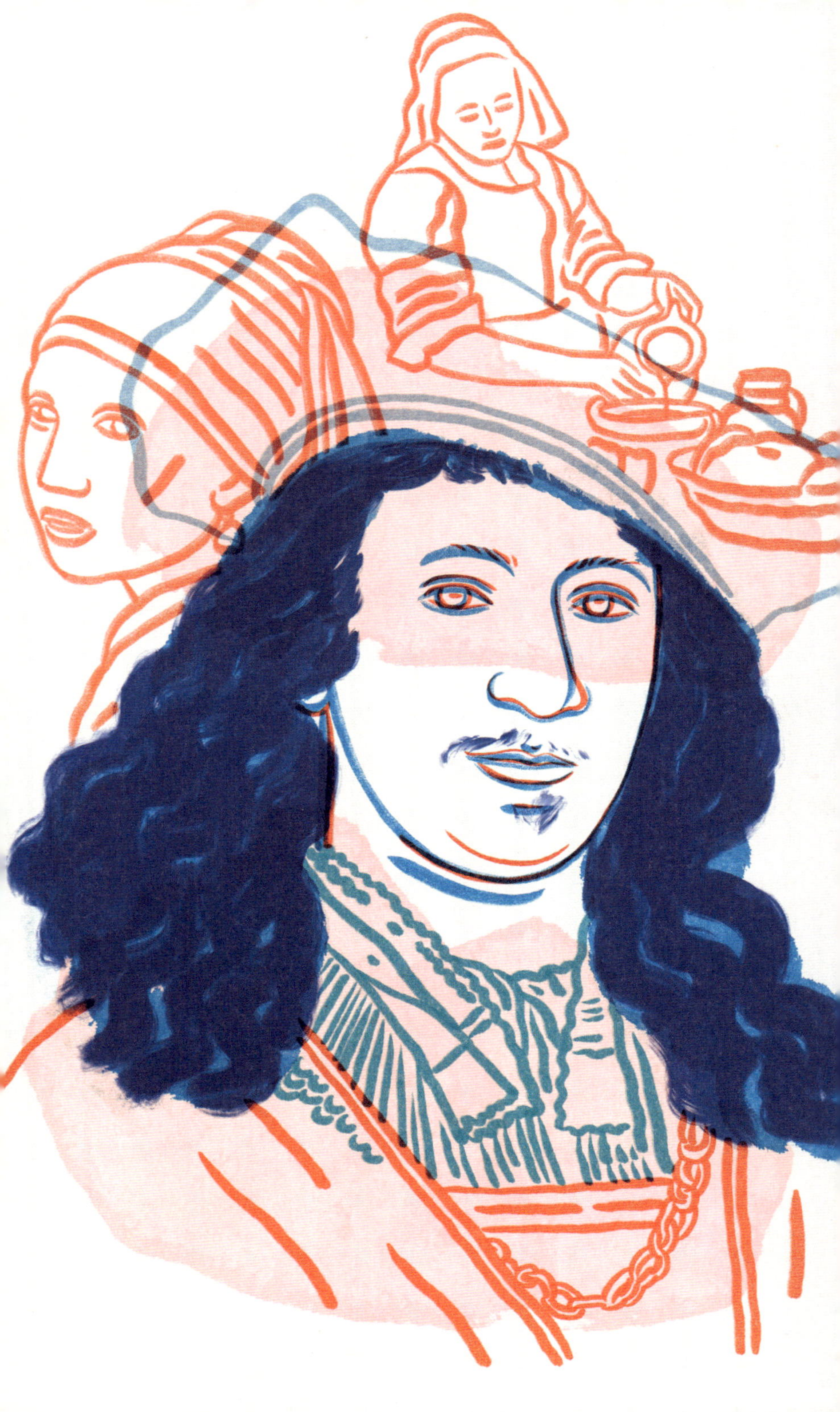

Johannes
Vermeer
1632–1675

Overlooked No More

irl with a Pearl Earring belongs to a rare species in history, an artwork that has become a cultural benchmark globally. It's creator, Johannes Vermeer, however, remains largely in the shadows. Known as the 'Mona Lisa of the North', the painting has effortlessly slipped into our shared consciousness despite the majority of people not knowing the name of the artist. What's more, scholars remain frustrated by the lack of information about the man who created jewel-like paintings that pulsate with light and detail. Dead by his early forties, Vermeer left almost no impression of himself and fewer than forty paintings. Unlike his fellow Dutchman Rembrandt who fell from the height of fame into poverty, Vermeer was never well known in his lifetime. He never left his home city of Delft, he had no pupils and no distinguished patrons. The fact that his work is so esteemed today, in fact valuable and desirable enough to create one of the largest forgery scandals of modern times, is one of the small miracles of art history.

Vermeer is an artist who made the ordinary extraordinary. Almost all of his paintings focus on domestic interior scenes, with the same light source, furniture and motifs appearing regularly. Ostensibly, he was painting his own modest domain, which in a poorer artist's hand could be dreary. In Vermeer's sumptuously lit paintings, his eye for realistic detail, compositional harmony and atmospheric use of space make his scenes exquisite windows into a parallel universe. His work is not grand, tragic, baroque or showy. Instead he shows us a lace maker intensely preoccupied with her work, a forlorn young woman reading a letter, a maid carefully pouring milk, a music lesson in progress. Nothing is sentimental, kitsch or didactic. The paintings are pioneering because they relate to the modern preoccupation for the simple pleasures of life and the beauty of those in-between moments.

The appeal of his work most likely resides in the special combination of factors that make them beautiful, technical, scarce and created by someone who remains unknown to us. The lack of information about Vermeer and his practice has resulted in an engaged enquiry from art historians as well as experts from other fields keen to somehow decode the majesty of his small oeuvre. Vermeer had a compulsive eye for detail and worked at a pace of only two paintings a year, an almost farcical rate when we compare that to fifty paintings completed in the same timespan by his peers. There is little evidence that he created drawings or used tracing in his final works and yet he was able to achieve an almost photorealistic finish. The British artist David Hockney has joined the ranks of scholars who have posited that Vermeer used basic technologies such as camera lucida, camera obscura and concave mirrors to assist him in the pursuit of a precise painting style. It is not known if Vermeer was formally trained as an artist apprentice, but we know that he was elected four times to be the Head of the Artists' Guild of St Luke. However, we shouldn't take this to mean he was financially secure. A collector once arrived at his home to see his work and was promptly sent to the local baker to whom he had given paintings on loan in exchange for much-needed bread. He certainly had a lot of mouths to feed. Vermeer's wife, for whom he converted to Catholicism, bore fourteen children, eleven of them survived beyond infancy.

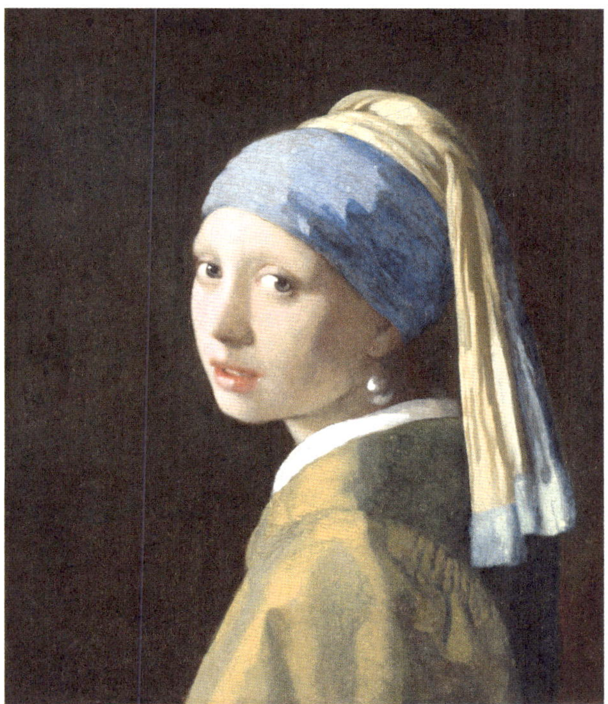

Girl with a Pearl Earring
Johannes Vermeer (1632–1675)
c. 1665, oil on canvas,
44.5 × 39 cm (17 ½ × 15 ¼ in),
The Mauritshuis, The Hague,
the Netherlands

The paucity of his output and tales of pawning paintings that would one day be worth millions could set the stage for the myth of a tortured, unfortunate artist. But Vermeer is a much more complex character than that. His mother-in-law was a wealthy woman and he converted to Catholicism, still a religion that had to be conducted out of sight, in order to marry her daughter. The conversion didn't occur just for the financial advantages the marriage brought, as Vermeer seems to have become a devout Catholic, and the introspective and tender portrayals of women in his work have led viewers to assume that he was a dedicated family man. He also inherited his father's art dealing business and was an inn keeper. He was smart enough to charge a high price for his own paintings, most likely to make up for their scarcity and had at least one regular local patron. He did not make any sacrifices in his art and was categorically unsparing in his choice of materials, employing the most expensive of pigments for his pictures that would normally be employed by more established artists and only when working on religious commissions.

Vermeer's untimely demise was not caused by disease or war but rather by the effects of the major financial crisis that occurred after the Year of Disaster in 1672. After the French invaded the Dutch Republic, the country was severely affected for a number of years. Like many citizens, Vermeer took out a loan in 1675 in order to steady the family. His wife described his death thus as she later tried to extricate herself from the debt: 'During the ruinous war with France he not only was unable to sell any of his art but also, to his great detriment, was left sitting with the paintings of other masters that he was dealing in. As a result and owing to the great burden of his children having no means of his own, he lapsed into such decay and decadence, which he had so taken to heart that, as if he had fallen into a frenzy, in a day and a half he went from being healthy to being dead.' Vermeer's illness was short and the exact nature of his stress-related death aged forty-three remains a mystery.

Vermeer's tiny body of paintings had to wait two hundred years to find their audience. Although in his lifetime he sold his work with moderate success, after his death his paintings remained overlooked and misattributed until 1860 when they were rediscovered and championed by the brilliant German museum director Gustav Waagen. The attention he brought to Vermeer resulted in the first exhaustive attempt to catalogue the artist's work, undertaken by the French scholar Théophile Thoré-Bürger, who published his research in 1866, at that time mistakenly attributing more than seventy works to him, the number now stands at a more conservative thirty-four. The timing of Vermeer's rediscovery was fortunate. France was hitting its stride as the new centre of the art world with a burgeoning middle class who appreciated art and a host of artists who would start to convey everyday scenes for the first time. Vermeer's world of pensive female figures engaged in their activities in contemporary surroundings was not so different from the approach taken by artists like Edouard Manet or Henri de Toulouse-Lautrec. By the 1930s the great Surrealist Salvador Dalí made work in direct homage to the Delft master, who was now in the international spotlight. It was also in this decade that Han van Meegeren, the most notorious art forger in history, began to make his own Vermeer paintings, even selling a work to Hermann Göring – a prized possession for the Nazi party that derided the avant-garde but idolized the quiet introspection of Vermeer.

Vermeer's paintings have that intoxicating combination of being somehow instantly familiar upon first viewing and remaining unknowable. He is an enigmatic figure, thwarted by financial ruin and yet uncompromising right to the end in both his painstaking execution and unsparing choice of luxuriant pigments. His penchant for portraying what we feel to be the authentic reality of the few rooms he and his enormous family shared make him a pioneer for a modern art world that would turn the lens away from religious painting, mythology and grand historical subjects to everyday people and scenes. Like Van Gogh and Modigliani after him, he would never know that his exacting meditations on the smallest of moments would not only remain forever suspended in time, but touch millions of people around the world.

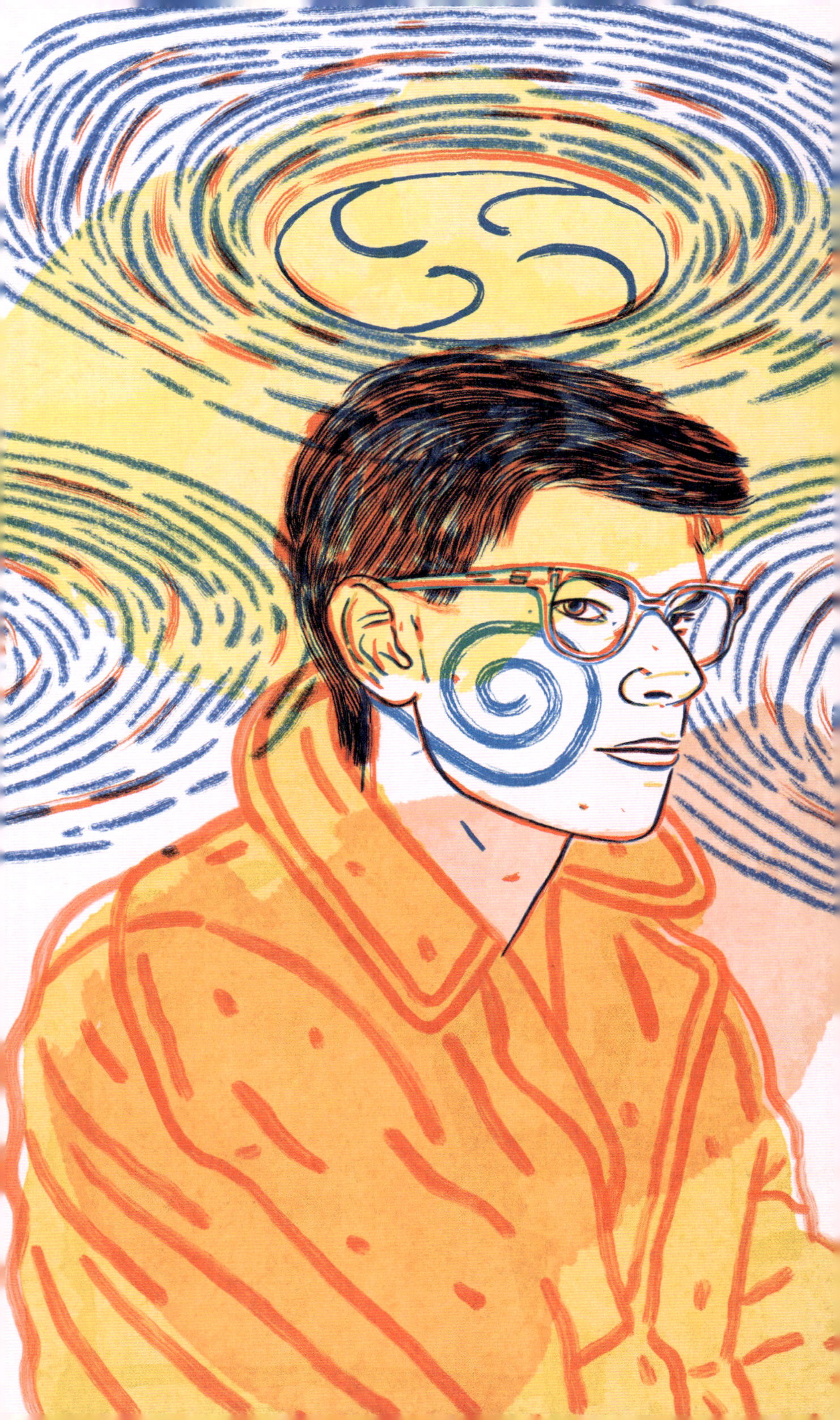

Robert Smithson
1938–1973

Master of the Land

Robert Smithson is the man behind one of the most important and influential artworks of the twentieth century, *Spiral Jetty*. Dating from 1970, it quickly entered the canon of art history and has become a touchstone for new ways of thinking about creating and displaying art. We often think of artists as belonging to a style or a period, their legacy attached to art history, not art in a singular fashion. It is even more unusual, then, that an artist who had a short career could, with time, become absolutely wedded to numerous, iconic artworks, such as *Broken Circle/Spiral Hill* and *Partially Buried Woodshed*. More staggering still is that an artwork that speaks for them, like the aforementioned *Spiral Jetty*, was lost from sight for decades and without serious intervention will inevitably one day disappear entirely.

A pivotal work of Land Art, *Spiral Jetty* was created directly on the northeastern shore of Great Salt Lake of Utah. The scale was unprecedented. Smithson arranged more than six and a half thousand tonnes of basalt rocks and earth from the site into the shape of a coil that measures fifteen feet wide and one and a half thousand feet in length. Leading from the shore into the water, Smithson's work was the very antithesis of the notion of art as a sanctified object that was made to last and be treasured at all costs. His alteration of the landscape was not precious; from the moment it was created it showed signs of deterioration. *Spiral Jetty* has never been fixed in time, it cannot physically be one thing, it is in a constant state of change and flux and ultimately one day will disappear. Smithson's great achievement with *Spiral Jetty* was the spectacular shorthand he created for revealing both the splendour and fragility of nature. The artwork was a thoroughly modern concept while physically and aesthetically sharing a great deal with prehistoric art, as close to Stonehenge as it was to art of Smithson's era.

Smithson came of age as an artist in the final act of Abstract Expressionism and Pop Art. He belonged to a generation of artists who would eventually turn away from these movements. The tide was turning towards less noisy and commercial kinds of art making, the new order was detached and thorough in its examination of what constituted art and how art should be experienced. Minimalism and Conceptualism would emerge as the dominant trends. Smithson embraced Minimalism's reductive aesthetic and use of industrial materials. A keen student of minerology, geology and the theory of entropy – the second law of thermodynamics that forecasts the eventual exhaustion and collapse of any natural system – Smithson's breakthrough was to take art out of the white cube of the gallery and into the natural world. The artist coined the term Land Art and also used the name Earth Art to describe what he and his peers were developing. In 1963 he married fellow artist Nancy Holt; she shared his preoccupation with the Great American West. It was Smithson, though, that would make the first masterpiece of the movement, confidently creating *Spiral Jetty* by using the earth as his raw material and the landscape as his canvas.

Land Art emerged alongside hippy culture but it had a machismo that saw the main figures competing to surpass previous notions of scale, physical feats and elements of risk involved in creating gigantic interventions. In this context, Smithson has become one of the most enigmatic artists of the last century. He broke down age-old boundaries and art traditions by creating one of the world's largest artworks in the middle of nowhere that was promptly subsumed by the landscape. His legendary status was sealed when he died three years after completing his masterpiece. While surveying the terrain for a new work, his plane crashed, ending his life at just thirty-five years of age.

Although Smithson did not have a long and full career like his wife Nancy Holt, who outlived him by more than forty years and remained committed to the principles of Land Art, he leaves behind an

"I'm not a reductive artist, I'm a generative artist"

extremely important legacy. Smithson was a theorist and great thinker about art and committed lots of his ideas to paper. These have become a huge source of inspiration for generations of artists. He has an almost mythical status in the art world today. So much so that in 2005 a tiny sketch the artist left behind of a boat tugging a small piece of Central Park around the Island of Manhattan was realized posthumously. *Floating Island to Travel Around Manhattan Island* (1970–2005) was an ingeniously simple premise, instantly reminding the viewer that

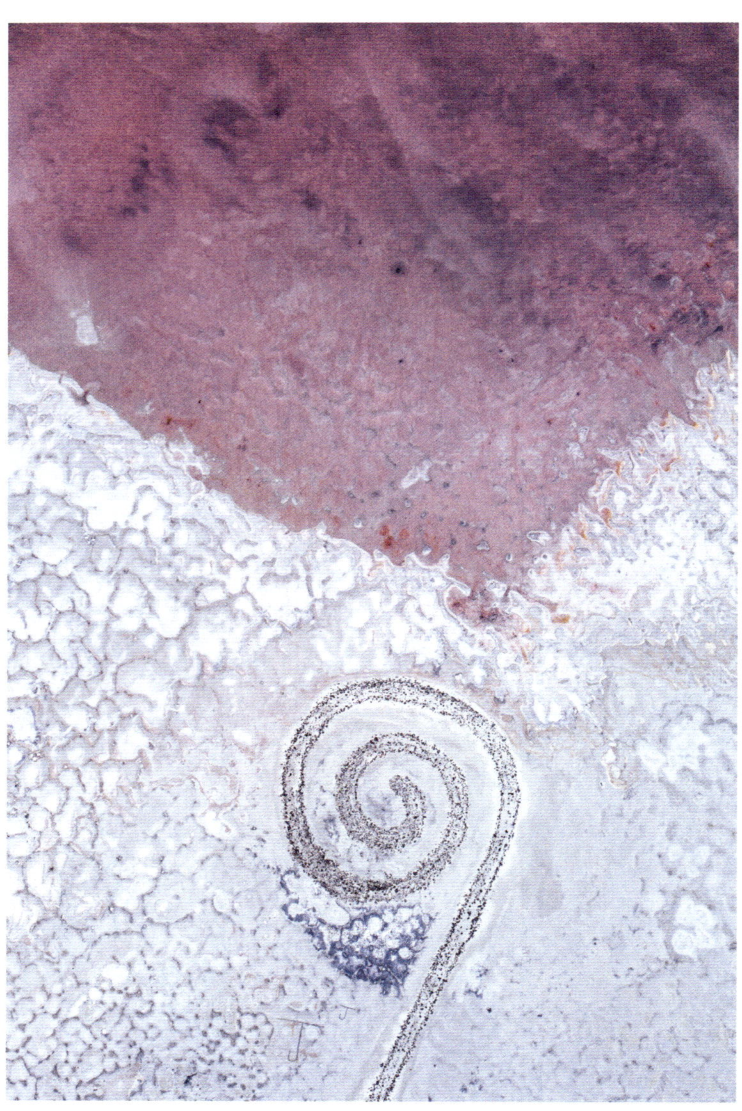

Spiral Jetty
Robert Smithson (1938–1973)
1970, black rock, salt crystals, earth, red water,
45,720 × 457.2 cm (18,000 × 180 in),
Great Salt Lake, Utah, USA

the New York urban jungle was indeed an island, often easy to forget, especially given how the island's infrastructure has seen the addition of several more bridges and tunnels since his death, not to mention mass construction.

As with all of Smithson's ideas and artworks, the realization of his concept resulted in a complicated relationship between the artwork and the viewer. Those who knew about the piece being staged to honour the deceased artist found good viewing spots across Manhattan, but many more New Yorkers may have witnessed an island being pulled around an island without any comprehension they were witnessing a historic moment. The artwork could never be completely seen or consumed; like *Spiral Jetty,* it was constantly changing and with each passing second the materials were resisting their new purpose and finding their way back to nature. Smithson saw the world as constant beautiful flux, in his universe the notion of a bronze on a plinth in a gallery was ludicrous. He was decades ahead of his time by emphasizing experience and the interconnectivity of all things. Today Smithson's influence underpins our current passion for experiential art installations and *Spiral Jetty* remains a site of almost sacred art pilgrimage, legally and culturally protected as if it was in fact a prehistoric wonder.

Four

Battles & Salvation

Although I have tried to untangle the age-old mythology surrounding the tortured artist in chapter two, I don't deny that the life of an artist is a very different kind to most. In many respects an artist *is* their work, which is a manifestation of how they see the world, how they think, feel and experience time at a particular moment. For some, art might be a place of refuge, a way to navigate difficult circumstances and find a kind of salvation.

As sick children, both Henri de Toulouse-Lautrec and Aubrey Beardsley found art a source of immense comfort and inspiration. Toulouse-Lautrec suffered a great deal in his life as a result of physical shortcomings caused by his parents being first cousins. His art would not only entertain him through his convalescences, but would become his passport to freedom away from a stifling aristocratic family. At the same time as Toulouse-Lautrec in Paris, in London in the 1890s Aubrey Beardsley would also be given an opportunity to shine socially through his art, despite being a sickly person. The spectre of tuberculosis hung over his short life, and eventually as the disease gained ground, he would throw himself further into his quest to make ground-breaking and shocking imagery. I can't help but speculate that without the illness that made them outsiders and conscious of their own mortality, Toulouse-Lautrec and Beardsley would not have made such radical, forward-thinking artwork. Perhaps knowing it was unlikely they would have long careers, they did not have time to lose nor the same regard for social expectations.

In Los Angeles in 2012, an ambitious young African American artist and curator, Noah Davis co-founded the Underground Museum. Not content to simply enjoy the success he was experiencing as a distinctive new voice in painting, Davis was determined to make real change in his community. The Underground Museum delivered art to a part of the city that was unserved by the cultural world. Davis was remarkable for bringing an unassuming space in what was considered the 'wrong neighbourhood' institutional recognition and support. Unlike Beardsley and Toulouse-Lautrec, Davis had always been healthy and had no knowledge that his life would be cut short. He spent his final months after his cancer diagnosis programming years and years' worth of exhibitions for the Underground Museum. Art was more than just an escape from his own illness, the museum had a clear mission. As his friend and colleague Helen Molesworth put it, it was 'the creation of a dream world that made space for other people's dreams too.'

Like Davis, Eva Hesse also died in her early thirties with little warning that cancer would cut her promising career short. After a traumatic childhood fleeing Nazi Germany, Hesse had long found making art a source of complex catharsis, producing enigmatic and strange sculptures using unstable and unconventional materials. Despite enjoying critical success, as a young female artist she risked being forgotten and I stress the importance of feminist scholar Lucy Lippard in securing her a place in the canon.

Like Hesse, Charlotte Salomon was a German Jew, but she was tragically not able to escape the Nazis and was murdered in Auschwitz aged just twenty-six. Unlike Hesse, who has long been studied and even cited as a great example of proto-feminist art, Salomon is still neglected by art history, despite producing one of the most passionate, expansive and 'total works of art' in the last century. Her masterpiece *Life? or Theatre?* was created in a fury of activity and is a pioneering form of art. Partly autobiographical, Salomon's work was a modern *Singspiel*, a kind of lesser German opera that featured hundreds of gouache paintings accompanied by text and musical instructions. It's compelling narrative, visual originality and dramatic pace makes me think of the work as a graphic novel ahead of its time. Although she created it as a refugee while hiding from the Nazis in the south of France, it is not the context of the Third Reich that dominates the artwork. Rather it is her own dark family secrets and her young love life. The artwork was a literal salvation, taking its title from the choice she posed to herself to either end her own life, as so many of her loved ones had done, or to create art from it. Art literally saved her and was a productive respite from the battles she endured with family, herself and Nazi persecution.

Salomon used art to fight depression and suicidal thoughts whereas other artists in this section employed their artistry in literal battles. Umberto Boccioni saw art as an instrumental tool in overthrowing the old order and celebrating the new modern age of speed and machines. Along with his artistic brotherhood, the Futurists, Boccioni idealized war as a cleansing process by which progress could be made. Despite being offered an alternative, Boccioni was an artist who sought out the battlefield and he died doing cavalry training exercises.

Gerda Taro was the first woman photojournalist to die in the field during the Spanish Civil War. Like Hesse and Salomon, she was persecuted by the Nazis as a young German Jew and sought refuge in Paris. She was eager to wield her camera as a weapon in the war in Spain, not out of any misplaced idealism like Boccioni, but because she knew first-hand the dangers of Nationalism and wanted to reveal the human cost that General Franco was inflicting upon Republicans and civilians. Like Salomon, it is extraordinary that her work survived the circumstances of her death, and slowly the legacy of both women is being secured.

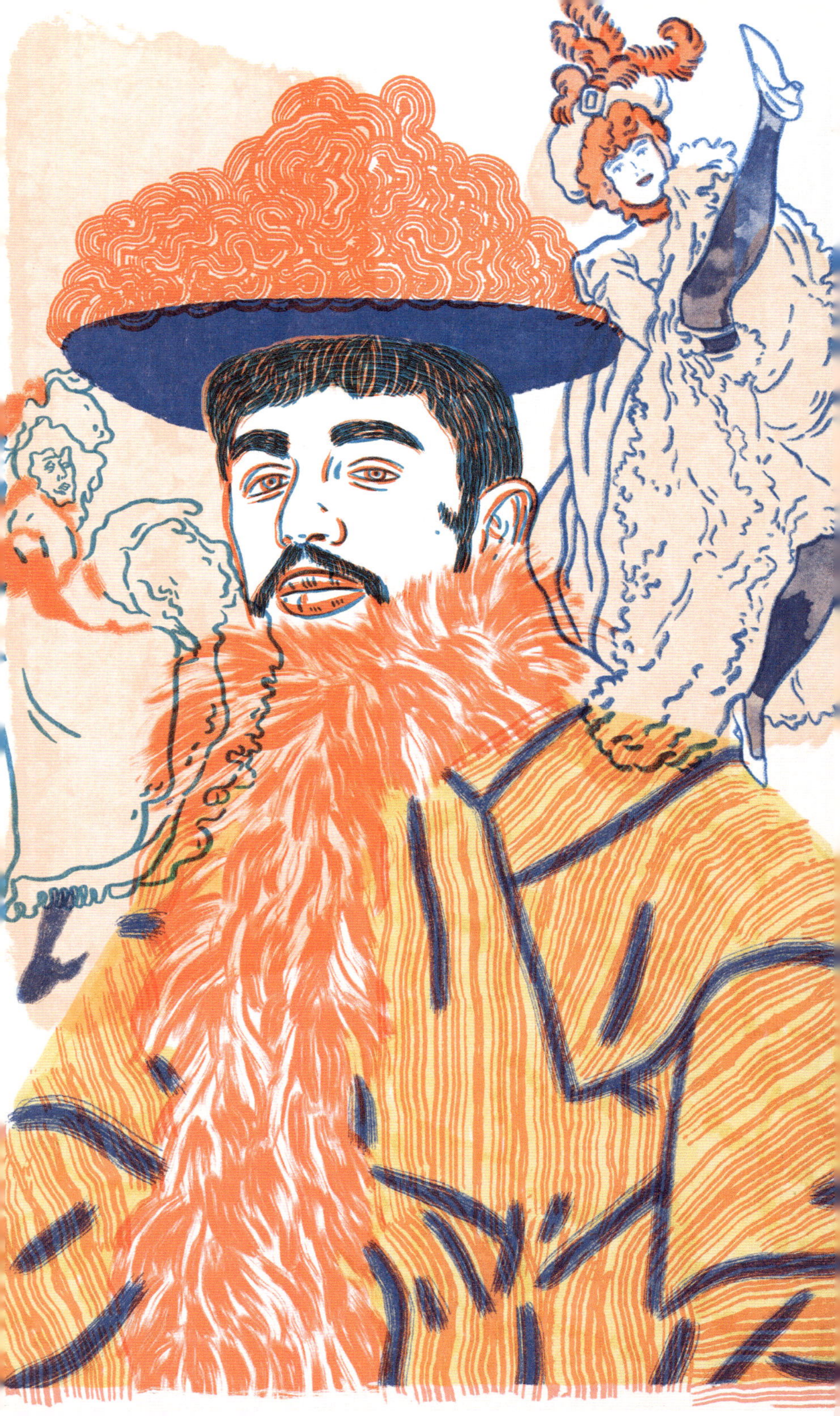

Henri
de Toulouse-Lautrec
1864–1901

Tender Bohemian

Henri de Toulouse-Lautrec was a star of *belle époque* Paris. The City of Light was at the centre of the world, brimming with a recently developed wealthy, middle-class population hungry for entertainment and a fine lifestyle. They were well provided for with the introduction of theatres, cabarets, parks and department stores, which were an immediate success, creating the beginnings of our modern indulgence – leisure time. Arriving in the city in 1882, Toulouse-Lautrec was a moth to the flame of Paris and he became one the period's most iconic chroniclers. His images of the Moulin Rouge thrilled the public in his own day and today they are downright mesmeric, almost torturing us with a longing to be able to time travel to witness this golden age for ourselves.

However, beneath the glamour and the bright lights lay an alternate reality, one that Toulouse-Lautrec was all too aware of. Paris at the turn of the century may have been thoroughly modern in some respects but it was also still unforgiving and harsh towards marginalized citizens. Those who were poor, unhealthy, considered immoral or outsiders were shunned. Toulouse-Lautrec's art has such staying power because he moved between worlds, a VIP of every theatre in town, he also skirted the margins of society as a lifelong victim of ill health, treated as a freak by bullies on account of his physical appearance.

Born to an aristocratic family with a lineage that could be traced back to Charlemagne, the young Henri should have been an object of jealousy, living in various fine estates in the south of France among a rich and indulgent dynasty, one day destined to take the title of Comte from his father. But his birthright was a curse, because to keep the lineage and its fortunes intact it had been a longstanding tradition to intermarry. Count Alphonse de Toulouse-Lautrec was a first cousin of his wife Countess Adèle Tapié de Celeyran, which resulted in genetic deformity for their children, Henri and his brother, who died aged one. As a child, Toulouse-Lautrec injured both legs and, as a consequence of the ill effects of inbreeding, never fully recovered. His bones ceased to grow and so he matured as an adult with child-size legs and a full torso. His full height was 1.52 metres, barely five foot, and it was painful to move, even supported by a walking stick. Toulouse-Lautrec's father was an eccentric, an obsessive huntsman who prized physical prowess above all and was disappointed in his bedridden only (surviving) child. Toulouse-Lautrec's mother was, however, doting to the point of suffocation and, despite her religious fervour, remained a lifelong supporter of her son. In his never-ending convalescence, Toulouse-Lautrec's passion and natural talent for drawing developed. Art would become his passport to escape an aristocratic world that crushed him with boredom and wanted to hide away one of their 'weak'.

Toulouse-Lautrec was just eighteen years old when he shunned his heritage – his father partially disowned him because of his artistic ambitions – and began a new life alone in Paris. He took formal instruction not at the traditional École des Beaux-Arts but in the studios of the modern-thinking artists, Leon Bonnat and Bernard Corman. Also enjoying Corman's experimental tuition was Vincent van Gogh, who became a subject for Toulouse-Lautrec in what is possibly the most moving, vital portrait of the Dutch artist ever created. Like the Impressionist painters he admired so much, Toulouse-Lautrec would draw from life and became a popular fixture sketching away while seated in a circus, theatre or bar.

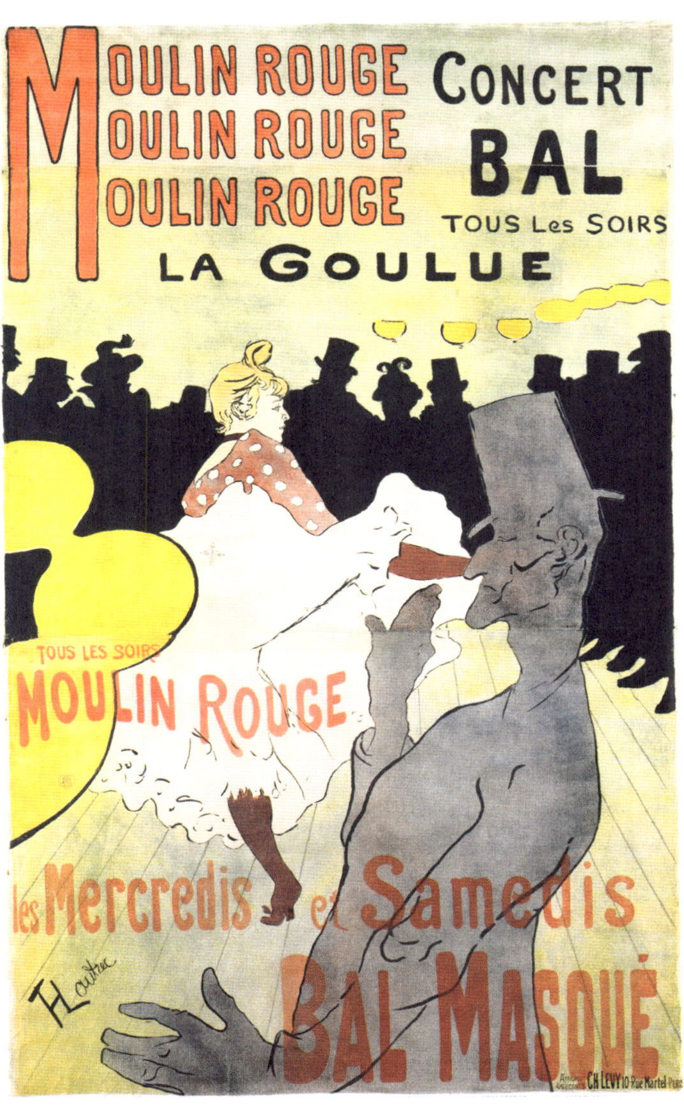

La Goulue at the Moulin Rouge, poster
Henri de Toulouse-Lautrec (1864–1901)
1891, colour lithograph,
1.7 × 1.3 m (5 ½ × 4 ¼ ft),
private collection

Despite his ongoing health issues, the young artist was an extremely charming, witty and well-loved character in Montmartre. Away from his mother he revelled in his freedom and was in a unique position to be erudite and well bred enough for the well heeled, while simultaneously a sympathetic figure to barmen, dancers, circus performers and prostitutes. Other artists were also portraying those on the fringes of society or with questionable moral conduct, but for Toulouse-Lautrec's art these were not simply appealing 'subjects', they were multi-dimensional characters. His tender work reveals them as the friends they were; as a fellow outsider he moved freely among them without suspicion. Elles is a series of coloured lithographs that, very uncharacteristically for the period, represent a broad definition of what a woman might be without a hint of judgement or exploitation, from circus performers, to lesbians to brothel girls. The artist tenderly and brilliantly captures womanhood in many forms, portraying his subjects with honesty and tenderness rather than lewdness. A small treasure of a painting, *In Bed* of 1893 must surely be the most intimate and warm piece of cardboard in the Musée d'Orsay.

Toulouse-Lautrec found himself in vibrant, bohemian Montmartre, and he helped others find it, too. In October 1891 his iconic Moulin Rouge poster was pasted around the streets of Paris more than three thousand times, making him an overnight celebrity. Not only did the poster drive people to the theatre, it also created a healthy market for his art. His work was so sought after that eager admirers would pull the posters down while the paste was still wet. Toulouse-Lautrec's imagery is so familiar to us now it's easy to overlook what a technical innovation his posters were. He was the first artist to really harness the power of the colour lithographic method, creating vibrant, complex imagery that borrowed flat forms from the contemporary trend for Edo period Japanese prints in Paris. His imagery synthesizes music, dance, shady figures, intoxicating crowds and beautiful strong dancers, forever suspending the magic of *belle époque* nightlife.

Toulouse-Lautrec was a cultivated, well-trained artist who cited Degas as his greatest influence, and yet he also made art that triumphed with the public, let loose from the gallery and on the streets in a manner comparable to Keith Haring a century later and Banksy today. He has unquestionably created the most significant posters in the history of art and helped to elevate the art of print making to museum status. Even in his lifetime his posters became collector's items and his reputation continued to soar, making him star a with a permanent seat reserved at every notable venue in the city.

Toulouse-Lautrec worked hard but he also played hard, taking full advantage of the culture of excess, bohemia and wildness that had taken him in and helped forge his name. He was a heavy-drinker-turned-alcoholic – absinthe was a favourite. Eventually his own weak body gave in to the effects of alcoholism as well as the syphilis he contracted from a prostitute as a younger man. In 1901 he suffered a stroke and was taken to his mother's estate. On his deathbed his hunting-mad father who had neglected his son appeared and the successful artist was rumoured to have uttered as his last words, 'I knew, Papa, that you wouldn't miss the kill.'

Toulouse-Lautrec died aged thirty-six and left behind an enormous body of work to represent his extraordinary twenty-year career as an artist, including more than seven hundred paintings, five thousand drawings, and the more than three hundred and fifty lithographic works that made him so famous in his lifetime. His doting mother left funds to open a museum in his name featuring more than a thousand works in Albi in the south of France. His popularity has never waned, largely thanks to the mythical status of the *belle époque* era and the modern language the artist developed that still appeals today. His technical innovations, ability to speak directly to the person on the street, uncanny sensitivity when depicting working-class women as well as starlets mark him out as a major influence for key artists who would follow in his footsteps. Andy Warhol, Diane Arbus and Keith Haring all walked through a door that Toulouse-Lautrec opened for them a long time before, he was truly one of the first modern artists.

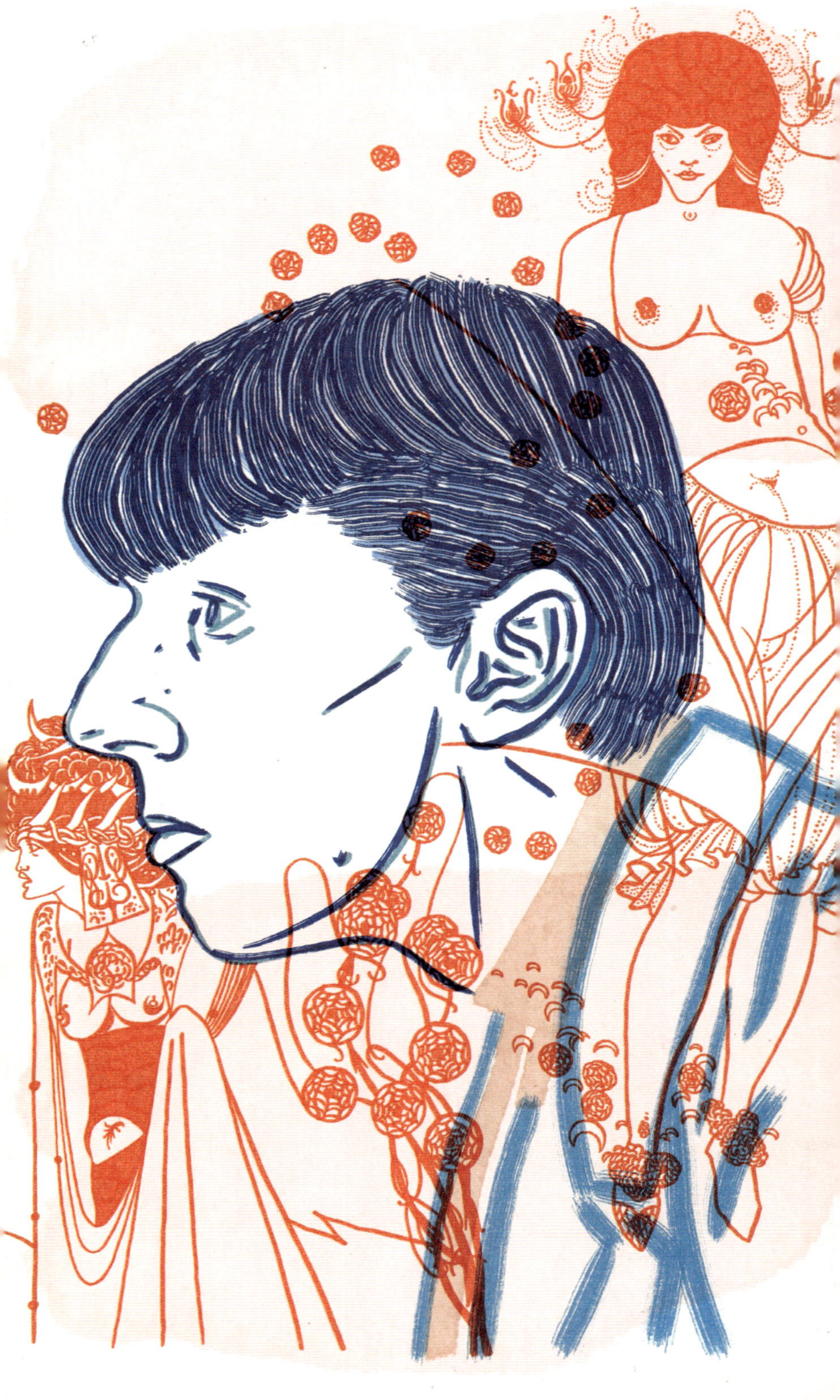

Aubrey
Beardsley
1872–1898

The Aesthete Terrible

Aubrey Beardsley was one of the many unfortunate people who succumbed to tuberculosis in Victorian Britain. The illness was commonly known in his era as consumption due to the way the afflicted would waste away as if the disease physically consumed them. His diagnosis aged seven meant that the aching knowledge of his own early demise hung over his entire life. Like Frida Kahlo, he spent much of his childhood confined to his bed in a fragile state of health, finding escape and solace in his art. Later as an established artist, Beardsley created work with the furious energy of someone with no time to waste and with the candour and nerve of someone who eyed the hypocritical prudishness of his day with deep suspicion. He was dead at the age of twenty-five; his artistic innovations survived long after he did and the explicitness of his sexually daring moral transgressions still warrant a warning.

Considered the *enfant terrible* of *fin de siècle* London, Beardsley knowingly pushed the boundaries of decency and morality. For an artist who found infamy exploring taboo subjects of sexuality, gender and the grotesque, his artistic beginnings were unlikely. He had grown up admiring the Pre-Raphaelites, whose paintings were anchored to the art of the medieval world – full of colour, morality and a kind of earnest beauty. The world Beardsley created for himself would come to be the antithesis of this. Nonetheless, his introduction aged nineteen to Sir Edward Burne-Jones proved a vital start, with the elder Pre-Raphaelite securing him a place at Westminster School of Art. Not long after beginning the course, Beardsley – who was considered something of a child prodigy – received his first commission, which would catapult his name into London society. With a sophistication and innovation beyond his experience, the young man illustrated *Le Morte D'Arthur* (1893) by Thomas Malory, leaving behind

"If I am not grotesque, I am nothing"

the bright purity of Pre-Raphaelite art in favour of a dark, monochromatic series of prints that relish in the demise of the medieval King Arthur and the Knights of the Round Table.

The manner in which Beardsley blended beauty with decay attracted the attention of one of the most significant cultural figures of the day, the writer Oscar Wilde. Wilde was a leading member of what has come to be known as the Decadent Movement, an informal group that believed that art should exist in its own realm, untroubled by social or moral concerns. They championed art for art's sake as a direct rebuttal to the moralizing plays and sermons in paint that had long dominated Victorian Britain.

Also referred to as Aestheticism, this was the countercultural milieu that Beardsley would find himself at home in in the mid-1890s.

In 1894 Beardsley created his masterpiece: sixteen plates illustrating the English translation of Wilde's notorious drama *Salome*. The play had been banned by Lord Chamberlain and Beardsley's sexual and macabre illustrations would add further fire to the flames of objection to the scandalous work. In one of the key works from the series, boldly named The Climax, Beardsley depicts the anti-heroine Salome as she lustfully kisses the severed head of St John the Baptist. She floats in space, not anchored to the morality of this world, and relishes in her wicked prize. Like a fiendish princess she cups his face in her hands as blood drips from his head into a deep black pool from which a flower grows. The grisly scene is beautifully rendered with rhythmic lines and background patterns to enhance the decadence of the moment.

The young artist was so successful in creating a powerful body of imagery that Wilde eventually came to fear that his text was in a merely supporting role, illustrating the illustrations. Beardsley's fetishization of the already risky narrative was scandalous and in fact several of his original artworks were rejected by the publisher who insisted he tame the imagery. One of the censored works portrayed Salome at her toilette with a naked young servant holding a tray of tea while another masturbates to Salome who is also pleasuring herself. Beardsley brazenly disregarded the strict moral codes governing women's behaviour and place in society, it was shocking enough to see them as murderesses let alone independent sexual creatures.

Wilde and Beardsley would come to blows over the illustrations in a public spat – Wilde even claimed he 'invented Aubrey Beardsley'. However, both men would have far worse issues to worry about once Wilde was put on trial for gross indecency. Their fall from grace was swift. Wilde was a condemned man and Beardsley was tarnished with the same brush (namely illegal homosexuality) by his association with Wilde, a situation not helped by his ambiguous sexuality and dandyish appearance. Before the trial Beardsley had been appointed art editor of *The Yellow Book*, a quarterly decadent magazine that challenged repressive Victorian attitudes and mocked conservative society in print. Although it was considered by its critics to be 'repulsive' it was hugely popular. After Wilde's arrest however, Beardsley was fired but his talent coupled with his notoriety kept him in high demand.

Sadly, his health could not keep pace with his career. He began haemorrhaging as the tuberculosis took hold of him once more. Determined to keep producing art, Beardsley remained as productive as he possibly could, defying expectations for such a sick man. He worked for another magazine, *The Savoy*, illustrated Alexander Pope's *The Rape of the Lock* (1896), produced dozens of artworks, travelled to Paris and even wrote and illustrated his own book, *Under the Hill*. He would spend his last months fighting his disease on the French Riviera finally succumbing on the 16 March 1898. In one of his final letters he lamented his impending death: 'such splendid things I had planned'.

Beardsley's great contribution to art was to reinvent the primacy of the black line. He resisted colour and even shading, using the latest printing techniques to allow him the deepest velvet-like blacks. In his final two years of life, Beardsley's style developed. His line became more elegant while his subject matter became increasingly erotic and shocking. It is almost as if the urgency of his medical position gave him a recklessness when it came to annihilating any sense of traditional moral values, he expertly detonated what was acceptable using the most beautiful, decadent and luxurious style. He may have been dealing with crudeness but he did it with exceptional style.

After his death, his approach to line and monochromatic directness became hugely influential for the Art Nouveau movement, as well as inspiring Pablo Picasso, Henri de Toulouse-Lautrec, George Groz, Charles Rennie Mackintosh and almost every modern designer thereafter. As for his compulsion to explore the taboo, Beardsley's art surged in popularity in the 1960s in London, when his countercultural message found a sympathetic

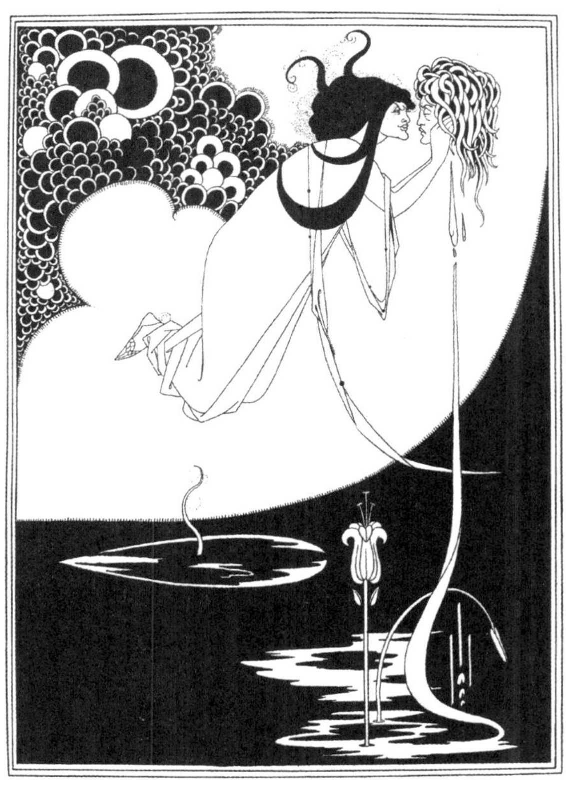

The Climax
Aubrey Beardsley (1872–1898)
1894, line block print on Japanese vellum,
34.2 × 27.2 cm (13 ½ × 10 ¾ in),
The V&A Museum, London, UK

audience, which was soon to gain mainstream ground. Beardsley defied his illness to become a thoroughly modern artist ahead of his time, presenting a seductive challenge that has simultaneously thrilled and horrified for over a century.

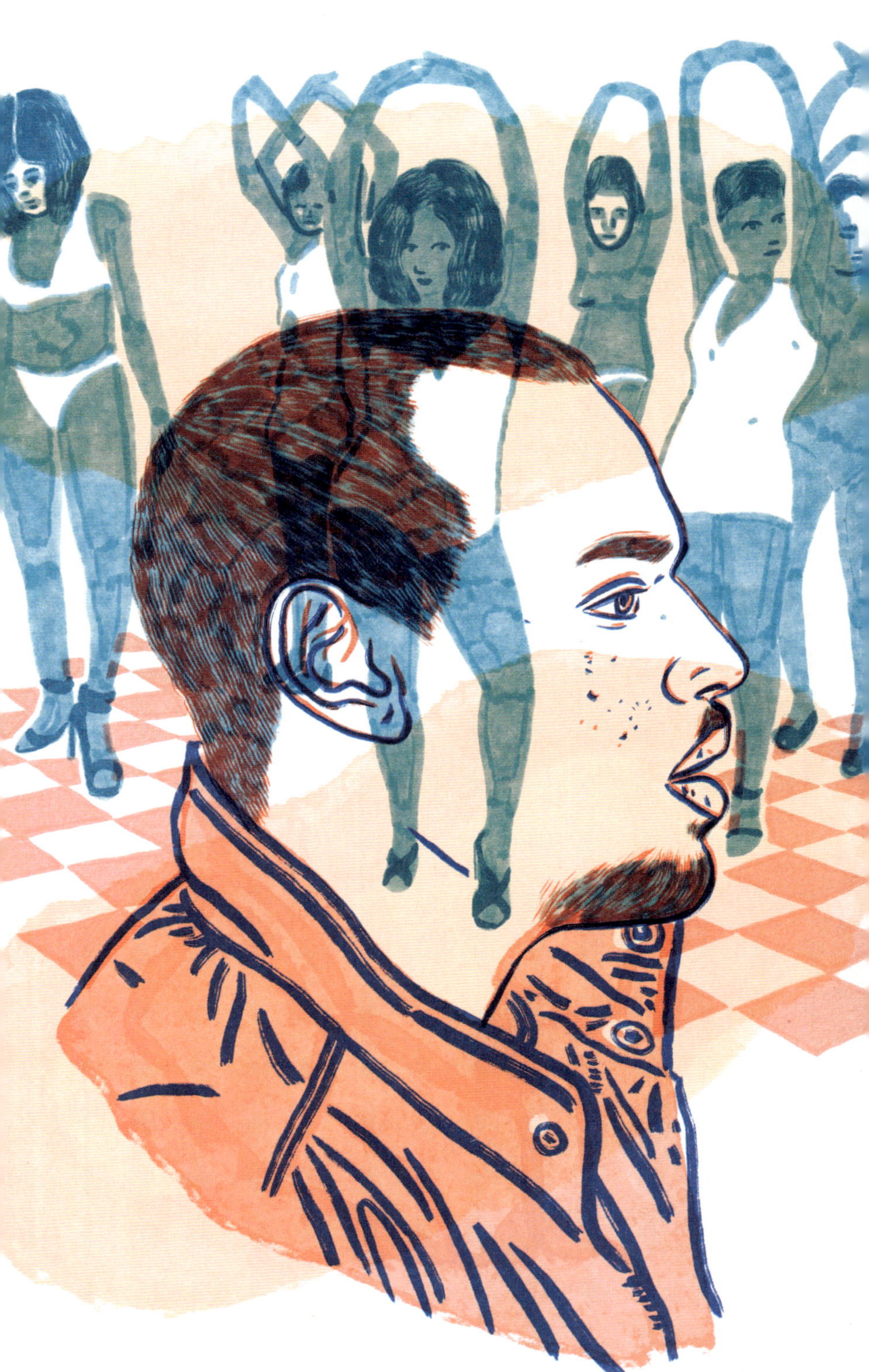

Noah
Davis
1983–2015

Energetic Painter and Curator

In the first years of the twenty-first century when new media and other non-traditional approaches to art reigned supreme, Noah Davis created a forward-looking painting language that was somehow new and urgent while also threading its way backwards in time through the pages of art history. In a career that spanned just over ten years, Davis leaves us with four hundred works and a haunting sense of what he could have gone on to achieve. He exhibited a voracious capacity for painting, often repainting finished works in order to instantly improve upon himself. His sensual work was rooted in the Figurative tradition but played with aspects of abstraction: he might present a recognizable domestic scene but with one aspect dripping away into a blurred obscurity, undermining the illusion of Realism. Although he is often described as an artist's artist (by which it is meant that he makes the kind of work that other artists admire), he was by no means caught up in a vacuum of art for art's sake. He had a deep interest in society and culture more widely and his work was firmly rooted in a humanistic approach. Davis exclusively represented African Americans in his paintings, expressing a motive to 'show black people in normal scenarios'.

Davis succeeded in representing a broad spectrum of figures going about their business, diving into a pool, reading on a sofa, smoking a cigarette, however his scenarios are not in the traditional sense of the word 'normal'. Instead, his paintings are a strange and complex blend of Domestic or Urban Realism with aspects of myth and Surrealism. Looking at *Untitled* of 2015, now considered one of the artist's masterpieces, we are presented with two women napping on a sofa. To the left we can see another person's legs and in the foreground a pair of shoes kicked off. As a viewer we walk through an open door that Davis has painted for us, so far it's a recognizable lazy Sunday afternoon. But the paint handling is undone, the solidity of the right female figure vanishes and we cannot make out her facial features. Above the women, Davis's homage to Mark Rothko drips down the wall as if he has defrosted art history. By playing with Realism and Abstraction, flatness and form, Davis created an uncanny ambiguity of time and place. The composition is in dialogue with Degas and Toulouse-Lautrec who painted snapshot scenes of women with similar intelligently cropped compositions.

Far from trying to obscure what he had borrowed and played with from other artworks, Davis was always quick to talk about artists he admired. Knowledgeable and open to new ideas, Davis had a confident and deep love of art history and would often paint with open art books around him. His sources were diverse and he was not so much interested in the socio-cultural or political position of the artist as their stylistic endeavours and how they broke new ground in painting. Born in Seattle, Davis studied art at The Cooper Union in New York and relocated to Los Angeles in 2004. He was already exhibiting work aged just twenty-four. As early as 2008, Davis's work was selected for inclusion in what became an acclaimed exhibition of black artists, '30 Americans' first shown at the Rubell Family Collection in Miami.

Although commercial galleries would give Davis opportunities to show and sell his work, the artist had an increasingly ambivalent relationship with the art market. It has come to be assumed that art production feeds

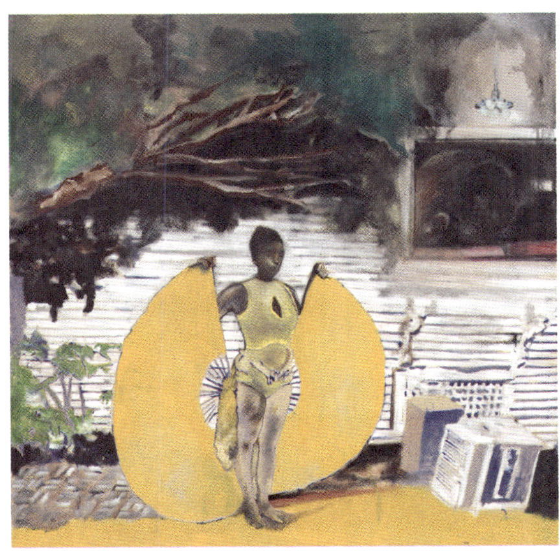

Isis
Noah Davis (1983–2015)
2009, oil and acrylic on linen,
121.9 × 121.9 cm (48 × 48 in),
David Zwirner Gallery, New York, USA

art consumption, but Davis was part of a ever-narrowing pool of artists who felt disillusioned with the rapacity of the market. Instead, inspired by artists such as Theaster Gates, who made a deep commitment to art activism in Chicago, Davis fostered plans to circumnavigate the elitism of the art world. In 2012, along with his wife the sculptor Karon Davis, his brother Kahlil Joseph and the film producer Onye Anyanwu, Davis founded The Underground Museum. Initially a humble operation, the experimental artist-run space also served as his studio. Located in Arlington Heights, a historically working-class African American and Latino neighbourhood, the endeavour aimed to foster creative dialogue in the middle of communities who were not being well served by the city's existing institutions.

In 2013 Davis staged the exhibition, *Imitation of Wealth*. Unable to secure any loans (his wife Karon joked museums and collectors were thinking 'we are not bringing this work to that neighbourhood'), the artist painstakingly recreated works by museum heavyweights such as Jeff Koons, On Kawara and Marcel Duchamp. He acquired the exact specification vacuum cleaner from Craigslist and installed it atop of fluorescent tubing inside a Plexiglass case exactly as Koons had done to great market and museum applause in the 1980s. By doing so, Davis raised questions about authenticity, audiences and the sanctification of art in approved locales. To anyone else it might have seemed absurd to expect museums to lend works to an unknown endeavour in an underprivileged neighbourhood. This did not stop Davis from writing letters. At the time the exhibition was barely viewed beyond the founders' close circle of friends, Kahlil described it as 'an experiment for himself' however it has now become legendary.

In 2014 Helen Molesworth, the Chief Curator of the Museum of Contemporary Art Los Angeles (MOCA), visited The Underground Museum and learned of Davis's ambitions. 'Everyone said no, and for completely legitimate reasons – the museum was three dingy storefronts on Washington. To be really honest, I don't know why I said yes. I guess I trusted the situation and I was looking for another way to work. I wanted a new, more diverse audience.' Their meeting would result in an unprecedented partnership between The Underground Museum and MOCA who began to lend major works to the embryonic museum. The first collaborative exhibition in 2015 was for the internationally respected South African artist William Kentridge, who veils politically engaged work with a kind of magical realism not dissimilar to Davis's painting.

Shortly after the exhibition opened, Davis's career was tragically cut short when he died of a rare form of soft tissue cancer aged just thirty-two. The artist would not allow his plans to be derailed though and before he died, he energetically mapped out a future programme of eighteen exhibitions, even curating with Molesworth and his fellow museum founders from his hospital bed. Molesworth described his determination under the 'incredible time pressure. As he got sicker time was becoming compressed and precious. He was trying to secure this roadmap his left us.' His art saw him through the darkest of hours and his ambition to fulfil on the early promise of the forward-thinking museum would not be dampened. Davis tasked everyone with different roles – to write to this artist, to obtain that particular permission, and Molesworth recognizes something profound in his vision, 'That is the genius of Noah. When I think of The Underground Museum as a work of art, as I often do, that's where I see Noah's authorship.' Today The Underground Museum is one of the LA's most beloved and successful spaces. Still showing experimental exhibitions, it is at heart a community focused space and is now a think-tank for leading black voices. The museum also showcases film and music, such as screening Barry Tompkin's film *Moonlight* and hosting Solange Knowles' listening party for her album *A Seat at the Table*.

As an artist, Davis has been crowned as one of the finest and most innovative painters of his generation. In 2020 the mega dealership David Zwirner Gallery in New York mounted the first posthumous exhibition of his paintings. The show included *Isis* of 2009, a painting that presents a young girl dressed in gold in a pose reminiscent of one of Degas' ballerinas. It is a powerful work, drawing in the viewer by sharp compositional devices that give way to several ambiguities – who is the child, does she have gold wings? If she does, why is she standing in front of what might be a dilapidated house. The title makes explicit reference to Isis, one of the greatest goddesses in Egyptian mythology. The painting, brimming with art historical references and a nearly obscured under-painting, is at once beautiful and uneasy, Davis has conjured a vision that is compulsive viewing because of the unresolved narrative. Paintings like these are not the work of an emerging talent but rather an experienced artist with a very nuanced, educated stylistic point of view. Davis did not die before he found his voice, he died before everyone could hear it. In his paintings and in The Underground Museum, a reconstruction of which formed a vital part of the Zwirner exhibition, his vision lives on.

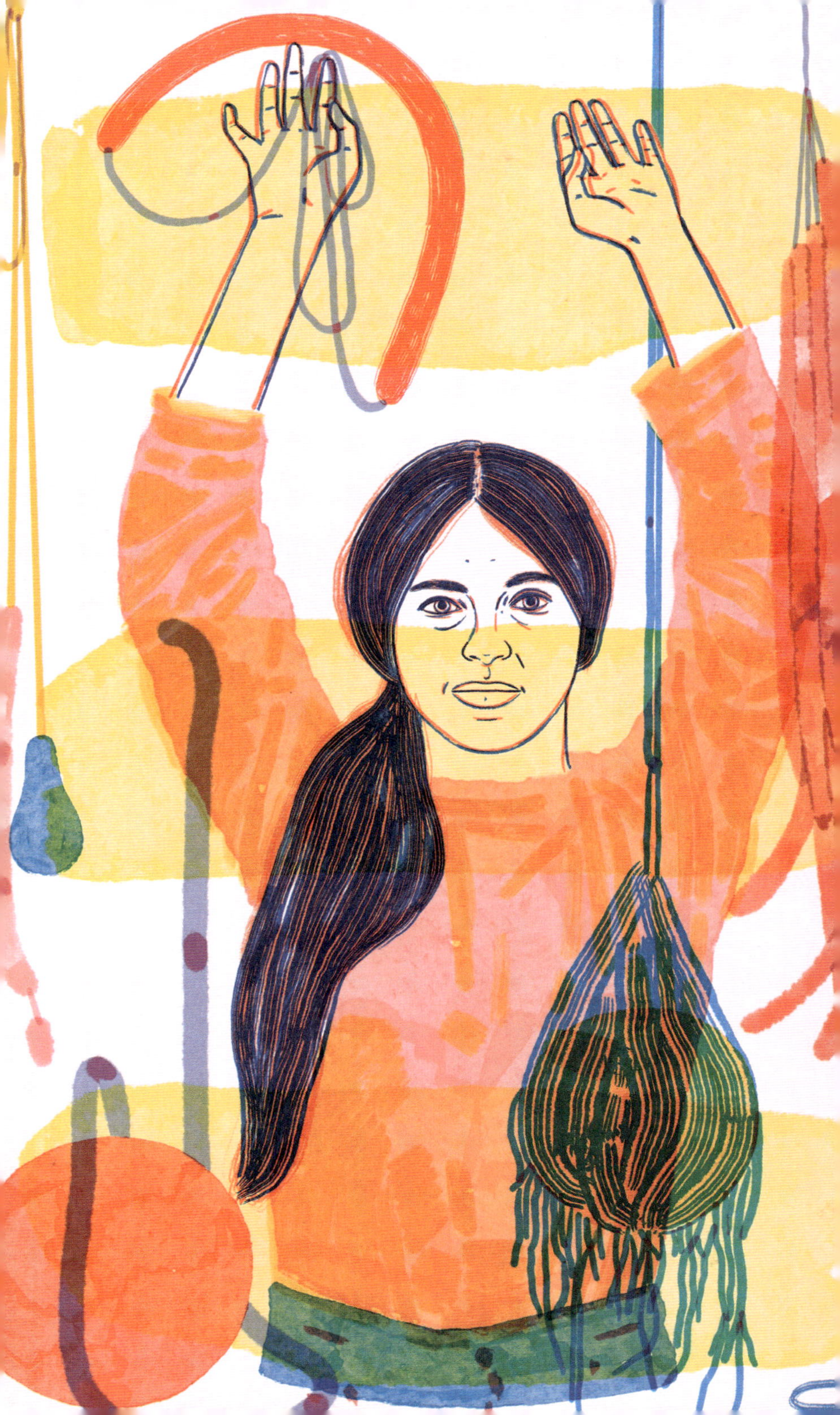

Eva
Hesse
1936–1970

The Master of Paradox

An icon of 1960s American art, Eva Hesse ploughed her personal demons into making powerful sculptural work that resists easy categorization. Hesse rejected the coolness of Minimalism that pervaded the New York art world, turning away from the discipline's logic, verticality, monumentality and rational 'building' of a volume-based sculpture. Instead, she concentrated on a more intuitive approach, drawing out strangeness, absurdity and organic associations in her creative process. Her non-traditional materials were unstable – latex, sawdust, copper, plastic, rubber, polythene, chicken wire and glue – and would degrade over time.

Paradox was at the heart of her ideas, which attempted to reconcile or at least investigate the boundaries between two supposedly opposite forces: femininity and ambition; softness and power; intimacy and grandeur; absurdity and seriousness; fixed matter and vitality; sensuality and revulsion; discipline and freedom; the organic and the industrial. Hesse's practice was the product of a restlessly enquiring mind and the works she created test the limits of both their unusual materials and the conventions of traditional sculpture. Although Hesse's career lasted only one decade, in the period directly after her death she became something of a deity for feminist artists and scholars and a touchstone for many artists of every generation since.

The enigmatic and paradoxical quality of Hesse's work has made her the subject of sustained critical enquiry and theory. The difficulties she experienced personally have also played into subsequent interpretations of her work. Born in 1936 to a German Jewish family in Hamburg, Hesse's first years were deeply affected by the Nazis. Forced to stop practising law, Hesse's father sent his two young daughters to a Dutch children's home on one of the last Kindertransport trains. Two-year-old Eva and her older sister were unable to see their parents for six months. Reunited, the family arrived in New York via England in 1939. Her mother suffered with depression and eventually left the family in 1944. After her father remarried in 1945, her mother committed suicide. Eva was ten years old. Although she was a deeply affected by this trauma, she was a bright and competent student. After attending New York's School of Industrial Art Hesse was awarded an internship at *Seventeen* magazine, a period in which she began to find a confident voice as a young woman despite her insecurities. The subject of a feature article, she said of herself as an artist aged eighteen, 'It means trying to understand and portray people, their emotions, their strengths and faults.' She went on to have a formative experience at Yale University under the guru teacher Josef Albers, also an exile from Nazi Germany with his Jewish artist wife Anni Albers. After graduating with her Bachelor's degree, Hesse pursued an Abstract Expressionist style of painting and was successful enough to be awarded a solo exhibition just two years later. She met and married the sculptor Tom Doyle in 1961. Her productivity slowed and her journal entries reveal her resistance to the gender conventions of the time. 'In his achievements I see my failures. Resentments enter most precisely if I need to be cooking, washing or doing dishes, while he sits King of the Roost, reading.'

Hesse's breakthrough came in 1965 when she left her promising yet unresolved painting career in New York to live temporarily in Düsseldorf with Doyle. Hesse's German studio was in a former factory and she became enamoured with the commercial and industrial materials left behind. Plaster and string would dominate the experiments she made in this pivotal year, which set the course for the work she remains known and celebrated for today. By the time Hesse returned to New York, she was firmly committed to her sculptural practice and was quickly recognized as an important new voice. The now-renowned writer Lucy Lippard included her work alongside Louise Bourgeois and Bruce Nauman in an influential group show and seminal text entitled *Eccentric Abstraction*. In 1966, Hesse's marriage ended and her father died. Grieving and emotionally untethered, Hesse threw herself into her work. Compulsively recording her thoughts, plans, ideas and progress, Hesse's journals and letters are fascinating adjunct to her practice. She believed there was 'only one art sin' and that was beauty.

In the late sixties she created her Accession series, which borrows the cube motif of a Donald Judd work and revises the geometric nature of the form. *Accession II* (1967–8) incorporates a strange soft lining made of multiple plastic tubes seemingly growing from the interior walls. Her work may have shared the language of reduction and abstraction with the Minimalists, but her endeavour was entirely different. *Accession II* also borrows from Surrealism, it conjures a mood, it is at once inviting and intimidating. Hesse's work can be seen as a development of Duchamp's readymade in that she takes industrial materials and makes familiar yet unsettling forms. *Expanded Expansion* (1969) in the permanent collection of the Guggenheim museum is considered a key work by Hesse but is now too unstable to be exhibited. The fibreglass poles determine the height of the piece and give the work a fixed point of reference which is contrasted with a delicate cheesecloth coated in rubber suspended between the poles. A riposte to the conventions of sculptural practice, the horizontal dimensions of the work vary due to its accordion-like shape. This mutability has been exaggerated by the decaying nature of some of the work's materials. Hesse was conscious of this ephemeral quality to her work, embracing, as

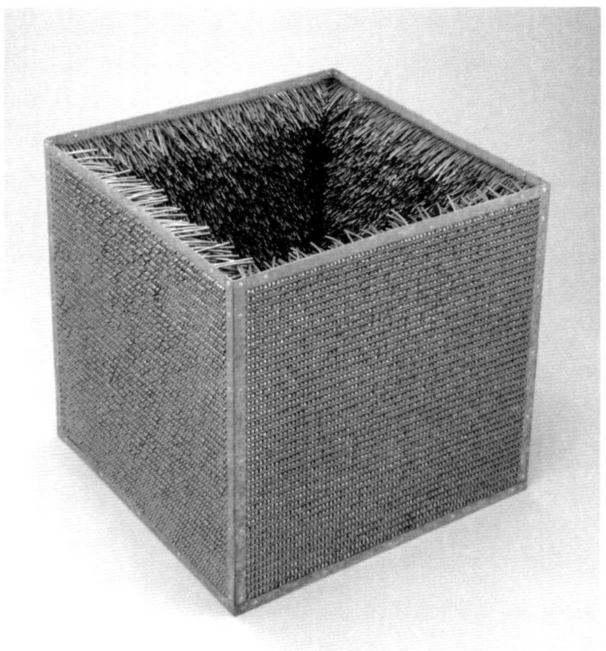

Accession II
Eva Hesse (1936–1970)
1969, galvanized steel and vinyl,
78.1 × 78.1 × 78.1 cm, 53.1 kg (30 ¾ × 30 ¾ ×
30 ¾ in, 117 lbs),
Detroit Institute of Arts, Detroit, USA

she put it, the 'absurd' and undermining the perceived preciousness and immortality of art.

The transient nature of Hesse's work is underscored by her early death. In October 1969 aged thirty-three she was diagnosed with a brain tumour. She underwent three operations which failed to save her and she died aged thirty-four in May 1970. Before her death she had gained a solid reputation in the New York art world – a year before her diagnosis she exhibited latex and fibreglass work at the Fischbach Gallery. Her work was also included in a group show at the preeminent Leo Castelli Gallery and selected for exhibit at the Whitney Museum of American Art as well as a landmark exhibition at the Kunsthalle Bern, *When Attitudes Become Form* (1969). Her work was well profiled including a cover story for Art Forum and her acclaim led to acquisition of work by MoMA.

Hesse died before the women's movement became mainstream and had made a seismic impact on the art world. But her work remained and became a touchstone for theorists on the female condition, the rejection of both beauty as well as masculine tropes and the cultivation of a distinctly 'other' and therefore possibly feminist way of making art. Lippard worked quickly to write a monograph on her friend after she died, fearing that her work may be forgotten if it was not properly recorded. The text, which she had to fight hard to get published despite Hesse's respected standing in the art world, remains seminal and was certainly a key part of securing a legacy for the work. Hesse is today a source of inspiration for innumerable artists including Rachel Whiteread, Kiki Smith, Rachel Kneebone and Rebecca Horn.

The words and creations that Hesse left behind stand as a testament to an artist who was prepared to take risks, to employ both strength and vulnerability and to rethink masculine conventions. She is understandably a huge figure for feminists, but her work does so much more than posthumously sit within a gender-specific context. She described her practice as a 'challenge to the norms of beauty and order', it both distorts and elevates the everyday, insists that we look again, inducing a fearful kind of pleasure, a weird spectacle. We cannot help but see her decaying sculptures in light of the tragedies of her short life, but we must remember that Hesse was an expert of paradox, and adjacent to every difficulty was a fierce refashioning of what she described as an 'absurd' salvation.

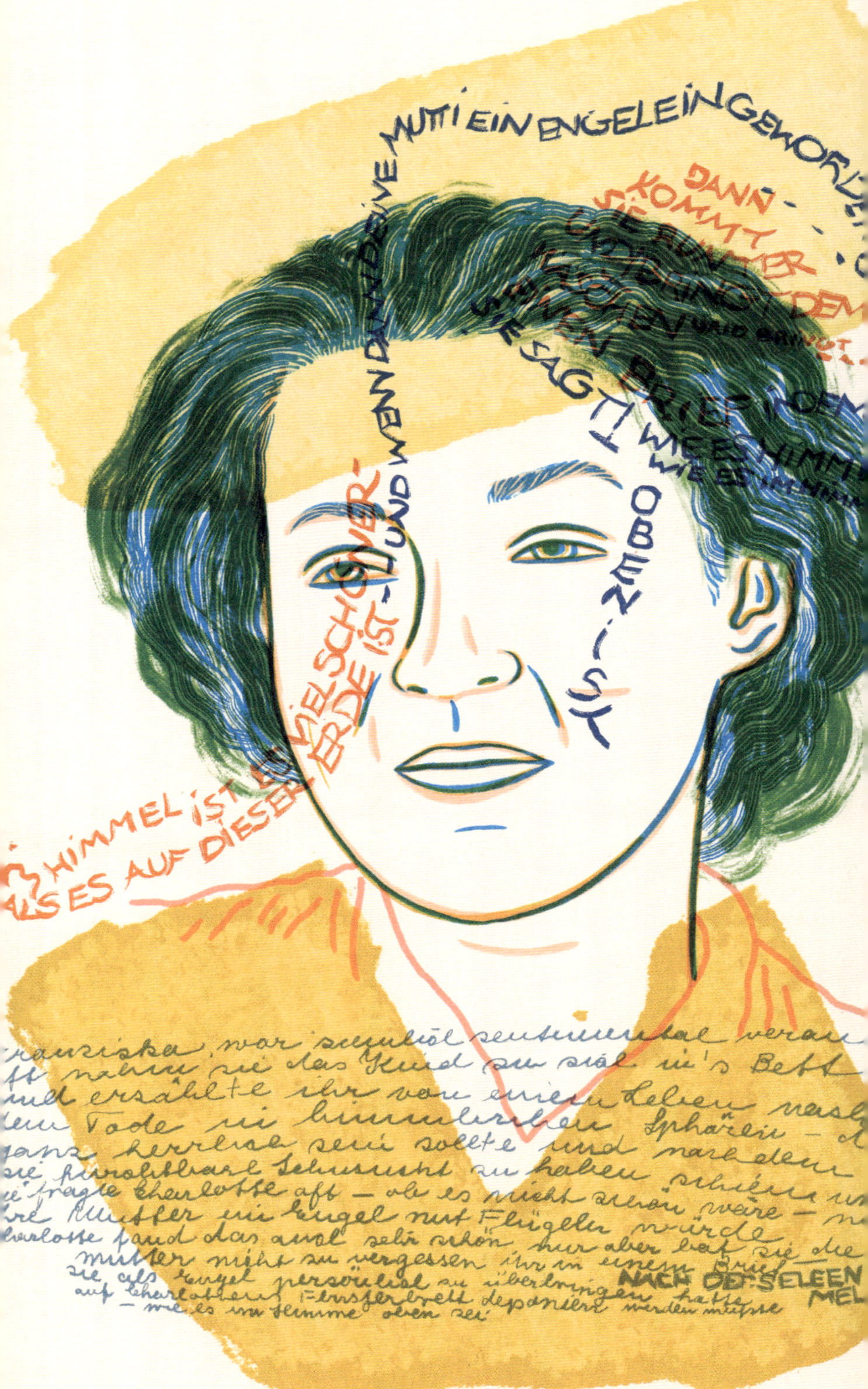
MUTTI EIN ENGEL EIN GEWORDEN
DANN KOMMT ER
SIE SAGT OBEN IST
HIMMEL IST VIEL SCHÖNER - UND WENN DEINE
UND WENN DIE ERDE IST - UND
IS ES AUF DIESER ERDE IST
NACH OBEN SEELEN

Charlotte
Salomon
1917–1943

Creating to Survive

Charlotte Salomon is one of the most important artists of the twentieth century and one who deserves to be better known. In the space of two years, she produced a revolutionary body of work that has a staggering power, urgency and presence nearly eight decades after her death. To spend time with her personal, poignant and dramatic art is to know and love the young woman who created it, and also to grieve for her. On 10 October 1943 Salomon, five months pregnant and aged just twenty-six, was murdered in the gas chamber upon arrival at Auschwitz. As a victim of the Holocaust her reputation as an artist has been largely defined by that darkest time in human history, but her art is transcendent. It does not live in Hitler's world, it lives and breathes and grows in her own.

Salomon began her magnum opus entitled *Life? or Theatre? (Leben? oder Theater?)* in 1941. The wholly unique work takes the form of a *Singspiel*, a kind of German play or lesser opera which was often comedic in nature and involved a love story. Salomon's appropriation of a historic art form during the Third Reich transforms what was long used as a vernacular expression of Germanic identity. In the hands of this supposed outsider, a young Jewish woman, the *Singspiel* is thoroughly modern, fantastical and yet personal. *Life? or Theatre?* comprises 769 gouache paintings that are all 13 x 10 inches in size, with 340 transparent script overlays and even includes notes from Salomon on what music would suit various scenes such as Nazi marching songs or Mahler. *Life? or Theatre?* is semi-autobiographical, with names and personas changed, and recounts her life story from the meeting of her parents to her time studying art through to the events of her adult life that led her to create the masterpiece. It ends by portraying a version of herself the day she began the artwork in Nice in 1941.

The title was born from a question the young woman asked herself, 'whether to take her own life or undertake something wildly unusual'. Years before the Nazis came to power in 1933, Salomon's family history was already well versed in tragedy and horror. Her mother's sister, who Charlotte was later named after, killed herself in 1913. Her mother became obsessed with death and when Salomon was in her twenties it was revealed to her that her mother did not die of influenza as she had been told when she was eight, but rather she, too, had committed suicide. She learned of this devastating fact shortly after she witnessed her grandmother end her life by jumping from the window. The connecting factor between the three women was Salomon's abusive grandfather. She wrote that 'Everything I did for my grandfather drove blood to my face... I was sick. I was constantly beet-red from mute rage and grief.' These are the words from her tragic nineteen-page confession. After suffering abuse for years, the young woman took the momentous decision to poison her grandfather with a barbiturate omelette. Salomon defied a history of suicide and pain, proclaiming 'I will live for them all' and painted her way out of hell. 'My life began ... when I found out that I myself am the only one surviving.' Her art was so intrinsic to her refusal to allow shame and depression to take hold that she even drew her grandfather as he died.

Despite the backdrop of Nazi persecution and family tragedies, Salomon created an uplifting and captivating work. *Life? or Theatre?* was a life raft, full of charm, wit, honesty and declarations of love. It didn't shy away from the difficulties of losing her mother, hating school, being

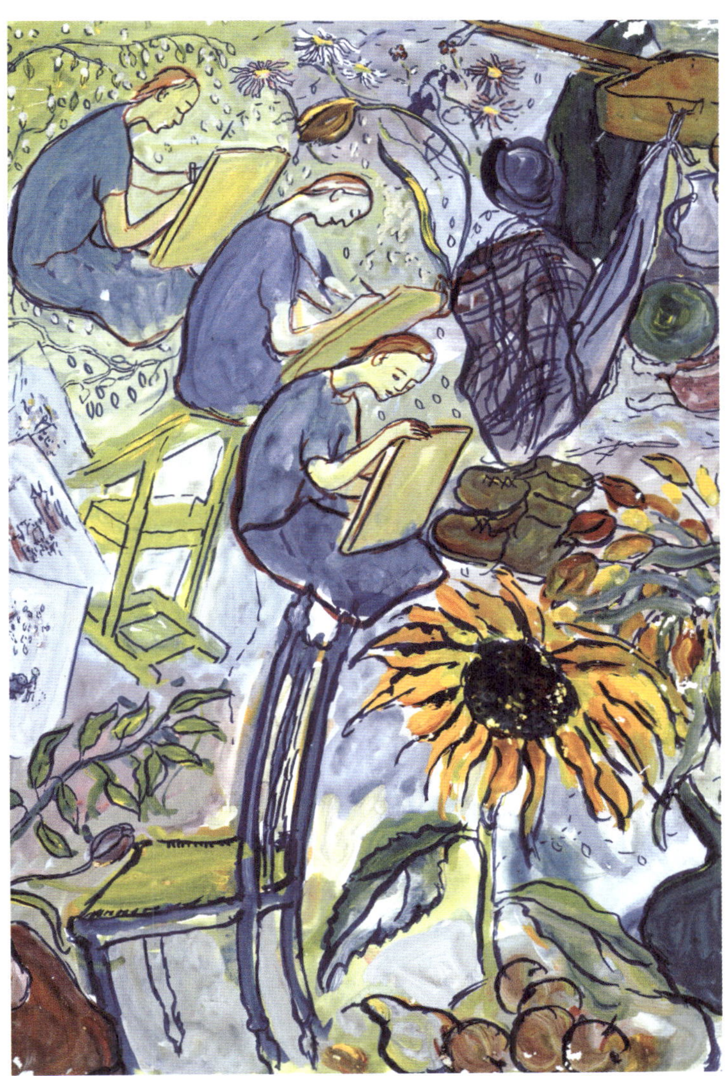

Gouache from *Life? or Theatre?*
Charlotte Salomon (1917–1943)
1941–1942, gouache on paper,
32.5 × 25 cm (13 × 10 in),
Jewish Historical Museum, Amsterdam,
the Netherlands

persecuted as a Jew or suffering abuse, but nor did it focus on them. They are episodes that are recounted alongside the joy of birthdays and Christmases, tormenting her governesses and the magic of love. As well as portraying a continuous affection for her father, Salomon enjoyed painting scenes that demonstrate how besotted she was with her stepmother, Paula Salomon-Lindberg who her father married in 1930. Salomon loved the well-known opera singer, whose social circle included Albert Einstein. Paula engaged a music teacher for Salomon and he would become the focal love story of the *Singspiel*. Alfred Wolfson, who appears in *Life? or Theatre?* as Amadeus Daberlohn, was twice her age, a supporter of her artistic talent and someone who opened the young woman up to great art, culture and philosophy. It was her lover's teachings that are echoed at the happy ending of Salomon's long work as she states that her heroine 'did not have to kill herself like her ancestors, for according to his method one can be resurrected – in fact, in order to love life still more, one should once have died.' So she was in fact the living model for his theories.

Taken in its entirety, *Life or Theatre?* is like a painted play, it has a distinct rhythm with a cadence that swings between moods. Salomon's work starts full of colour and detail and as the episodes come closer to her present life, it becomes more expressionistic and muted in palette. The compositions are masterful. She compresses several connected scenes to show multiple narratives on one page, a device that borrows from the cyclical layout of Italian Renaissance fresco cycles. The scenes include the night her father leaves for the war and when she lay in bed with her depressed mother who talks to her about heaven. Her treatment of the figure is evocative, often portraying male figures in a state of dismay or grief as solid, lumpen shapes in the shadows. Her female figures are fluid and share a rhythm on the page. Her mother's suicide is painted as if a ballerina has acted out the jump from the window in a crushing finale, and the accompanying text takes a similarly desperate shape of a broken form.

The fact that *Life? or Theatre?* survived is a small miracle. In November 1938 her father was imprisoned and tortured at Sachsenhausen

Concentration Camp. His wife was able to use her connections to secure his release. Having lost half his body weight, he acted quickly to remove his daughter Charlotte from Germany, sending her to stay with her maternal grandparents, who had fled to the Côte d'Azur several years earlier. They benefitted from the protection of a remarkable American woman of German parentage, Ottilie Moore. She heroically housed many Jews during the war and later escaped to Portugal with a car full of Jewish babies and children. Salomon spent most of the war years living at Moore's property, L'Ermitage, and dedicated *Life? or Theatre?* to her. Three months after her

"My life began … when I found out that I myself am the only one surviving"

grandmother took her own life in June 1940, the French surrendered to the Nazis and Salomon and her grandfather were imprisoned for several weeks at a Vichy-run concentration camp. (The only mention in her work of the horrific experience in a camp with no running water where disease was rife and food was rotten was to say that she would rather sleep in a crowded train car than alone with her grandfather.) Soon after their release, Salomon moved by herself to a hotel in Saint-Jean-Cap-Ferrat where she worked furiously on her masterpiece, making several gouaches a day and barely eating or sleeping for months. After poisoning her grandfather in February 1943, she settled back at L'Ermitage and married Alexander Nagler, a Romanian Jewish refugee who she met through Ottilie Moore. Several weeks after their wedding – which confirmed their names and address with tragic consequences – Salomon wrapped the paintings, transparencies and confession letter into brown paper packages. She pleaded 'Take good care of it, it is my entire life' as she handed it to a trusted local doctor who had treated her grandmother's depression and advised Salomon to paint to stave off her own. On 23 September 1943 the Gestapo arrived at L'Ermitage and bundled Salomon and Nagler into a truck. They were sent to Auschwitz two weeks later, the transportation list documenting Salomon as a 'graphic artist'. As a pregnant woman Salomon would have entered the gas chamber the day she arrived; her husband, condemned to slavery and starvation, later died of exhaustion.

When Moore returned to her home L'Ermitage after the war, the doctor kept his word and safely delivered the extraordinary packages to her. Moore then passed them along to Salomon's parents, who had survived the Holocaust in hiding in Amsterdam. They preserved the astonishing creation in red boxes, showing it only to their friend Otto Frank, who in turn revealed his daughter Anne Frank's diary to them. Ten years later the Salomons donated the entire contents of the boxes to Jewish Historical Museum of Amsterdam, although the confession letter concerning her grandfather was not made public until 2011.

Although the contents of *Life? or Theatre?* are staggering in their artistic ambition, personal accomplishment and psychological drama, Salomon remains in the margins of art history. The dominant names of Modernist art are white men, for decades written about and collected by white men. Although her work has been on permanent exhibit in Amsterdam and has travelled internationally, Salomon has been denied the attention that befits the magnitude of her achievement because there are no works on the open market, and she has been contextualized largely in terms of the Holocaust. In 1998 an exhibition at London's Royal Academy was a huge success, surpassing all expectations. In more recent years her oeuvre has found a wider audience more in tune with her creative endeavour. Thankfully, we live in an age where the traditional boundaries of art and the criteria for exhibiting it are relaxing – her work is breaking out of her categories of unknown, female, Jewish, graphic artist. It has been reappraised in terms of its extraordinary vision, its intellectual reworking of the historic *Singspiel* and as a modern Wagnerian 'total work of art'. The celebrated art historian Griselda Pollock described *Life? or Theatre?* as 'an event in the history of art'.

Salomon created beauty from horror and succeeded in living for everyone who had passed away in a way she could never have anticipated. Before her grandmother took her own life, Salomon pleaded with her, something which she recounts in her work, proposing to her that 'instead of taking your own life in such a horrible way... why don't you make use of the same powers to describe your life. There will surely be some interesting material that's weighing on you, and by writing it down you will liberate yourself and perhaps perform a service to the world.' In an act of unfathomable bravery and hope, Salomon took her own advice where her grandmother could not and defied a world that tried to erase her, her art was her salvation and through it she lives on in her own terms.

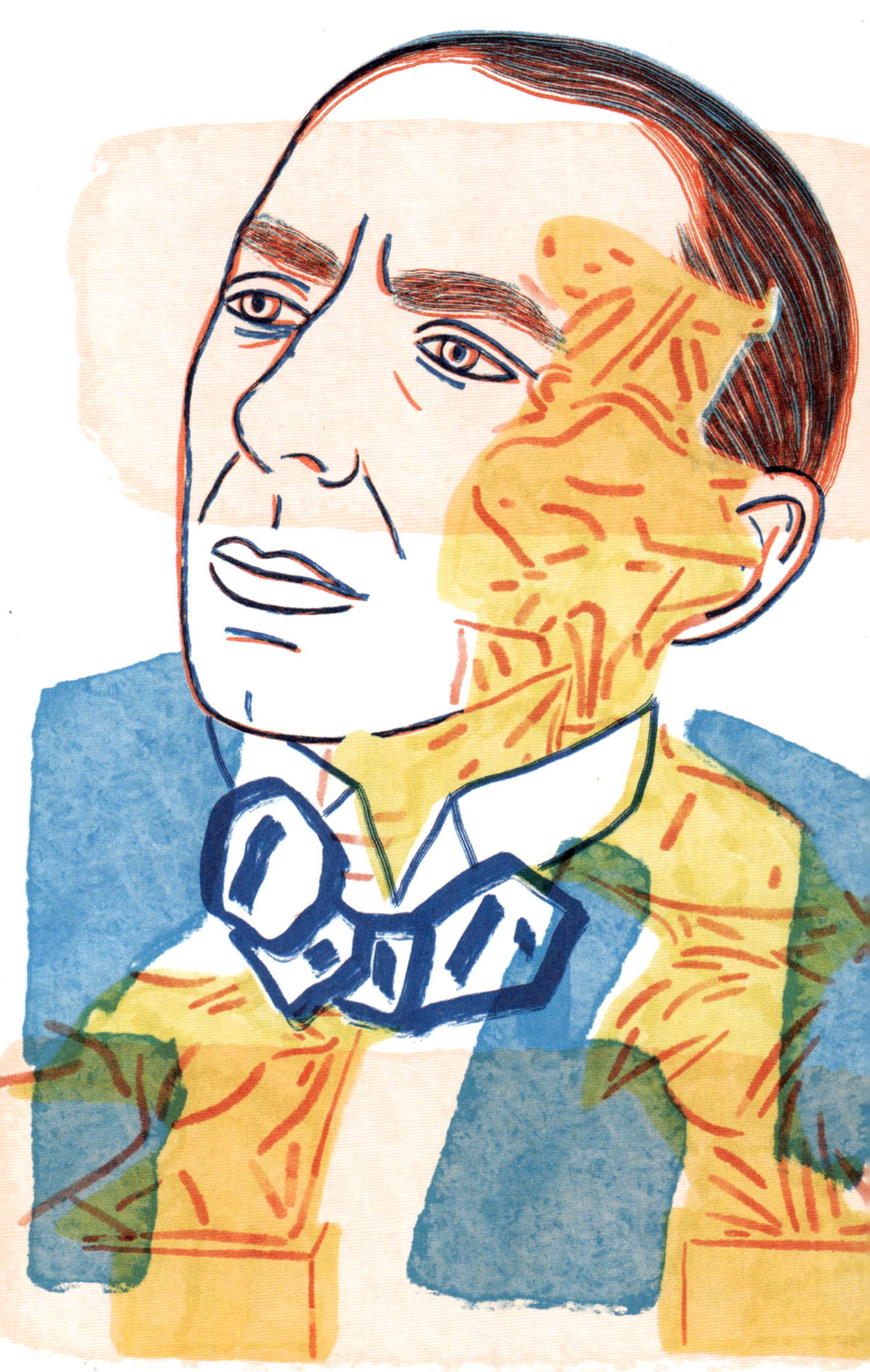

Umberto
Boccioni
1882–1916

The Idealist Fighter

Futurism was the first cultural movement to promote the modern world at the direct expense of the past, comparing Italy's museums to cemeteries, and archaeology to gangrene. It was anarchic, its manifesto of 1909 avowed that 'We want to demolish museums and libraries, fight morality...'. The movement celebrated all that was new and modern in the urban world, worshipping technology, speed and youth. The group had a particular appreciation of cars, planes and trains and were desperate to harness the power of incessant motion and flux. On paper these ideas were revolutionary and even admirable, in so far as they wanted to clear away the bondage of agricultural poverty to allow a youth-orientated Italy to emerge triumphant into the modern era.

Founded by the poet Filippo Tommaso Marinetti, on paper Futurism had an arrogance, wit and bite that would be hard to commit to canvas. The principles of worshipping the machine age and celebrating speed were rather at odds with the traditional and static mediums of painting and sculpture which were bound up with the weight of art history that the idealistic men were desperate to destroy. The disconnect between Futurism's words and the movement's artistic responses was most successfully navigated by Umberto Boccioni who is today regarded as the most significant artist to emerge from the era. His masterful sculpture *Unique Forms of Continuity in Space* (1913) presents a powerful figure striding with speed, as if fighting against magnificent winds. It plays with time and space in a way never managed before in art, the boundaries are so blurred we can hardly tell where the movement ends and the form begins. It's the apotheosis of Futurist art: dynamic, youthful, modern and a revolutionary way of creating sculptural form.

Boccioni was born in rural southern Italy in 1882 and moved to Rome in 1901 to train in classical art. He met Marinetti nine years later, attracted to the principles of Futurism in its embryonic phase largely because he felt that young artists were being consistently overlooked in Italy. As well as exhibiting across Europe with other artists in the group including Gino Severini and Luigi Russolo, Boccioni also contributed to further manifestos and penned his own theoretical texts such as *Technical Manifesto of Futurist Painting* of 1910. With a speed that the group must have relished, Futurism quickly found its way into the newspapers with its boisterous rhetoric.

Boccioni's subject matter was not still life, as had been largely the case with Cubism, to which the movement owed a clear stylistic debt, but rather the more impossible endeavour of depicting objects in motion. *The City Rises* (1910) aims to convey the flux of the Milanese urban landscape. As the title suggests, the city seems to rise up and with a sense of frenetic motion it is almost closing in on itself. In the background, construction is celebrated, and the foreground depicts horses racing furiously, the extreme perspective putting the viewer in the heart of what feels like a potentially violent moment. The painting is hailed as Boccioni's first Futurist painting and it is also sadly an eerie premonition of his own death that would follow six years later.

The outbreak of war in 1914 seemed to be a fulfilment of all that the group had hoped for, they prophesized that the age of machines would eradicate the weight of the past and, inspired by Nietzsche, they hoped

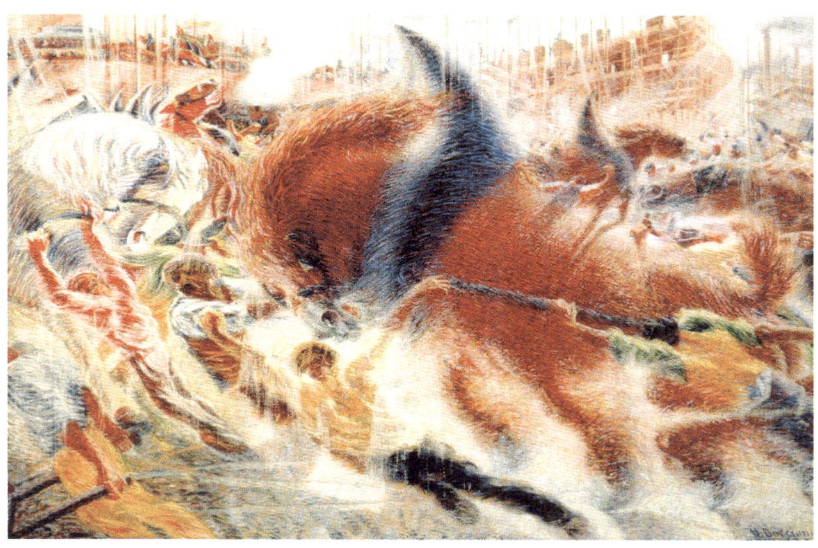

The City Rises
Umberto Bocconi (1882–1916)
1910, oil on canvas,
199 × 301 cm (78 × 119 in),
The Museum of Modern Art, New York, USA

for the birth a new mankind. Having written about war and violence in romantic terms, many of the group's members signed up to the army. Bocconi joined a Volunteer Cyclist Brigade, which gave him ample material for his ambition to pin down the velocity of moving wheels in his work. In July 1916, when Italy first entered the war, Boccioni was offered release but he was determined to fight at the front. His death was not at the hands of the enemy, or even a machine, but rather caused by falling from a horse during a cavalry training exercise. His horse, named Vermiglia after the red beast in *The City Rises*, threw and then dragged the young artist. He died from his injuries on 17 August aged thirty-three. Looking again at the painting, it's almost as if he prophesized his own death.

Marinetti stayed true to the movement's disdain for tradition as he commenced his speech at his friend's posthumous retrospective exhibition, 'Let us not offend Boccioni with a funeral eulogy.' The movement celebrated war and derided old age, and so in his death Boccioni became

"When we are forty let younger and stronger men than we throw us in the wastepaper basket like useless manuscripts!"

a tragic mascot for Futurism, frozen in time as a young, modern hero. The movement's greatest artist fulfilled its ideologies but his death would also mark the beginning of a decline that distorted revolutionary thought into ugly alliances. Futurism's glorification of war, machines and a modern Italy was extremely attractive to Mussolini who hired Marinetti as a speech writer. The words and imagery of Futurism would be subsumed into Mussolini's Fascist rhetoric in the decade following Boccioni's death. Without Boccioni, Futurist art would suffer enormously, he was the most artistically progressive as well as being one of its keenest theorists.

In the decades that followed the Second World War, Boccioni's reputation was untainted by the tarnish of Fascism that left a shadow over the work of his friends. His art found an international audience, particularly in the United States. *The City Rises* was acquired by MoMA in 1951 and several casts were made of *Unique Forms of Continuity in Space*, which allowed it to be acquired by collections such as the Tate Gallery. Boccioni had been opposed to bronze casts in his lifetime due to their associations with tradition, but these editions have secured his place in the canon of art history. It is ironic that Boccioni believed in his twenties that the relevance of him and his colleagues should be time sensitive, 'When we are forty let younger and stronger men than we throw us in the wastepaper basket like useless manuscripts!' Boccioni did not live to see forty, nor was he discarded. As a young idealist, he fetishized battles that indirectly cost him his life and he may not have believed in museums or libraries, but regardless they have carefully preserved his legacy for over a century.

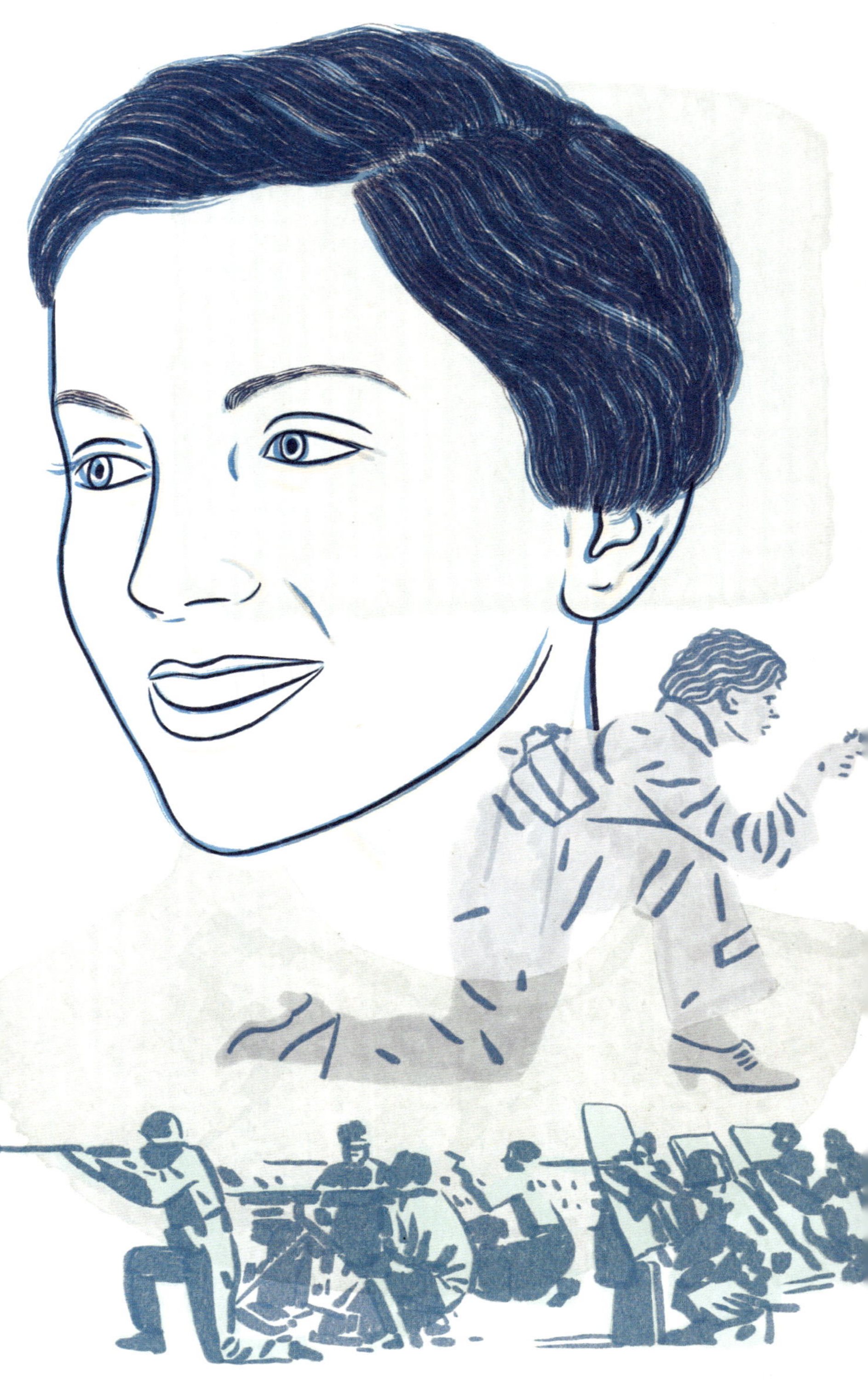

Gerda Taro

1910–1937

Finding Humanity in War

Gerda Taro's imagery of war is ferocious in its pursuit of honesty. Her eye for vulnerability was precise, artful and well developed despite her young age. She distilled the complexity, brutality and senselessness of the Spanish Civil War into quiet, important images that single out one gesture or moment of humanity: a militia soldier running with his back to us and his legs lifted from the earth as if leaping in a playground; a sleepy child refugee from Malaga bare-bottomed and missing one shoe; three handsome soldiers gently raising the enemy flag above their heads with the tip of their bayonets creating a makeshift canopy; an orphaned boy of about nine years of age eating soup, directly confronting the viewer with wide eyes too knowing for his young years. Throughout her short career Taro would take herself closer and closer to the action, capturing the plight and efforts of the Republicans loyal to the Left-leaning Spanish Republic against the Fascist Nationalists led by Franco.

Taro's commitment to document the fight against Fascism was not orchestrated as a photo-journalist career move, it was *her* war, too. Born as Gerta Pohorylle to bourgeois Jewish parents in 1910, she was a fiercely intelligent émigré who fled to Paris with a fake passport in 1933. In Germany she had been distributing anti-Nazi leaflets under the cover of darkness and was arrested and interrogated by the Nazis who suspected her of supporting a Bolshevik plot to overthrow Hitler. When she arrived in Paris, she was given support from a network of Communists because, despite only being twenty-three years of age, she was already an experienced activist. As she built a new life for herself, she met the Hungarian-Jewish photographer Endre Friedmann. A fellow liberal who would become her mentor, she fell in love with him despite her better judgement, describing him as a 'rogue and a womanizer'. The outsiders suffered hardship in an increasingly hostile environment for Jewish émigrés. Despite often having to pawn his camera, Friedmann schooled Taro in the basics of photography and she devoured the work of others in the Alliance Picture Agency where she worked. Recognizing the growing antipathy for foreigners in Paris, together they invented an American persona, Robert Capa who they claimed was a visiting photojournalist. Friedmann's work was ascribed to the fictional photographer with a pleasingly international sounding name and he successfully sold to newspapers for far greater sums than anything in his real name ever did. Their ruse was eventually discovered but Friedmann remained as Robert Capa and Gerta Pohorylle now became Gerda Taro, another outsider protected by losing their name.

Brave from reinvention, Capa and Taro travelled to Spain in 1936 just two weeks after the outbreak of the Spanish Civil War. The atmosphere was electric and, like other cultural figures, such as the writer Ernest Hemingway, they were not there to be neutral, they arrived in conscious support of the Republican resistance to the Fascist rebels. Together they worked tirelessly and in increasingly dangerous circumstances to photograph the path of the war. Capa's reputation as a preeminent photojournalist was established quickly and, in a climate unsympathetic to women, work created by Taro would often sell under his name or a joint by-line. Taro would return numerous times to Spain, eventually travelling

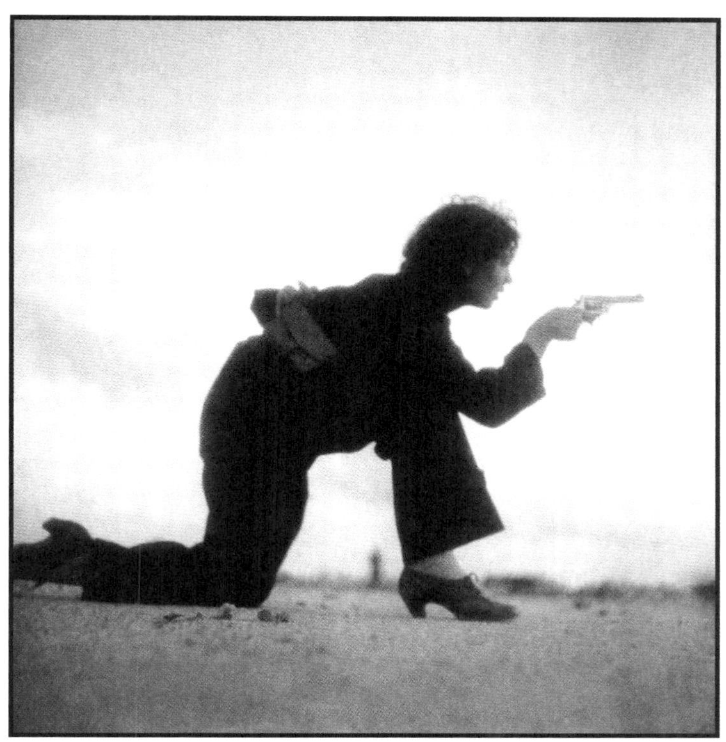

***Republican militiawoman training on the
beach, outside Barcelona***
Gerda Taro (1910–1937)
August 1936, black-and-white photograph,
International Center of Photography/ Magnum

without Capa to pursue her own vision. Her camera was her only weapon in an increasingly violent and chaotic series of battles. Galvanized by her experience of the Nazis, Taro's eye was always trained on the realities of what it was to be a civilian fighting for liberty and the consequences suffered by the population at the hands of Franco's rebels.

In July 1936, she travelled to Brunette, fifteen miles west of Madrid with a Canadian journalist who would become her last lover, Ted Allan.

The pair fell in love and as the war became more intense, they defied a ban on journalists. Bombs dropped around them on the front line and Taro, undeterred, would click away with her camera held high as Allan tried to protect them both from shrapnel. Her mentor Capa had famously said 'If your pictures aren't good enough, you're not close enough,' and she seemed to be taking the advice to its most extreme. On 25 July, the couple escaped from a foxhole and hitched a ride on the running board of a retreating vehicle carrying the wounded as planes overhead continued to drop bombs. The car was hit by an out of control Republican tank and

"If your pictures are not good enough, you're not close enough"

Taro was thrown to the ground. She was transported to a hospital where she was reported to have asked if anyone saved her camera and died from her injuries hours later aged just twenty-six.

Taro's funeral in Paris was organized by the French Communist party and attended by tens of thousands of people, including Allan who survived in Brunette, and her closest companion, Capa who held himself responsible for her death. She was the first woman photographer killed in action and in death she was a hero and powerful symbol in the fight against Fascism. Despite this status at the time of her death, her work fell into the shadows of history for decades. After her death, her legacy would be drowned out by the outbreak of the Second World War, which saw her family killed in the Holocaust. Later her work would also suffer from conflation with Capa's; his internationally renowned status cast a large shadow over her reputation.

Incredibly in 2007 a suitcase containing thousands of negatives by Capa and Taro was discovered in Mexico. That the works surfaced is something of a miracle. Capa had tried to smuggle the negatives out of France during the war and after he failed, the suitcase fell into the hands of a Mexican ambassador for protection. He returned home with it and evidently forgot he had it. Nearly five decades later his descendants unearthed the suitcase and contacted the International Center for Photography in New York, founded in 1974 by Capa's brother. Known as 'The Mexican Suitcase', it quickly acquired an almost folkloric status and provides an incredible portal to the past. The treasure trove of more than five thousand images finally allowed Taro to be distinguished from Capa, and for her work to be given the independent appraisal by experts that it long deserved.

Taro worked in an age when photography was not yet considered a fine art form and was believed to be a mechanical snapshot of a single reality. Taro shrewdly exploited that assumption to ensure that the images she sent home spoke clearly of the devastation and horror caused by the war. But like all modern photographers now revered in global museums, she knew the camera could be as adaptable as a paintbrush in its ability to allow the artist their own visual identity and unique perspective. Nearly a century later her style allows us to feel that this was partly a personal battle. We see her anger, astonishment and enormous empathy for her subjects when we look at the powerful photographs that would eventually cost her life.

Five

Unfinished Stories

art of the motivation for writing this book was to work out how artists who had such short careers were able to have some kind of artistic legacy. Most artists do not secure permanent museum recognition or carve out deep relationships with the right people until their career is a few decades advanced, if at all. Another motivation was the realization that there are several artists I greatly admire whose reputations are not yet secured for future generations. It is my hope that through various future endeavours, and by including them here, they will increasingly be recognized, and the light of their talent can be allowed to shine even brighter.

Three of the artists in this section do not enjoy ample recognition now, despite having been established and widely respected in their lifetime. Joanna Boyce Wells, Pauline Boty and Helen Chadwick carved out serious careers and yet after their death, their reputations have suffered, at least partly as a consequence of being women artists. Boyce Wells managed to work within a Victorian art system and society that fundamentally opposed the concept of a professional woman artist. Even though she was lauded by the greatest critics and male artists of the day, Boyce Wells is not a name commonly associated with the Pre-Raphaelite Brotherhood, an art movement that excludes women through its very title. An exhibition in London at the National Portrait Gallery, *Pre-Raphaelite Sisterhood* (2019), shone a light on the untold stories of the women who were fundamental to the movement as muses, models and most importantly as artists. Although the artist and poet Elizabeth Siddal is better known and written about (largely as a result of being the model for her husband Dante Gabriel Rossetti's paintings) to my mind Boyce Wells is a more interesting artist because of the psychological burdens she faced in her career. She was so much part of a system that supressed the desires of women and denied them autonomy, that she had to wrestle her own guilt over her wish to paint professionally. After she died, small steps were made towards increasing rights for women artists, but they were too modest to make much impact and sadly gender bias was compounded by the rise of art history as a discipline, initially written by, and for, men.

Pauline Boty also suffered as a result of being a woman artist in a man's world. Nicknamed the Bardot of Wimbledon, she was a star of London's swinging sixties. Despite being an instrumental part of the Pop Art movement in London, her fame and beauty counted against her after she died young. Like Gerda Taro, Boty's work also fell out of view entirely and was salvaged literally by a twist of fate. An influential art historian, who as a teenager had fallen under the spell of Boty's work, would later track down her lost paintings. The works not only stood the test of time but offer a key insight into the era from the perspective of a woman at the centre of the action. Boty deserves to be widely celebrated in the British art establishment and today has loud champions in fellow pop artist and friend Peter Blake, the journalist Alastair Sooke and the author Ali Smith. In an era that is being held accountable for lack of representation for women, hopefully Boty's practice will be given the space it deserves.

Like Boty, Helen Chadwick was an established name in London's art scene. In the eighties she was a pioneer in a fledging contemporary art scene and by the time Cool Britannia reigned supreme in the nineties she was a leading artist of her generation and a source of inspiration for younger artists. It could be argued that these artists, known as the Young British Artists (the YBAs), borrowed some aspects of Chadwick's complex practice, most especially her adoption of visceral materials such as blood, urine and rotting vegetables. Despite being the first woman nominated for the Turner

Prize, exhibiting internationally and breaking visitor attendance numbers, after her death perhaps Chadwick's practice was seen as too theory-heavy in an art world that became increasingly commercialized with a tendency for reduction. Two decades later, we are in an era where nuance is cherished and we are now better placed to engage with the complexity and sensitivity of Chadwick's practice, which wrestled with ideas surrounding the female body as a political object, the act of making and social expectations.

The two most recently deceased artists in this section are Khadija Saye and Bartholomew Beal. Beal is probably the least well known of all the artists in this selection, but those who encountered his work and character, are left with a lasting impression of a great talent who emerged fully formed. He is an artist whose legacy means a great deal to me personally as one of the people who worked closely with him and now advises his estate. There was a particular poignancy to writing this chapter, not just because this is the only artist in the selection that I knew personally, but because he was alive and well when I started the manuscript. Before he died aged thirty of the brain tumour that hung over his adult life, Beal quickly developed a mature painting style and achieved impressive feats including a museum solo show and sold out exhibitions even as a young graduate. He lived life with remarkable gusto and his ten-year career is a shining example of the power of art to give direction and meaning to life.

The youngest artist in the selection, I included Khadija Saye not just because she is such an inspirational figure, but because I believe her small body of work to be of exceptional quality and heartbreakingly full of great future promise. Against all the odds for a young black woman from a disadvantaged background, Saye found a celebrated place in the art world that would surely have been the start of something global, visionary and spectacular. Her time was cut brutally short by the 2017 Grenfell Tower fire in London, just weeks after she had been lauded at The Venice Biennale. In a landscape where artists must seriously reckon with the challenges of diversity and inclusion, Saye's story and mesmeric work are vital and, thankfully, her champions are loud and many.

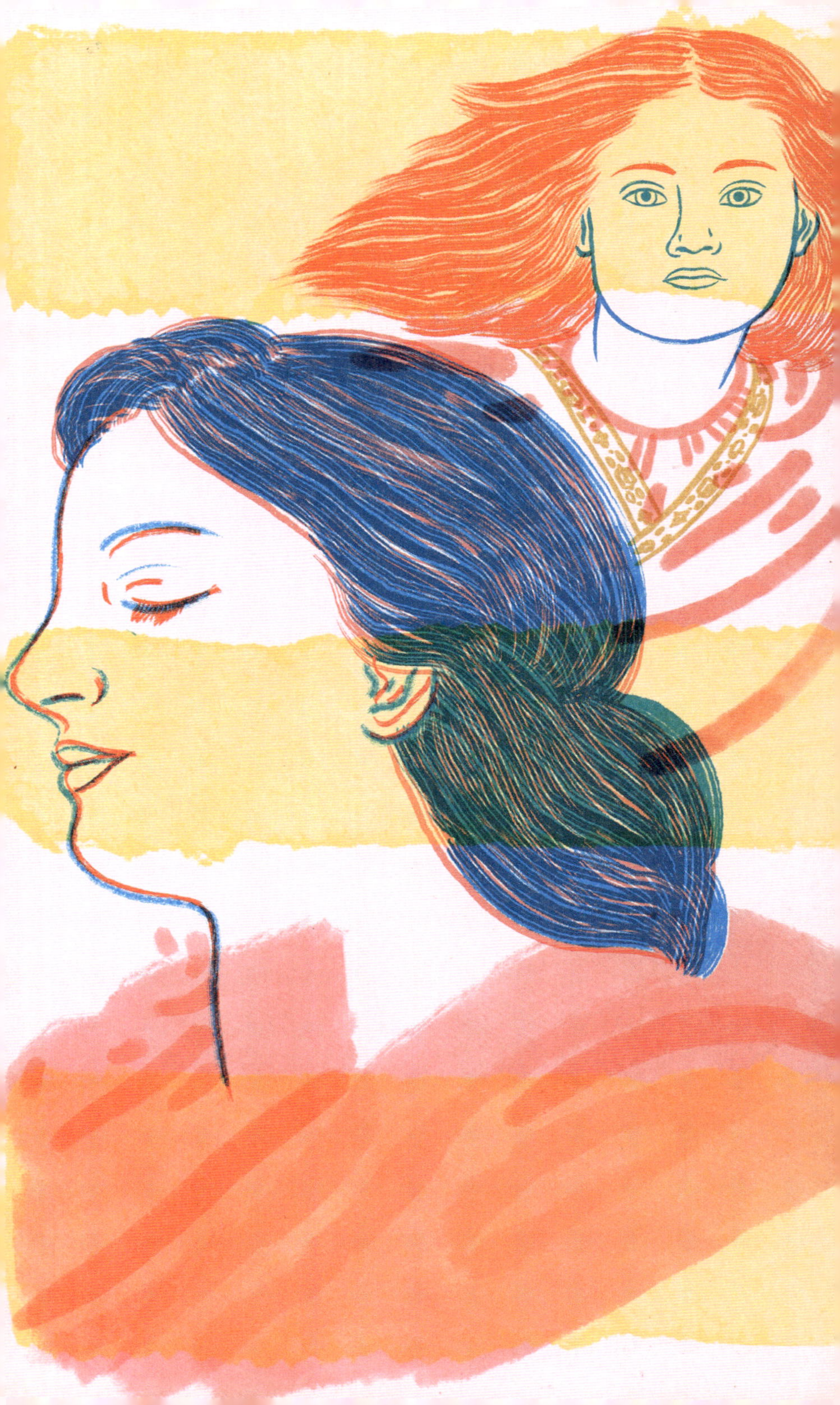

Joanna Mary
Boyce
1831–1861

Pre-Raphaelite Sister

n 1848 a group of three young painters studying at the Royal Academy of Arts reacted against what they perceived to be the unoriginal history of painting championed by the institution. Their secret society rejected the artwork of Raphael as the apotheosis of Western art and proclaimed they would go back further to the Italian medieval world for inspiration. They strived to create art that was clear, authentic and morally serious. Formed by William Holman Hunt, John Everett Millais and Dante Gabriel Rossetti, the defiant artists called themselves the Pre-Raphaelite Brotherhood (PRB). The choice of the word brotherhood was very deliberate: an exclusively masculine preserve, evoking medieval monasteries and selectivity. Despite this macho ringfencing, women were fundamental to the movement not only, as we might expect, as muses, models and sitters, but also as artists and poets in their own right.

Joanna Mary Boyce (later Wells) was one such artist who struggled with the prevailing Victorian attitude, which dictated a controlled sphere of activities for women. It was socially acceptable and increasingly fashionable to be a woman who painted, but she was destined to be a hobbyist whose work was kept within the domestic realm to which the female was culturally confined. To have aspirations to move beyond this into the art world proper by seeking an arts education, exhibitions, patrons and association with male painters broke too many strict rules of polite society.

Unusually, Boyce was supported by her father and brother in her aspirations to become an artist. (Her brother Henry was also a painter, though of considerably less note than his gifted sister.) Boyce's diaries and letters reveal a lifelong conflict between being confident in her abilities and passionate about pursuing her career, while also being fearful of the social repercussions of appearing immodest. Joanna Mary Boyce was sixteen when the PRB, as the group would anonymously sign their paintings at first, was formed. Soon after, she would seek out her own arts education and training and, as she did so, the ideals and principles of the group would come to align with her own artistic philosophy.

Women students were prohibited from attending the Royal Academy; instead Boyce took courses at Cary's and Leigh's Art academies in London. In 1852 she visited Paris with her father. Now aged twenty she was beginning to develop a keen eye for art and confident opinions of her own. She derided the majority of the French art she viewed, describing it as 'disgusting in colour, false in feeling, theatric in attitude'. In the same year, in London, she was entranced instead by the clarity and authenticity of Millais' paintings. Her *Self Portrait* from this period demonstrates that Boyce rejected much of what she had seen in Paris and synthesized what she admired with that of the PRB. It is an honest, lucid painting with an elegant colour palette, with enough detail to interest the eye without breaking the harmony of the easy repose Boyce captures in her own face.

A year later Boyce painted what might be her strongest work, *Elgiva*. In what would come to be something of a preoccupation, Boyce chose a strong woman from history to portray. Elgiva was an Anglo-Saxon queen who was persecuted, disfigured and ultimately murdered. Boyce presents the resplendent queen deep in studied contemplation moments before her disfigurement. The leading art critic of the day John Ruskin was full of praise for the work, 'The dignity of all the treatment – the beautiful imagination of faint but pure colour, place this picture, to my mind, among those of the very highest power and promise.' In Boyce's capable hands the subject was treated with solemnity and the style effortlessly evokes late medieval Italian art of the kind the PRB saw as the gold standard. Ruskin saw the work at the RA the year after it was painted; the delay was a consequence of Boyce being too nervous to submit the work. Her father had just died, and she was feeling especially anxious about how her career might appear to others, believing it was her 'plain duty to give up all hope of improvement in painting rather than in any way neglect Mamma'.

Thankfully Boyce's confidence returned, and she continued to paint and seek out her own arts education, travelling to the Netherlands and again to Paris to see the Exposition Universelle. Paris would get under her skin and in 1855 she would relocate there for a time to join a women-only class at the studio of the successful artist Thomas Couture. For the first time Boyce's day was entirely free from the domestic world inhabited by her mother, a woman Boyce found it difficult to love. In Paris her time was her own and it was happily spent studying, making, viewing and writing about art. She was commissioned to write reviews of what she saw in Paris for the London readership of the *Saturday Review* and was not afraid to speak her mind, even lambasting the acclaimed artist Jean-Auguste-Dominique Ingres and asking 'How has he attracted such a crowd of worshippers?'

After Paris, her career continued to develop, with several works selected for inclusion at the RA Summer Exhibition and an invitation to the all-important exhibitor's party, which she reluctantly turned down for fear of appearing immodest. Boyce had long held the opinion that marriage was entirely incompatible with her ambitions to be an artist and turned down a proposal from fellow artist Henry Wells when she was twenty-three. He persisted and Boyce continued to decline his offers letting him know in no uncertain terms that, for her, love was inferior to her career, brilliantly citing great women from history such as Catherine the Great and asking what love had ever done for them. After repeatedly outlining her commitment to her art she finally accepted Wells' proposal on the grounds

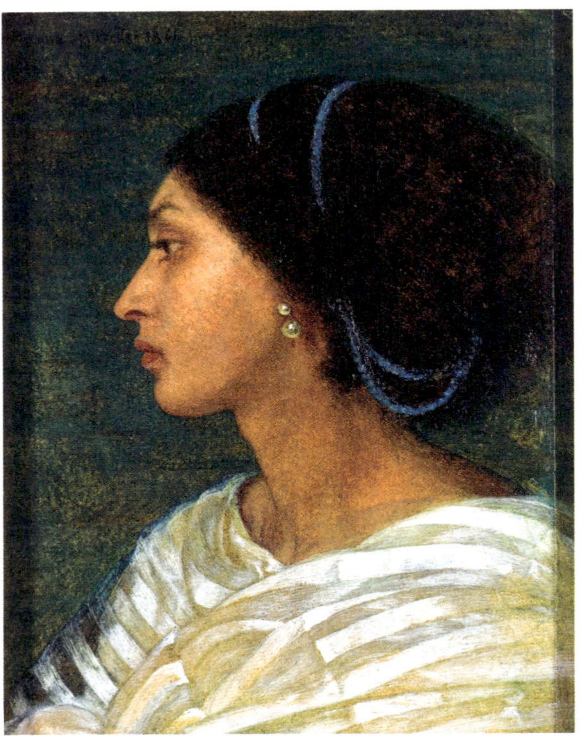

Fanny Eaton
Joanna Mary Boyce (1831–1861)
1861, oil on paper laid to linen,
17.1 × 13.7 cm (6 ¾ × 5 ½ in),
Yale Center for British Art, New Haven,
Connecticut, USA

he would honour her career and they were married in Rome in December 1857. Wells, having never given up, was rewarded with a happy marriage and was his wife's most faithful and ardent supporter, never breaching their agreement that her art must not be sidelined in favour of wifely duties.

She continued to enjoy success after the birth of her first child, receiving praise in *The Spectator* and selling work to PRB collectors. She was known to many of the Brotherhood by now and Ruskin followed her career closely. By 1860 she had two young children, and in 1861, in a period of increased rather than decreased productivity, she gave birth to another daughter. She fell ill directly after the birth, and like so many other women of the time, she died from a fever caused by lack of hygiene. Her husband asked Millais to fulfil the Victorian custom of creating a deathbed study the same day, 15 July 1862. His tender drawing confers the same dignity that Boyce bestowed upon her quietly heroic women. Millais may have formed a distinctly masculine brotherhood in his youth but by this time he was certain of the special and still overlooked value of women painters, and lamented that Boyce was a 'great artist sacrificed to bringing more kids into the world, as if there were not other women for just that'. Boyce's paintings are a valuable testimony that, despite lack of opportunity and pressure to conform socially, women were still capable of producing great art that could be considered equal in merit to that of their male peers. Her words are a reminder of the trying circumstances she fought against and the frequent internal battle she endured with herself, fearful of both giving up and diving in. Had she lived a few decades longer, she would have seen the situation slowly ease for her female colleagues as more progressive art schools such as the Slade opened, allowing women students from the start. In many respects, women like Boyce who persisted against all odds to paint professionally in the mid-nineteenth century are the godmothers of every female artist working in Britain today.

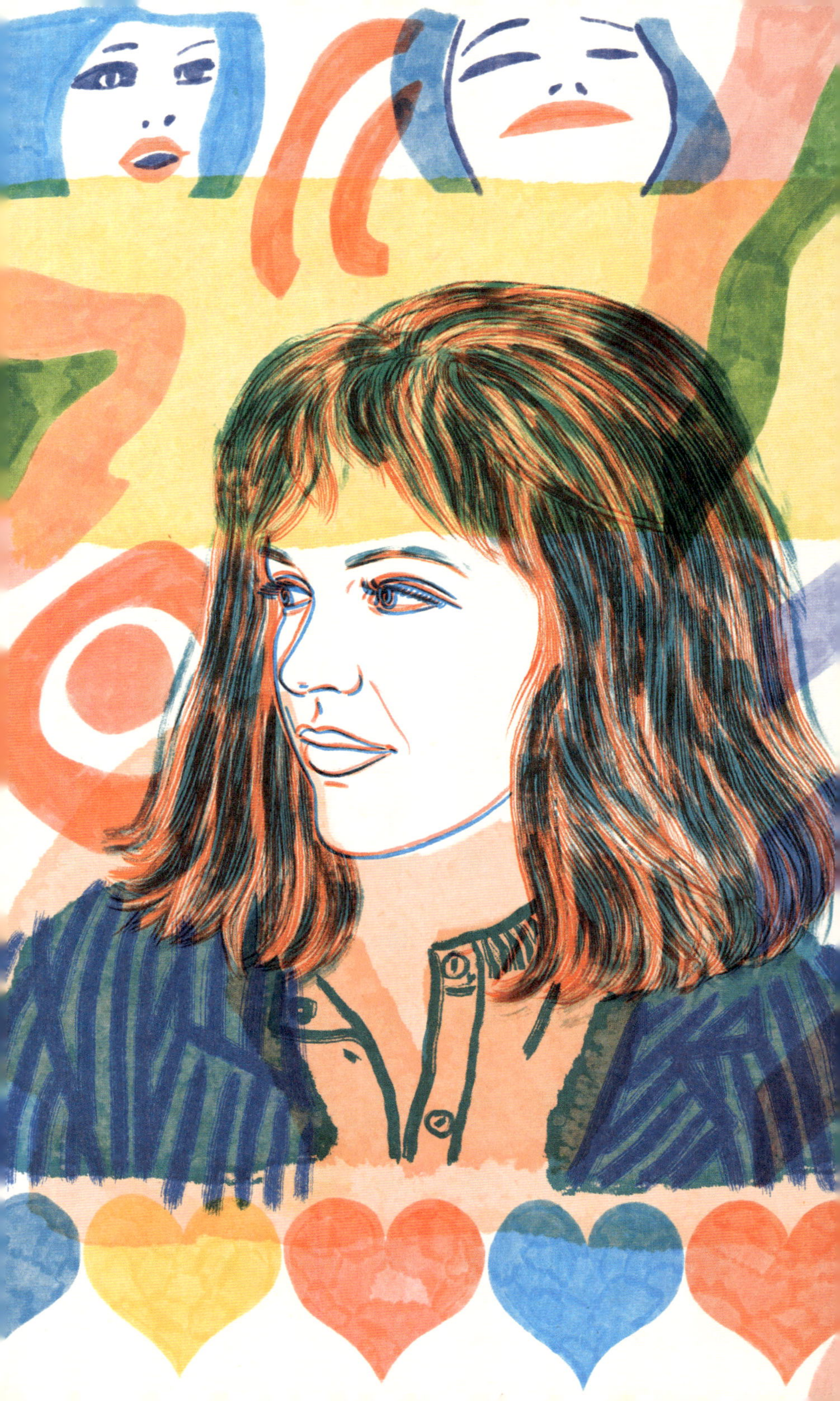

Pauline
Boty
1938–1966

Grand Dame of Pop Art

Imagine the thrill of rediscovering lost artworks, unwrapping canvases that haven't been seen for decades but that still pulsate with the energy of the era in which they were made and helped to define: London's Swinging Sixties. The artworks were created by a charismatic persona who typified the era: socially lauded, sexually liberated, moving between the worlds of television, fashion, photography, art and film. Featured as an actor in the blockbuster movie *Alfie* (1966) as well as interviewing the Beatles on television, their cool factor was so high they were also asked to escort Bob Dylan around his first visit to London in 1962. The same magnetism found its way into the paintings: the innovative compositions ooze wit, colour and charm and their maker was instantly designated as a founder of a new, thrilling art movement for Britain, Pop Art.

The rediscovery took place in a barn in Kent, UK, after dedicated art historian David Alan Mellor had conducted a passionate search. He was not just looking to bolster an existing body of work, but actually unearth the entire career and revive the reputation of the late artist. Because, despite the evident brilliance of the paintings and the vitality of their creator, they had been wilfully ignored for decades because of one issue:

gender. The works were created by a woman, Pauline Boty who died in 1966 aged just twenty-eight. Had Boty have been a man she would have been memorialized as the James Dean of the Pop Art Movement, an extraordinary artistic force who, before dying tragically young, helped shape a new era for British art alongside Peter Blake, Eduardo Paolozzi and Richard Hamilton. Instead, Boty was ignored and her legacy is still striving for oxygen half a century after her death.

Nicknamed the Bardot of Wimbledon, Boty symbolized the new woman of the sixties: liberal, modern, glamourous, talented and vocal. An engaging personality, she was high profile and proto-feminist, once proclaiming on screen 'All over the country young girls are starting, shouting and shaking, and if they terrify you, they mean to and they are beginning to impress the world.' Sadly, Boty's beauty and magnetism counted against her after she died; it was too much to ask that this kind of woman also be seen as intelligent and culturally relevant beyond her lifetime. Ironically then, her posthumous reputation suffered from the popularity she had enjoyed while being the talk of the town. She was at the centre of the vibrant sixties' cultural scene alongside writers, actors, musicians, activists and filmmakers, many of whom wanted to harness her star power for collaborations. She was decades ahead of her time for moving between these creative worlds.

Despite her openness to cross pollination as true 'pop' spirit, it was her art above all else that defined and drove her. Born in 1938, she grew up in Carshalton, a suburb of Croydon and fought against the wishes of her conservative father to be able to attend art school. She enrolled at Wimbledon Art College aged sixteen, and it was there she earnt her Bardot nickname. Boty belonged to a generation of women artists who faced systemic sexism – in 1958 she graduated to the Royal College of Arts where she was told to enrol in the stained-glass department, not the competitive painting classes, because she was a woman. But this didn't hold her back, not only did she find her way into the painters' slipstream, her work also benefitted from her course. Boty's pop paintings divided the canvas into sections, not dissimilar to stained glass windows, and allowed her to

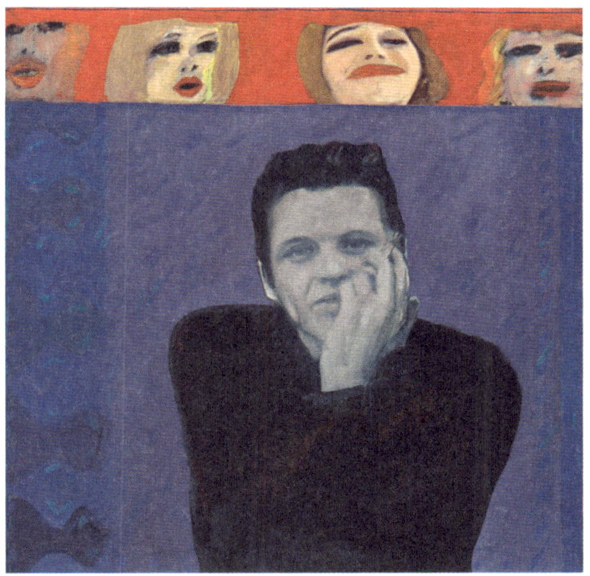

Portrait of Derek Marlowe with Unknown Ladies
Pauline Boty (1938–1966)
1962–1963, oil on canvas,
122.2 × 122.4cm (48 × 48 in),
Tate, London, UK

create painterly collages. Her imagery was drawn from the contemporary world around her, presenting motifs from 'low' culture such as magazine clippings and pin ups, then elevating them to 'high' status by harnessing the power of painting.

Portrait of Derek Marlowe with Unknown Ladies (1963) is a deceptively complex painting. On the surface it's not dissimilar to a piece of fan art, presenting a glamourous portrait of the young writer, laconically cool with cigarette and boyish good looks. Behind him sit a strange chorus line of generic women with bold red lipstick. Boty seems to have transcribed these figures from magazines, Marlowe could be stolen straight from a brooding black-and-white photograph. He is projected forward against a bold flat surface of blue and red, an unbelievable space that becomes more surreal in the stained-glass-like section that hems in the women who are purposefully rough in execution. The contrast between the treatment of Marlowe and the women raises the painting to an astute piece of social commentary. Boty has weaponized crude painting to raise the question of gender politics. Marlowe is depicted in a photorealist style, all the better for the viewer to share eye contact with this charismatic star. Whereas the 'unknown women' of Boty's telling title fight for room in the work, and what might have appeared to be beautiful women upon first glance fade away into rudimentary almost nightmarish faces. Boty's work is a critique of her era, a sophisticated game that plays with the rules of painting and source imagery by an artist who would ultimately herself be resigned to the status of the 'unknown women'.

That she was relegated to the margins of art history is even more shocking when we learn that Boty's work was instantly recognized as important. In 1961, the year she graduated, she headlined an exhibition that has come to be known as a significant, if embryonic, moment for British Pop Art, *Blake Boty Porter Reeve*. She had already featured in the seminal documentary film by Ken Russell, *Pop Goes the Easel*, which presented her work to the nation on the BBC. Her first solo show was held in 1963, less than two years after graduating, quite a feat, especially for a woman artist at this time, and the exhibition was critically well received. In the same year she married the literary agent and film producer Clive Goodwin after a ten-day romance, a radical decision, but one that she justified on the grounds that 'he accepted me as a human being, you know, with a mind, he accepted me intellectually which men find very difficult'. Not surprisingly, Boty's marriage did not dampen her creativity, rather she and her husband were a powerful couple in the art world. Boty continued to paint the world around her, never losing sight of the value of the female perspective. Her home was plastered with clippings from newspapers and magazines that might find their way into one of her painted collages.

Just as her work was becoming increasingly political, including a now-lost painting centred on the Profumo affair, Boty was diagnosed with cancer. At a routine four-month pregnancy scan a tumour was discovered and she was advised to terminate the pregnancy and commence radiotherapy. Boty refused and delivered her daughter, Katy Goodwin in February 1966. It was an enormous sacrifice; treatment was deemed ineffective after the birth and she spent her last months in bed smoking marijuana to ease her pain. During this time, she still manged to sketch her visitors, including the Rolling Stones, and died a few months later in July 1966 aged just twenty-eight. Her husband died twelve years later, making an orphan of their young daughter Katy.

With Goodwin also gone, there was no partner to champion Boty's paintings after her death, instead some time would pass until she was sought out by a younger generation. Mellor had been transfixed by Boty as a young man after watching Ken Russell's ground-breaking *Pop Goes the Easel* documentary. He included some of Boty's rediscovered work in his 1993 show at the Barbican, *The Sixties Art Scene in London*. This marked the start of a revival of interest in the 'Unknown Woman' of Pop Art. Since then, Boty has been consistently revealed to be fundamental to the entire movement and yet entirely ignored by those documenting and exhibiting it. Art history books present one singular, male-dominated narrative of this era. In many ways Boty saw this more clearly than anyone, one of her standout works is even titled *It's A Man's World II*. As someone who was vocal about gender inequality and who made it a staple part of her painting, Boty was not just at the core of Pop Art, but also paved the way for later artists such as the feminist icon Judy Chicago, who burst on to the scene in the seventies, and Tracey Emin in the nineties. The author Ali Smith included some of Boty's life story in her novel *Autumn* (2017) stating her relevance as vital: 'Boty blows the canon away – and that's why it's so important that we have her back.' If Boty was alive today she would be the Grand Dame of the British art world; as it stands there is still much work to be done to correct decades of neglect.

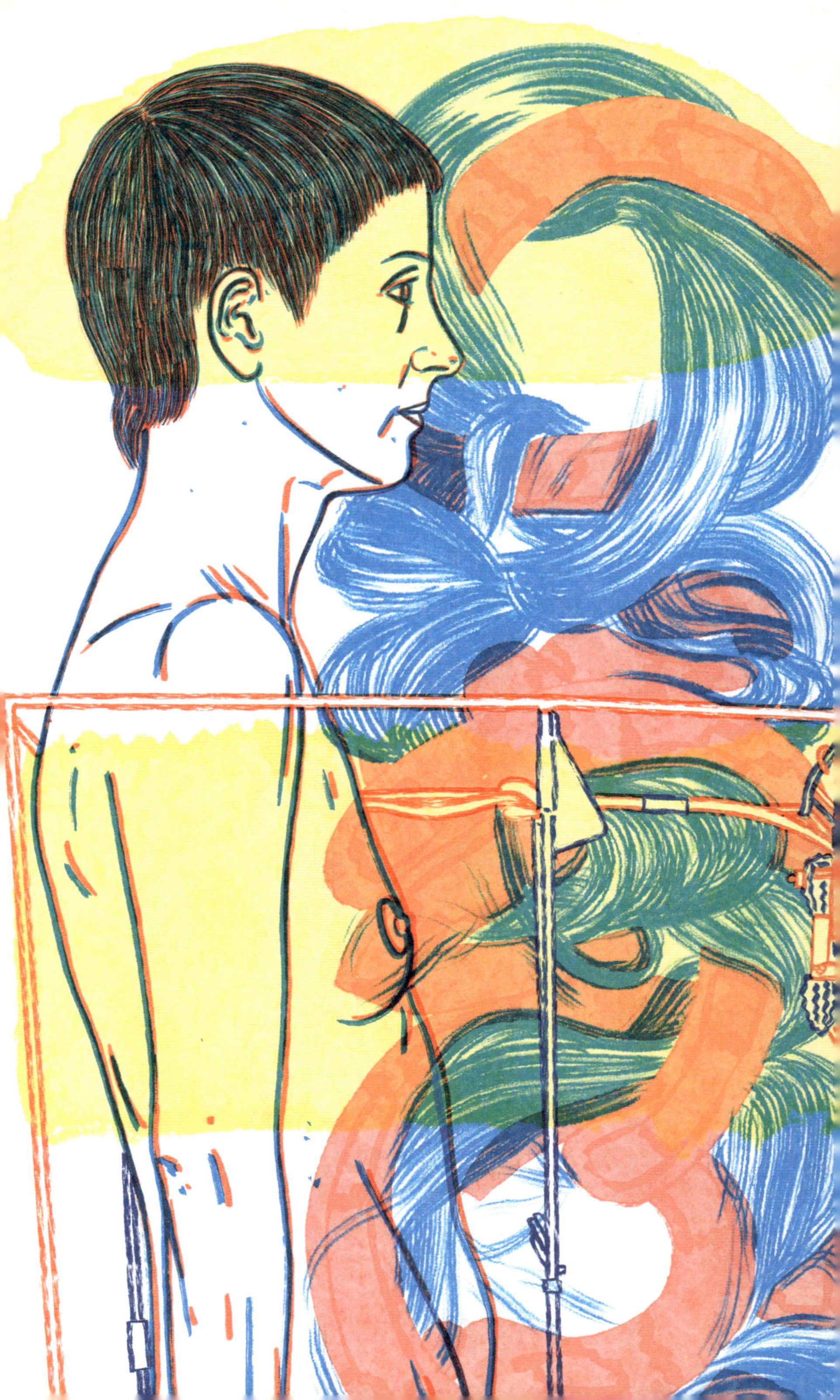

Helen
Chadwick
1953–1996

Navigator of the Body Politic

I t is peculiar to think that artists can fall victim to bad timing. We rarely consider that great art might be set a sell-by date or allocated a small zeitgeist window where it can best flourish and then, later, be cruelly unnourished and overlooked. What's even stranger to consider is artists at the peak of their powers then falling out of fashion, as happened to names even as internationally celebrated as Rembrandt and Botticelli, both of whom had scaled the greatest heights only to die broke and be relegated to obscurity for a serious length of time. This often occurs because the artist represents the Old Guard and seems out of touch when a new wave emerges. For Botticelli it was the muscular High Renaissance that cast his sensual beauties into the shade until they were rediscovered by the Pre-Raphaelites 350 years later. In the case of the British artist Helen Chadwick in the 1990s, it was that Sensationalism and Conceptualism became fetishized, overshadowing her theory-based work. Chadwick was the first woman nominated for the Turner Prize and her Serpentine Gallery exhibition broke visitor attendance records, yet she is an artist that critics tried to sideline shortly after her death in 1996. She risked being relegated to the footnotes of art history but two decades on, the relevance of her approach and ethos can no longer be denied. Instead of marching forward, art history has, as in the case of Botticelli, come around in a circle to better listen to what Chadwick and her generation were saying.

Chadwick was a great teacher and influence for a generation of artists that would become more famous than their elders as the Young British Artists. In her nineteen-year career Chadwick used urine, meat, faecal-like chocolate, nudity and bodily fluids and cells to create her complex work. For Chadwick, the unconventional materials that would find their way into the YBA era were not simply employed to instigate disgust, rather they were intricately and intrinsically linked to the arena of the body politic that she had been grappling with since art school. Born in 1953 in Croydon, Chadwick came of age during the second-wave feminism in the 1970s. Her artwork was an attempt to deconstruct the male gaze and interrogate the idea that a woman's body was in any sense owned or indebted to the exacting standards expected by society. By using herself as her subject, Chadwick not only rejected long-held cultural values surrounding what was expected of women's bodies, but interrogated what the 'body' even was. After receiving what is now considered unfair criticism for perpetuating stereotypes by using her own body in her work, in the late 1980s Chadwick moved away from herself as a subject. She worked in a complicated and exacting age for women's art and argued her case, 'I felt compelled to use materials that were still bodily, that were still a kind of self-portrait, but did not rely on representation of my own body.'

Often, she played with involuntary aspects of the human body and externalized what should be private and not seen such as *Piss Flowers* of 1991. While on a residency in Canada with her future husband David Notarius, she urinated into the snow and cast the negative space. Her stream was fast and hot, creating a penile form, meanwhile Notarius's was slower and cooler, creating a flat petal shape. Their bodily functions had unknowingly inverted the expectations of what is deemed masculine and feminine. The subsequent twelve bronzes of the pair of casts were joined together to create what she humorously titled *Piss Flowers*.

In 1994 she created *Donor/Donee,* which extended the parameters of the body debate greatly by inviting the public to use their own bodies, and more specifically, blood to create the piece. She distributed cards with the word 'Donor' on them, and participants would fulfil the promise of the artwork by going to a blood donor bank and receiving a signed 'Donee' card after giving a pint of blood. Chadwick removed her specific body and instead, by making blood visible and measured, instigated a conversation

"I felt compelled to use materials that were still bodily, that were still a kind of self-portrait"

about the mutability and impermanent nature of our bodies. In both *Donor/Donee* and *Piss Flowers* Chadwick creates engaging dualities, using the tools of playfulness and repulsion to create a dialogue about things that are intrinsic, beautiful and serious.

The standout work of Chadwick's solo exhibition in 1994 at the Serpentine Gallery was *Cacao.* A fountain of molten liquid chocolate, the piece delighted with an intoxicating aroma that could be smelt as visitors entered the gallery from the surrounding park. Delight quickly made way for more ambivalent or disgusted responses upon seeing the source: a large round vat of mud-brown, faeces-like gloop with a penile fountain recirculating the slopping, bubbling liquid. It was a spectacle of sensory overload, an untrustworthy chocolate mud-bath that was simultaneously beguiling and off-putting. The exhibition welcomed a record number of visitors and attracted mainstream newspaper coverage.

Chadwick had alighted upon a winning combination of wit, irony, revulsion, beauty and seduction. International success followed with a rare invitation to exhibit at MoMA in New York in 1995. She was an extremely well-read artist and multi-faceted theory permeated all of her practice, from the philosophies of Georges Bataille to the mythical labours of Hercules to obscure architectural principles. Chadwick died aged forty-two from a sudden heart attack. At the time of her death she had been inundated with requests to travel, exhibit, collaborate and was working at her usual unrelenting pace. Had her career had more time, there is no doubt she would have continued to make powerful investigations into the arena of the body politic and continued highly charged conversations about selfhood, identity and cultural expectations and norms. Less than ten years after her death a large retrospective toured from London's Barbican to three other European museums. Critics largely sidelined her contribution to British art, viewing the work as suddenly irrelevant for its theory-heavy approach; in 2004 *Frieze* Magazine described her art as 'at best, a vivid souvenir of an art world long gone, and at worse a vaguely hysterical irrelevance'. Fifteen years later, it is the critics that seem to be the souvenir of an art world long gone, not Chadwick. In today's highly politicized climate when gender has taken on an increasingly nuanced and public form, Chadwick could have been a vital voice. Looking back, her work seems extremely prescient and should be more widely exhibited and discussed.

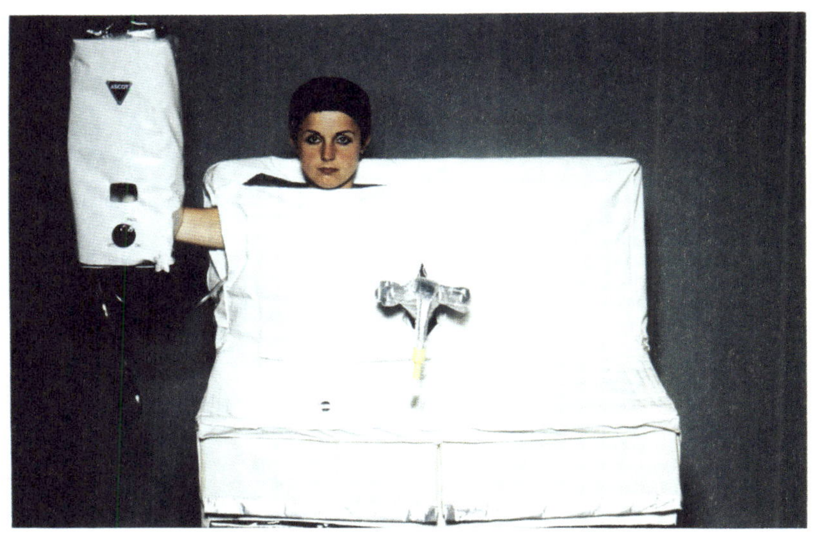

In the Kitchen
Helen Chadwick (1953–1996)
1977, photograph,
Leeds Museums and Galleries (Leeds Art
Museum), Leeds, UK

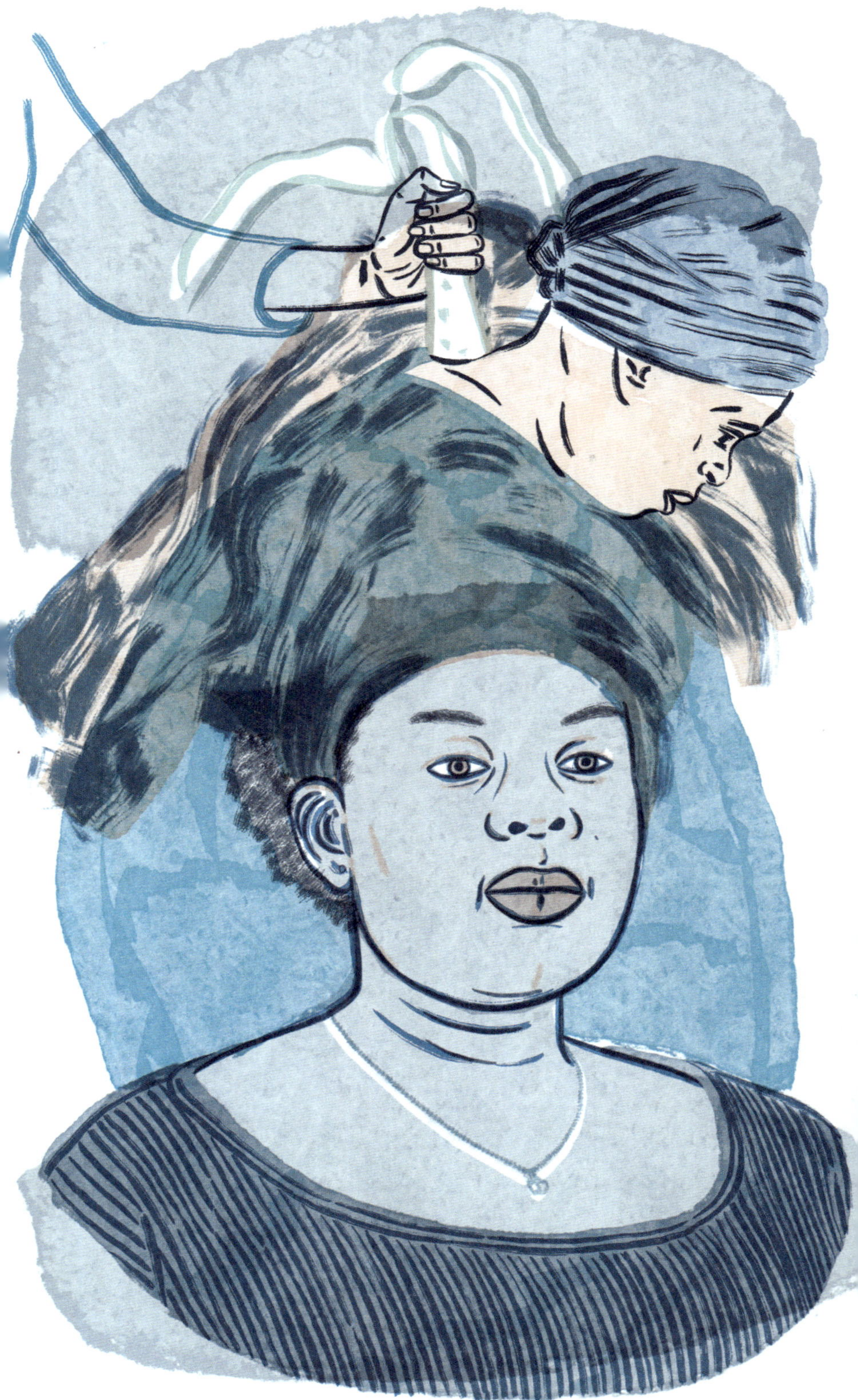

Khadija
Saye
1992–2017

Quiet Energy, Huge Inspiration

It is an almost impossible task to break through to the inner chamber of the notoriously cliquish and unfairly opaque art world. With more artists working than ever before, only truly authentic and determined voices will be heard. Khadija Saye broke through invisible, but nonetheless powerful, barriers and was recognized as a compelling new talent aged just twenty-four. The fact that she did so as a Black woman without financial or social privileges, living on a very modest income in a council-owned block of flats is even more extraordinary. Khadija Saye enjoyed the shortest career of any artist in this book, but she will be remembered for beautifully interrogating contemporary social issues in a personal, nuanced and historically sensitive way.

Saye's parents moved to the UK from The Gambia and Saye was born in London in 1992. She had a quiet determination to make artwork from a young age and from the age of seven attended the summer holiday Notting Hill Carnival Club making art and costumes. Her mother recognized her ambitions, taking her to an excellent after school club, IntoUniversity that supports children from underprivileged backgrounds. Through this programme she won the Arnold Foundation scholarship at age sixteen to attend the prestigious Rugby School Sixth Form whose alumni included Neville Chamberlain, Lewis Carroll and Salmon Rushdie. Saye would later remark that it was a shock to see the students exercise such high ambitions and expectations about their place in the world. Although she would continue to navigate her own insecurities throughout her short career, she would also assert herself and her right to make work and be heard. Her friend and fellow young artist, Lubna Ashraf felt a kinship with Saye: 'We had a commonality as we were neighbours and she was also from a conservative family background where being an artist was not considered a "normal" choice.' She fondly remembers Saye as 'a real hustler unwilling to allow circumstance to hold her back in her attempts to keep building her profile as an artist.'

It was this assertiveness that led to an important relationship with the artist Nicola Green. Green was a guest judge for the ING Discerning Eye exhibition in 2014, which Saye applied to after graduating with a photography degree from the University for the Creative Arts at Farnham. After selecting her series Crowned (2013) for inclusion in the exhibition, Green met the young artist who quietly stood by her work all night with her mother. Saye was direct with Green, asking how an artist went about making a living. At the time she was working in a care home like her mother, and although she was delighted to have been selected for the exhibition, she was anxious about how to financially support her artistic ambitions. Green admired Saye's unusual combination of vulnerability and directness and would become her mentor, inviting her to work part-time in her studio. Whilst still taking shifts at the care home, Saye was now working in a professional artist's studio and hungrily applying for workshops and other internships such as the arts organisation PEER where she was a Creative Access intern. Ashraf remembers Saye booking them both on to the same courses and feels that 'there was a real sense of urgency in Khadija's approach to seek out opportunities that would allow her to keep creating. It was important for her to be a part of intergenerational conversations that were taking place about the future of representation in art.'

In 2015 the curator David A. Bailey received funding to take a group of young curators from diverse backgrounds to visit the Venice Biennale, and Green sourced funding for young artists to join them; including Saye, Lubna Ashraf, Ray Fiasco and Kelvin Okafor. It was a revelation: Saye tweeted about a life-changing moment where she saw the artwork of one of her artistic heroes, Lorna Simpson, in the flesh. Ray Fiasco remembers the intensity with which Saye absorbed everything around her, describing her as 'having a quiet energy, she didn't need to say much to be loud and very present.' Having visited the Biennale, Saye knew that there could be no higher exhibition accolade than to be selected to show work at Venice, the epicentre of the contemporary art world.

Wonderfully, just two years later, Saye's work was exhibited at the 57th International Venice Biennale. She was selected to make work for the Diaspora Pavilion, a new and overdue rebuttal to the nation-centric organizational approach of the Biennale. Co-founded by David A. Bailey, Nicola Green, Peter Clayton and David Lammy, and co-curated by David A. Bailey and Jessica Taylor, the exhibition showcased nineteen British-based diasporic artists including Yinka Shonibare, Isaac Julien and Hew Locke. What made the endeavour more special was the platform it gave for emerging artists to exhibit alongside these museum-level names. Although she had only had one exhibition before, Saye was included on the strength of a powerful proposal that explored her cultural roots.

Saye had a longing to, in her own words, consider the 'migration of traditional Gambian spiritual practices.' In a series of nine self-portraits entitled, Dwelling: in this space we breathe (2017), Saye presents herself holding spiritual objects that belonged to her mother and father. The young artist placed herself in the position of healers in The Gambia and carefully reconstructed the poses of sacred ceremony. Okafor, one of the good friends she made in her first Venice trip, described the series as 'spine tingling' and admires 'the way she was able to take the influence from her family, and everything she felt inside, all the contradictions, and externalize it in such a powerful way.' The potent choice of objects is heightened by

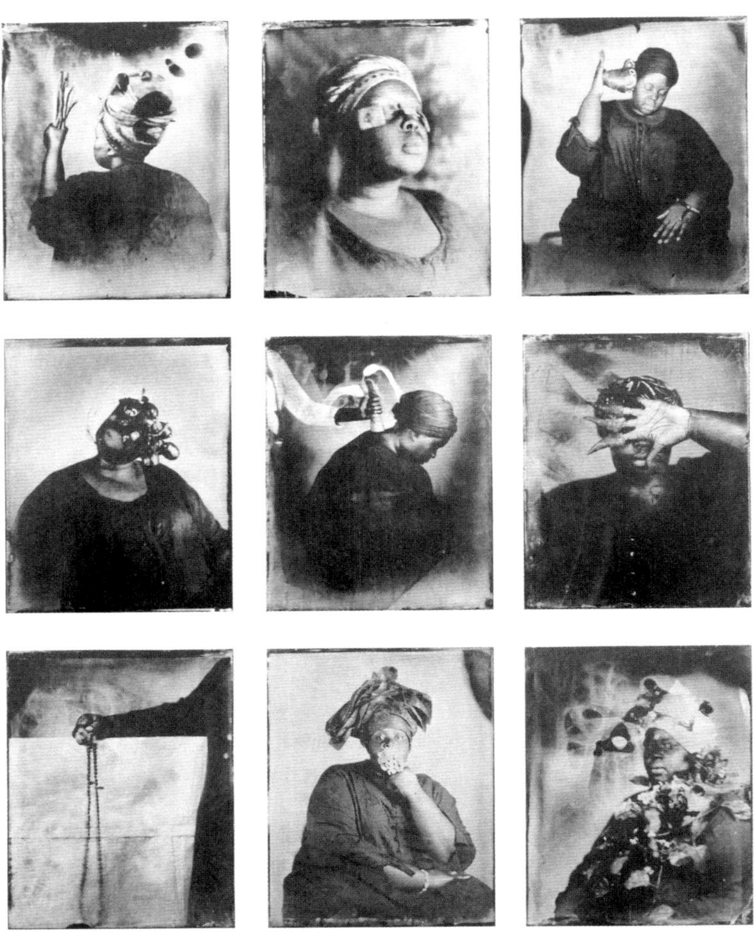

Dwelling: in this space we breathe
Khadija Saye (1992–2017)
2017–2018, nine silkscreen prints,
Each print: 61.3 × 50.2 cm (24 × 19 ¾ in),
courtesy of the Studio of Nicola Green
and Jealous © The Estate of Khadija Saye

Saye's medium: wet plate collodion tintypes. This throwback to historic image-making situates Saye's imagery in another century, underscoring the potency of her endeavour by reminding us of the relative scarcity of images of Black women in previous eras. Saye wrote that she had taken 'inspiration from the development of portraiture in the fifteenth century. I wanted to investigate how a portrait could function as a way of announcing one's piety, virtue, soul and prosperity.'

In a digital age of easy photography, her chosen medium was fraught with risk. Developing the plates in silver nitrate is time sensitive and does not allow for total control. Embracing the volatility of the medium, Saye exploited the liquidity of the process and the fragility of the light-sensitive plates. Far from the contrast-heavy world of film or digital black-and-white photography, the grey tones achieved are painterly, like a velvet X-ray. Saye's choice of medium insists on patience, a dance with the unknown and an intensity that is lacking in most modern image-making. She told Okafor that she was inspired to make work about the things that were difficult to talk about, 'She used to feel directionless, that society was saying this was going to be too hard for her, and then she put that into the work and it was so special.' Okafor touches upon something which I think sits at the heart of this series, Saye's work is deeply personal without being sentimental and fiercely tender without compromising its independence from the viewer.

At Venice, Saye's artwork was instantly compelling, attracting remarkable levels of attention for someone so young. On receiving a sneak preview, the seasoned collector Mark Wadhwa 'instantly knew they were something different, strong, beautiful' and asked to acquire the series. Although she was the least experienced exhibitor, Saye spoke to the eagerly assembled audience on opening night, 11 May 2017. Her poignant series was picked out from thousands of artists on display at Venice in the press reviews including by the arts broadcaster and critic Waldemar Januszczak, who described her as an artist who 'heaps poetry and sadness onto her imagery.'

Venice opened doors for Saye. Back in London in June the thrilled young artist met with Andrew Nairne, Director of Kettle's Yard, the University of Cambridge's modern and contemporary art gallery. Nairne remembered first seeing the work at Venice and asking 'Is Khadija Saye here?' When I came across Saye's photographs I immediately wanted to meet the artist. Who was the creator of this series of astonishingly compelling, poetic and mysterious images, which seemed to confront the viewer in the present, while appearing to be photographs from the Victorian era? Here was photography exposed as a vehicle of racism and exclusion, and here too were beautiful images, self-portraits of the artist, represented through light and shadow, both subject and witness.' Nairne was seriously engaged with Saye's work and had decided to include it in a future exhibition. The day after this important meeting the early promise and bright future for the young artist who had fought to find a place for her talent was cruelly stolen. Saye lived on the twentieth floor of Grenfell Tower with her mother and was not saved from the flames of the murderous fire that swept through the building on the night of 14 June 2017, killing seventy-two of its residents.

Only a month before Saye was being celebrated in Venice and the devastating news of her death sent shockwaves through the artworld. Her friend and mentor Nicola Green was determined that Saye would be remembered not just as a remarkable artist at the start of an exciting career, but as a role model. In July 2020, Green launched the Khadija Saye IntoArts Programme with IntoUniversity, which provides support and mentoring for young people from disadvantaged communities to explore the arts. Green describes the programme as a 'continuation of the work Khadija had already started so passionately. Khadija was an activist and had already begun teaching and mentoring other young people from similar circumstances to herself.' Kaye's work continues to be exhibited and draw new audiences, her work was included by Nairne as planned in the reopening show at Kettle's Yard in 2018 and in an exhibition curated by the artist Isaac Julien at Victoria Miro Gallery, *Rock My Soul*, in 2019. For Julien, 'to be in the presence of Khadija's art, one can see what an exceptionally gifted artist she was, whose extraordinary promise, although tragically cut short, shines bright eternally.' In 2020 her work was exhibited as part of an outdoor art programme *Breath is Invisible*, founded by Eiesha Bharti Pasricha and curated by Sigrid Kirk, on the walls of Notting Hill, less than a mile away from the ruins of Grenfell Tower. In 2021 Saye's work was exhibited in a solo exhibition at the British Library as well as the group show, *Unfinished Business: The Fight for Women's Rights*. Fellowships and paid internships have been set up in Saye's name at both the London Transport Museum and PEER where Saye was an intern.

No sense can be made of the death of Saye, it is too cruel for words. But it is absolutely imperative that lessons are learned from her remarkable tenacity to carve out a space for her practice. Ray Fiasco remembers her as 'quietly amazing, I carry the intensity of her with me everyday'. Okafor recalls feeling that 'there was no blueprint for artists like us, but Khadija surprised herself with her confidence. She knew she had to make art and in speaking her truth in that way she found power.' Understanding, sharing and acknowledging Saye's journey as an artist is a fundamental part of changing and opening up the artworld. As her mentor Green puts it, 'Khadija's story is inspirational, it needs to be told so that other young people in the world hear it – that is the important legacy of her incredible story.'

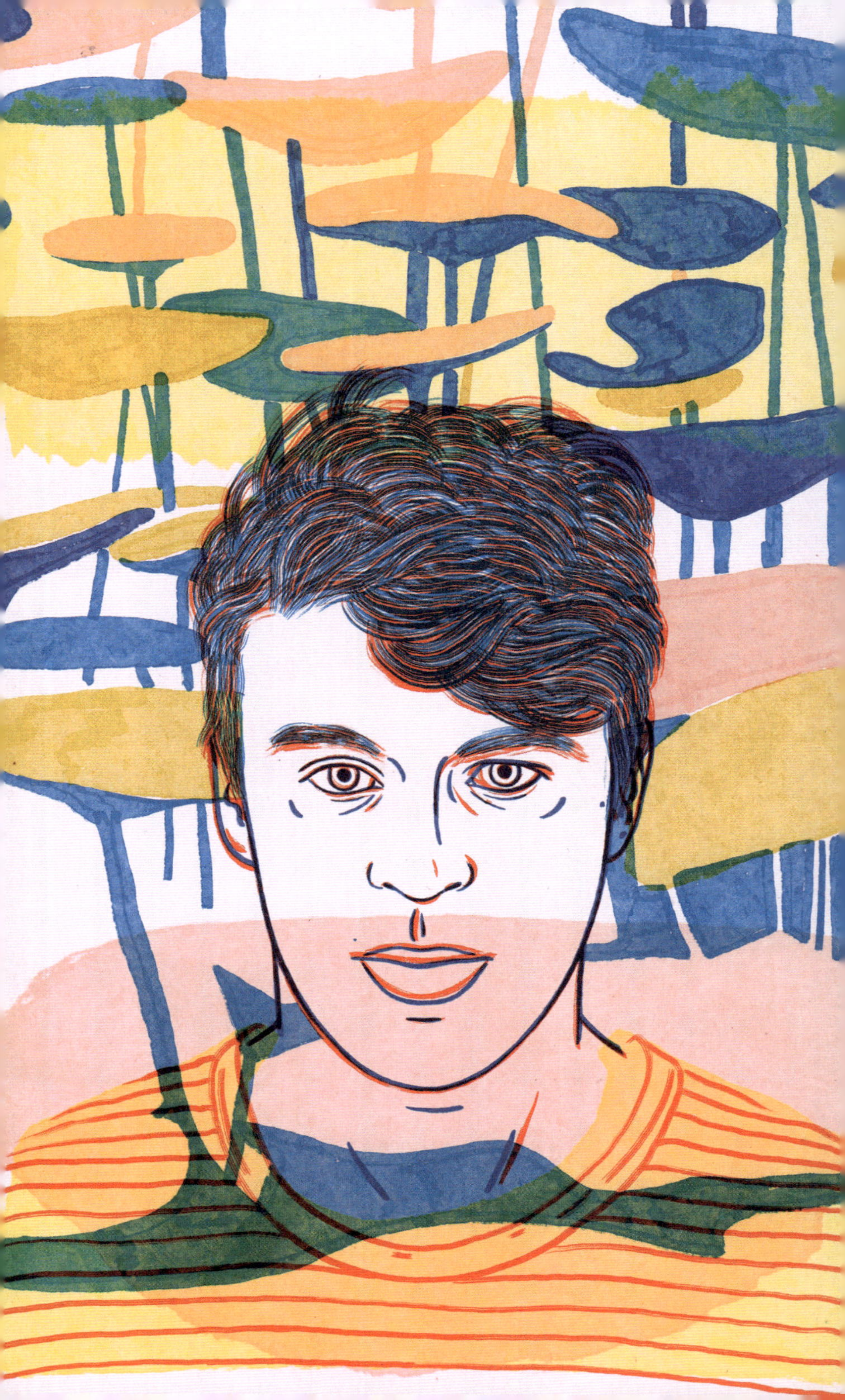

Bartholomew Beal
1989–2019

Literary and Vibrant Painter

Great painting is measured not by appearances but by feeling. How you feel standing before a canvas is the ultimate test. Does it conjure something, does it overwhelm you with an atmosphere or force an emotive response from you, even when you were unprepared to deliver one? This is something that first occurred to me as I took in the British artist Bartholomew Beal's large painting, *The Drowned Sailor* in 2014. It is a painting I longed to own and although it slipped away from me, it occupies a special place in my mind, a work I can recall and think about without a visual prompt. An older man, bald, but with a long-unattended white beard, stands quarter profile with his hands in his pockets, lost in his own thoughts. His crumpled blue shirt is the colour of the ocean in sunlight and his white trousers fade away into a ghostly nothing. Although he is at least part apparition, we imagine his feet are planted on the bottom of the seabed. Hovering in and out of reality, his skeletal boat rests almost within him, stripped bare by the force of nature. More like a thrilling stage set than a nightmare, red lines lead the eye upward like promising balloon strings, arriving in a festival of colour. Abstract shapes play across a black scene, some painted out, some

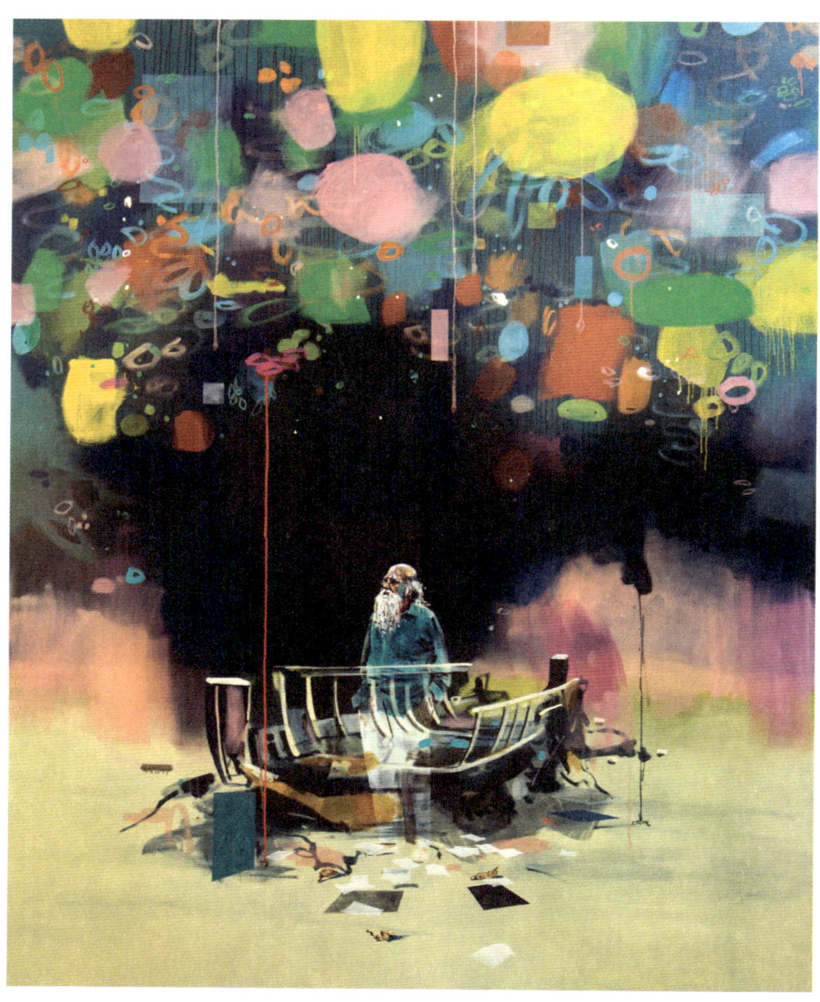

The Drowned Sailor
Bartholomew Beal (1989–2019)
2014, oil on canvas,
185 × 225 cm (72 ¾ × 88 ½ in),
courtesy of the Estate of Bartholomew Beal

repainted back in, a blanket of possibilities. The joyful colour palette above doesn't undo the poignancy of the painting, it is allowed to sit quietly side by side with something very deep, complex and tender.

The Drowned Sailor is emblematic of Beal's great achievement: to create paintings with a distinct sense of mood without forcing a singular narrative upon the viewer. More than that, his paintings depict people, spaces and time of his own conjuring which are never straightforward in their beauty. As a young artist coming of age in a robustly conceptual and newly digital art world, Beal stood by figurative painting with an innate sense that it still had plenty to offer. A decade later and museums and galleries are again full of figurative painting; painters like Beal reminded us that we gave up too much when we singularly obsessed over new media. His entire body of work can be characterized by his mature use of space: like a set designer, stage director and painter rolled into one, combined with his unending empathy for people, consistently presenting figures with whom we connect as viewers. Even if there are multiple bodies in a scene his subjects are always ultimately alone, the closest they come to unison is a contemporary kind of *sacra conversazione*. Despite their indeterminate surroundings they feel real, as if the artist has cared enough to lend all of his creations emotional and intellectual specificity. Beal's poetic painting was intimately linked with his love and knowledge of literature and he would often paint life lessons as gleaned from T.S. Eliot, William Shakespeare, Seamus Heaney and Samuel Beckett.

After graduating in fine art from Wimbledon College of Art in 2012, Beal won a much-coveted position to be Artist in Residence as part of the Jonathan Vickers Fine Art Award in Derby. He wasted no time and spent his year producing a significant body of work that was then then displayed at the Derby Museum and Art Gallery. Not only was Beal's first solo show out of art college in a museum, but he subsequently became the youngest artist to have a solo show at The Fine Art Society in London in 2014. The gallery had been on New Bond Street since 1874 and, as its director of contemporary art, I was instantly impressed with the work and awarded Beal the opportunity. He would become the first recent graduate I would champion. The fact that he was well read and energized by things written a long time ago made his work even more special. His exhibition was a considered and subtle response to Eliot's *The Waste Land*, taking the viewer on an esoteric journey through Beal's interpretation of the text. Although his source material was a classic piece of literature nearly a century old, Beal's paintings had an unquenchable, youthful energy. In their exuberance they were like songs as much as paintings and an exhibition of his was like a great soundtrack. A later show drew on the poetry of Seamus Heaney, his poem 'Postscript' inspiring *Catch the Heart Off Guard* (2017–19) a full-length portrait of his fiancée. In personal works like this he could achieve a rare feat in art, to make romantic work that was not sentimental.

His success is all the more exceptional when we consider that Beal was diagnosed with a brain tumour aged just twenty-two. He lived with this tumour for nine years. Most people who encountered him, including myself, had no idea of his condition. Beal did not consider himself an ill person, nor allow these circumstances to define him, in fact he seemed to have an almost alarming disregard for the brutality of his diagnosis. Instead of living mournfully like his days were numbered, he lived with such joy and appetite for the world, it was as if he had solved the meaning of life. He touched everyone who worked with him, from major collectors to gallery interns.

Despite his love for his craft, he was a tough critic of his own work. Beal's paintings hide an immense labour, and he would often repaint works he was unhappy with. This quest for improving the works later became part of his style, sometimes leaving ghostly traces to add another level of meaning to the work. A wise head on young shoulders, he painstakingly produced elegiac paintings that get to the heart of what it is to be alive, to be worried, to be sad, to be lonely, to be beautiful, to be flawed. He could paint a young woman with her hands shielding her face as if he himself had long graceful fingers. He could paint a soulful old man with hunched shoulders as if he himself was eighty years old.

But, tragically, along with the other artists in this book, he didn't get to live until he was eighty, and he should have. Bartholomew Beal died smiling at the age of thirty, surrounded by family on Boxing Day after his condition worsened at the end of 2019. His last solo exhibition was still on display and selling well and he had been energetically painting in the weeks leading up to his death. In his paintings Beal lived hundreds of lives, I feel him inhabiting every single piece of canvas and every little drawing. He is a great example to young artists, showing that an exceptional career can be made in less than a decade and that to seize every day possible to make art is a great gift. His unapologetic lust for life, bounteous capacity for thought and feeling and pursuit of poetic beauty irradiate in the work Beal leaves us.

All of the artists in this Unfinished Stories section deserve to be widely celebrated, exhibited and cherished into the future. Although there is an argument that their legacies are the most fragile in this wider selection of artists, we should caution against complacency. I believe all of these thirty artists to be great and yet, in reality, not one of them is exempt from art history's perversity: artists' legacies are subject to prejudice, whim and accident. Although it might feel that right now we are addressing the canon, by revising a narrative that we realize is exclusionary (as is the case with women artists or those from minority backgrounds) and sometimes careless with talent (as is the case with Vermeer) we should remember that taste is forever changing, quietly eroding reputations before we realize someone has left the room. Those who manage estates are engaged every day in keeping an artist's practice vital, relevant and meaningful as time passes. For all the artists in this book – even if they are household names in this century – we must protect the flame of their legacy into the next. History is unstable territory and so the work must be a permanently ongoing endeavour. As viewers in any form, we share a collective responsibility to keep art alive on behalf of its maker and ensure that what speaks so beautifully to us is not lost to future generations.

Index

A

Abstract Expressionism 25, 134, 162
Abstraction 156
Aestheticism 151
Albers, Josef and Anni 162
Allan, Ted 183–4
Andre, Carl 69–70, 74
Aristotle 49
Art Nouveau 109, 152
Ashraf, Lubna 210, 211
Avant Garde 88, 112, 122

B

Bacon, Francis 112
Bailey, David A. 211
Banksy 20, 101, 147
Basquiat, Jean-Michel 7, 8, 13–14, 22–9, 41, 100, 112
Beal, Bartholomew 189, 216–21
Beardsley, Aubrey 139, 140, 148–53
Bernard, Émile 50
Beuys, Joseph 99
Blake, Peter 188
Boccioni, Umberto 141, 174–9
Bonger, Jo 10, 50, 51–2, 53, 89
Bonnat, Leon 144
Botticelli, Sandro 203, 204
Boty, Pauline 8, 10, 187, 188, 196–201
Boyce, Joanna Mary 187–8, 191–5
Brancusi, Constantin 56
Burne-Jones, Sir Edward 150

C

Capa, Robert 182–3, 184, 185
Caravaggio 8, 11, 13, 14, 15, 30–5, 48–9
Cézanne, Paul 31, 51, 116

Chadwick, Helen 10, 187, 188–9, 202–7
Chagall, Marc 119
Chigi, Agostino 81
Colen, Dan 38–9
Conceptualism 134, 203
Corman, Bernard 144
Cubism 56, 176

D

Dada 38
Daley, Sandy 104
Dalí, Salvador 131
Davis, Karon 157, 158
Davis, Noah 140, 154–9
Decadent Movement 150–1
Degas, Edgar 51, 146, 156, 159
Dickens, Charles 48
Doyle, Tom 162, 163
Duchamp, Marcel 38, 41, 74, 158, 163

E

Earth Art 134
Egan, Victor 125
Eliot, T.S. 219, 220
Emin, Tracey 112, 119, 201
Expressionism 116

F

Fauvism 116
Fiasco, Ray 211, 215
Figurative art 155
Freud, Dr Sigmund 110
Friedmann, Endre *see* Capa, Robert
Futurism 141, 175–9

G

Gallo, Vincent 27
Gates, Theaster 101, 157
Gauguin, Paul 49, 50–1, 88, 116, 117, 122
Gentileschi, Artemisia 7, 34
Girouard, Tina 99
González-Torres, Félix 44–5, 72–7

Goodden, Carol 99
Goodwin, Clive 200, 201
Green, Nicola 210, 214–15
Groz, George 152
Guillaume, Paul 57, 58

H

Hammons, David 95
Haring, Keith 7, 9, 13–14, 15, 16–21, 27, 45, 100, 147
Heaney, Seamus 219, 220
Héburterne, Jeanne 57, 59
Hendrix, Jimi 14, 28, 104
Hesse, Eva 10, 140, 141, 160–5
Hockney, David 128
Holt, Nancy 134, 135
Holzer, Jenny 25, 88, 112, 119
Horn, Roni 101
Hughes, Robert 20

I

Impressionism 49, 50, 57, 122, 144

J

Joplin, Janis 28
Joseph, Khalil (Davis) 157, 158
Judd, Donald 74, 99, 163
Julius II, Pope 80, 81, 83

K

Kahlo, Frida 119, 123, 149
Kandinsky, Wassily 119
Kapoor, Anish 95
Keith Haring Foundation 21
Kentridge, William 158
Kerouac, Jack 104
Klee, Paul 119
Klein, Yves 85, 91–5
Klimt, Gustav 109–10, 112
Koons, Jeff 158
Krauss, Rosalind 10, 62
Kruger, Barbara 25

Acknowledgements

Thank you to everyone who helped with the creation of this book. I would especially like to thank Nicola Green, Andrew Nairne, Isaac Julien, Lubna Ashraf, Ray Fiasco and Kelvin Okafor, who generously gave their time and words about Khadija Saye. To Amanda Silk and Bartholomew Beal's family, learning of Barley's death after I had begun this book was devastating, and I have found some small comfort in being able to write about what a special artist he was. Likewise, I am also grateful to the Estates of Noah Davis and Dash Snow for reviewing those chapters. Thank you to the impeccable Australian artist Janet Laurence for suggesting Gordon Matta-Clark, who I am now obsessed with. Another helpful conversation was with the critic Louisa Buck, who prompted me to include Helen Chadwick when we bumped into each other on the Northern Line. It was extremely kind of Dr Maria Balshaw, Director of Tate to write a quotation for the cover, kept in fine company by my art loving friend Noel Fielding no less. Thank you to Alice Graham, my dedicated editor and everyone at Quarto, including Joe Hallsworth and Melody Odusanya.

I won the lottery with my family and would like to include them here. My endlessly lovely mother, Nonna Poppins, keeps the whole house from falling down, metaphorically and literally, while I pursue art at all costs. To my father Gary Soden, I have so enjoyed your own writing and am so grateful to have inherited something of your immense curiosity and enthusiasm for life. To Jenny Harris, the world needs to invent a word for the special bond we have but until then, I love you my Spermster. Gina Soden, a gifted artist herself and a perfect auntie alongside Uncle Mike, thank you for everything but most especially babysitting. Timotei and Zoetei Soden: Team Broden for life. The Cappers still motivate me to get chapters written on time so I can take Sunday off to play. I also seem to have lucked out with my work family, so thanks to everyone at Soho House, Sky Arts and Storyvault Films. A special thanks to Sara Terzi for being the greatest colleague and kindest friend. And, of course, a mention of my fine Judgementals, Kathleen Soriano and Tai Shan Schierenberg, who are always willing to have a good look at a rogue word document I put underneath their noses.

I wrote the majority of this book whilst on maternity leave with my daughter, Juno. Three months after she was born, I began to take a couple of days a week to research and write which was an immense pleasure alongside the joys of motherhood. I will forever treasure memories of breastfeeding at my desk while she playfully hit the keys, deleting a precious paragraph or two. Of course, none of my many endeavours would be possible without my husband, James Bryan. You continue to astound me with your love and dedication to our family, thank you a million times for redefining what I ever thought was possible.

Picture Credits